Ethical Space – *Journal with a difference: Celebrating 20 years Volume 1.*

2023 marks the 20th anniversary of *Ethical Space: The International Journal of Communication Ethics*. Yes, we have come through! In our first editorial, in early 2003, we stressed that ES was 'an academic quarterly with a difference. At its core are the academic papers which over the years will embrace the diverse disciplines and issues that fall under the substantial communication ethics umbrella. But it is also committed to keeping abreast of the news in the field and providing a space for lively, opinionated pieces on topical subjects'. The journal was to be inter-disciplinary, international, philosophically and theoretically eclectic and rooted in a determination to approach in original ways the pressing communication, political, cultural and environmental issues of the day.

Drawing on papers published over those years, this volume's 27 chapters tackle a wide range of topics under five headings: 'Communication ethics: Philosophical reflections', 'New media, new ethical challenges', 'Professionalisation and media ethics: Beyond the rhetoric', 'Communication ethics and pedagogy' and 'Speaking out on ethics'.

In a profoundly reflective Foreword, Clifford Christians, one of the world's leading media ethicists, describes *Ethical Space* as 'an inspiring model of ethical realism'.

A second volume, appearing later in 2023, will cover 'Directing a critical spotlight on the mainstream', 'Alternative voices', 'Public relations: Beyond propaganda' and finally 'Speaking out on ethics'.

- **Ethical Space – *Journal with a difference: Celebrating 20 years, Volume 1*, edited by Tom Bradshaw, Sue Joseph, Richard Lance Keeble and Donald Matheson, will be available from abramis.co.uk.**

The International Journal of Communication Ethics

Aims and scope

The commitment of the academic quarterly, *Ethical Space*, is to examine significant historical and emerging ethical issues in communication. Its guiding principles are:

- internationalism,
- independent integrity,
- respect for difference and diversity,
- interdisciplinarity,
- theoretical rigour,
- practitioner focus.

In an editorial in Vol. 3, Nos 2 and 3 of 2006, the joint editor, Donald Matheson, of Canterbury University, New Zealand, stresses that ethics can be defined narrowly, as a matter of duty or responsibility, or ethics can be defined broadly 'blurring into areas such as politics and social criticism'. *Ethical Space* stands essentially at the blurred end of the definitional range. Dr Matheson observes: 'As many commentators have pointed out, a discussion of ethics that is divorced from politics is immediately unable to talk about some of the most important factors in shaping communication and media practices.'

The journal, then, aims to provide a meeting point for media experts, scholars and practitioners who come from different disciplines. Moreover, one of its major strands is to problematise professionalism (for instance, by focusing on alternative, progressive media) and highlight many of its underlying myths.

Submissions

Papers should be submitted to the Editor via email. Full details on submission – along with detailed notes for authors – are available online:
www.ethical-space.co.uk

www.ethical-space.co.uk

Subscription Information

Each volume contains 4 issues, issued quarterly. Enquiries regarding subscriptions and orders, both in the UK and overseas, should be sent to:

Journals Fulfilment Department
Abramis Academic
ASK House
Northgate Avenue
Bury St. Edmunds
Suffolk
IP32 6BB
UK

Tel: +44 (0)1284 717884   Email: info@abramis.co.uk

Your usual subscription agency will also be able to take a subscription to *Ethical Space*.

For the current annual subscription costs please see the subscription information page at the back of this issue.

Publishing Office
Abramis Academic   Tel: +44 (0)1284 717884
ASK House   Fax: +44 (0)1284 717889
Northgate Avenue   Email: info@abramis.co.uk
Bury St. Edmunds   Web: www.abramis.co.uk
Suffolk
IP32 6BB
UK

Copyright
All rights reserved. No part of this publication may be reproduced in any material form (including photocopying or storing it in any medium by electronic means, and whether or not transiently or incidentally to some other use of this publication) without the written permission of the copyright owner, except in accordance with the provisions of the Copyright, Designs and Patents Act 1988, or under terms of a licence issued by the Copyright Licensing Agency Ltd, 33-34, Alfred Place, London WC1E 7DP, UK. Applications for the copyright owner's permission to reproduce part of this publication should be addressed to the Publishers.

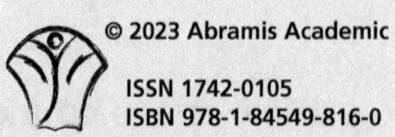

© 2023 Abramis Academic

ISSN 1742-0105
ISBN 978-1-84549-816-0

ethical space

The International Journal of Communication Ethics

Contents
Special issue: Indigenous communication landscapes

Guest editorial

How Indigenous narratives are embedded within, emerging from and calling across landscapes – by O. Ripeka Mercier, Beth Ginondidoy Leonard and Debra Harry — Page 3

Papers

Speaking into the silences: American Indian representation and negotiation in news media – by Melissa Greene-Blye — Page 11

We are not your offensive mascots: Knowledge surveys exploring US national coverage and comments about Native people – by Victoria LaPoe, Sarah Liese, Candi Carter Olson, Cristina Azocar, Benjamin R. LaPoe II, Bharbi Hazarika and Julia Weber — Page 24

Missing women news coverage and implications of standpoint theory – by Grace James, Victoria LaPoe, Benjamin R. LaPoe II and Alesha Davis — Page 43

Pouwhenua: Marking and storying the ancestral landscape – by Margaret Forster and Peter Meihana — Page 62

Tautitotito – Kama'ilio: Talking story – Health storytelling between relations – by Ashlea Gillon, Samantha Keaulana-Scott, Kiri West and Mapuana Antonio — Page 82

Shijyaa haa research: Reflections on positionality, relationality and commonality – by Charleen Fisher and Nina Nikola Doering — Page 100

Traversing Indigenous communication landscapes: Translation, uptake and impact of Māori research – by Tanya Allport, Tom Johnson and Meretini Bennett-Huxtable — Page 119

Ngā taonga tuku iho: Intergenerational transmission using archives – by Peter-Lucas Jones, Keoni Mahelona, Suzanne Duncan and Gianna Leoni — Page 137

Kia tangata whenua: Artificial intelligence that grows from the land and people – by Peter-Lucas Jones, Keoni Mahelona, Suzanne Duncan and Gianna Leoni — Page 153

Future visions for te taiao: Re-imagining environmental governance and political communication through film – by Ellen Tapsell — Page 170

Examining how *Reservation dogs* and *Rutherford Falls* critically craft community narratives: Indigenous storytellers celebrate non-stereotypical designs – by Benjamin R. LaPoe II, Victoria L. LaPoe, Sarah Liese, Hannah Ötting and Julia Weber — Page 183

Reviews

Sue Joseph on *We come with this place*, by Debra Dank; Richard Lance Keeble on *An admirable point: A brief history of the exclamation mark!*, by Florence Hazrat; David Baines on *Violence*, by Toby Miller and Richard Lance Keeble on *Listen world!: How the intrepid Elsie Robinson became America's most-read female*, by Julia Scheeres and Allison Gilbert — Page 201

Editorial Board

Joint Editors
Donald Matheson — University of Canterbury, New Zealand
Sue Joseph — University of South Australia
Tom Bradshaw — University of Gloucestershire

Emeritus Editor
Richard Lance Keeble — University of Lincoln

Reviews Editors
Sue Joseph — University of South Australia
David Baines — Newcastle University

Editorial board members
Raphael Alvira — University of Navarra
Mona Baker — Manchester University
Jay Black — Founding editor, Journal of Mass Media Ethics
Antonio Castillo — RMIT University, Melbourne
Saviour Chircop — University of Malta
Clifford Christians — University of Illinois-Urbana, USA
Raphael Cohen–Almagor — University of Hull
Tom Cooper — Emerson College, Boston, MA
Roger Domeneghetti — Northumbria University
Deni Elliott — University of Montana
Chris Frost — Liverpool John Moores University
Theodore L. Glasser — Stanford University
Paul Jackson — Manchester Business School
Mike Jempson — Hon. Director, MediaWise Trust
Cheris Kramarae — University of Oregon; Centre for the Study of Women in Society
John Mair — Book editor
Ian Mayes — Former *Guardian* Readers' Editor
Jolyon Mitchell — University of Edinburgh
Colleen Murrell — Dublin City University
Kaarle Nordenstreng — Tampere University
Manuel Parez i Maicas — Universitat Autonoma de Barcelona
Julian Petley — Brunel University
Ian Richards — University of South Australia, Adelaide
Simon Rogerson — De Montfort University
Lorna Roth — Concordia University, Montreal
Karen Sanders — St Mary's University
John Steel — Sheffield University
Ben Stubbs — University of South Australia
Miklos Sukosd — University of Copenhagen
Barbara Thomass — Ruhruniversität Bochum
Terry Threadgold — Centre for Journalism Studies, Cardiff University
Stephen J. Ward — University of British Columbia
James Winter — University of Windsor, Canada

GUEST EDITORIAL

O. Ripeka Mercier
Beth Ginondidoy Leonard
Debra Harry

How Indigenous narratives are embedded within, emerging from and calling across landscapes

In Western academia, ethics are often framed as 'societal obligations', whereas values are seen as individual in nature. However, for many Indigenous peoples, values and ethics converge as responsibilities towards community take precedence over individual 'rights' (see, for example, the Ubuntu ethic 'we are, therefore I am'). How does this dual obligation play out in the many different media spaces and landscapes that Indigenous people occupy and use? What are the most important stories for us to tell? How does Indigeneity shape an ethic of communication practices within Western milieu? What are Indigenous peoples' modes of communication, and how are landscapes being reimagined and recreated within Indigenous hands? Significant questions addressed by papers in this issue include these and other, deeper ones: how are Indigenous peoples engaging ethics? And, in turn, how do ethics impact on Indigenous peoples?

Among the 1000s of nations in existence worldwide we, the editors of this special issue, hail from three distinct Indigenous nations. We do not promote ourselves as 'the' experts on Indigenous studies; rather, we have an interest in amplifying Indigenous voices. We are thankful for the expert reviewers who submitted extensive, constructive comments on the draft manuscripts (some of them quoted here with their permission) and the authors who spent many hours addressing comments and suggestions for revisions. We conducted an open review process that acknowledges an ethic of relationality between and among Indigenous peoples. We heeded author preferences and found accommodating space within this journal.

O. Ripeka Mercier

Beth Ginondidoy Leonard

Debra Harry

How this issue came about

The invitation for this publication came from *Ethical Space* co-editor Professor Donald Matheson, who emailed Māori media studies scholar Associate Professor Jo Smith (Kai Tahu, Kāti Mamoe, Waitaha) in January 2021 to offer a special issue on Indigenous media. He wrote:

> Probably the best place to start is what Indigenous groups and scholars would want from a journal like ours and what structure would work best for bringing work together. Because we're a small, self-published journal, we've freedom to make decisions about that and can vary the number and kinds of pieces, languages used, intellectual ownership, review processes, editing practices and the rest, so it's fairly wide open how we do this. The journal is international, so my initial sense is that the journal would be a good place to bring together a range of Indigenous perspectives (personal communication, 25 January 2021).

Jo reached out to Associate Professor Ocean Mercier (Ngāti Porou) to join this effort, as we had worked together as co-editors of a 2012 special issue of *New Zealand Journal of Media Studies*, on the film *Boy* (2010). We then brought our colleague, Dr Rebecca Kiddle (Ngāti Porou, Ngapuhi), lead of the project *Imagining Decolonised Cities,* onto the team. We appreciated the flexibility offered by *Ethical Space* to tailor publishing conventions.

Jo came up with the touchstone of 'Indigenous communication landscapes' as a theme for the issue, a notion that Māori film-maker and scholar Barry Barclay (Ngāti Apa) coined in the 1990s. Jo led the drafting of a call for proposals, describing Indigenous communication as an emergent quality of place: 'Barclay's notion of "communication landscapes" draws attention to how storytellers of the Indigenous world share narratives as embedded within, emerging from and calling across landscapes.' Jo and then Becky subsequently shifted from their academic positions, so Ocean reached across the seas, to other landscapes, to her friend Professor Beth Leonard (Deg Xit'an/Athabascan), and then Associate Professor Debra Harry (Numu/Northern Paiute) to join in editing the special issue.

We received 11 manuscripts, and are excited to be able to share all of them here. Practitioners and scholars seemed to appreciate situating their work in terms of 'Indigenous communication landscapes' and our call for proposals presented the following questions as food for thought:

- How do we, as Indigenous people, maintain continuity and connection with the communication landscapes of our ancestors?
- What strategies have we devised to create and maintain ethical space in communication landscapes?
- How do political, philosophical, institutional and physical structures shape an Indigenous ethics in communication?

- How are these practices and ethics different from mainstream systems and what are our responses and strategies to maintain our voices as Indigenous communicators?

Responses to these provocations were wide-ranging, saturated with in-depth discussions about language, heritage, relationality, sovereignty, the impacts of colonisation – past and present – racism, decolonisation, Indigenising, collaboration, storytelling, humour, creativity, accountability, responsibility, identity and more.

The first three papers in this collection are presented by Native American scholars, who confront news media in North America, analysing mainstream media's treatment of Indigenous stories and public reception of narratives about Indigenous peoples. The next four papers describe contemporary Indigenous landscapes in Alaska, Hawai'i and Aotearoa, spanning historical physical lands, Indigenous research collaborations, non-Indigenous allyship and sovereignty in Indigenous research. The final four papers in the collection share contemporary possibilities offered by new technologies, enriching the work of Indigenous story keepers and tellers. These include digital archives for heritage language and culture, Indigenous artificial intelligence, digital film and television. Insights are shared on how they can support authentic, inter-generational and joyful presentations of Indigeneity.

Contribution summaries

'Speaking into the silences: American Indian representation and negotiation in news media' by Melissa Greene-Blye (Miami Tribe of Oklahoma) synthesises key sources in Native media around current challenges e.g. No Dakota Access Pipeline (NoDAPL) and the Indian Child Welfare Act (ICWA). She gives an overview of the cultural history of journalism/cultural materialism and discusses how journalism shapes historical and contemporary narratives in America. Greene-Blye notes that historically, the press is 'a major instrument of nation-building' by defining 'American'. This history exacerbates current challenges in naming/labelling Indigenous peoples of the Americas and reporting of stories, as Greene-Blye notes: 'When a Native-centric story makes national headlines, it is typically because it is part of a larger non-Native narrative.' She also points to systemic failures of inclusion in the press, which fail to recognise that 'Native journalists are journalists first, meaning they share the same training and skill-set as a non-Native journalist and are equipped to report any story, is ultimately another way of silencing them, particularly when Native individuals are disproportionately missing in the employment stats of most newsrooms'. She, thus, introduces a media landscape impoverished by lack of Indigenous representation.

Victoria LaPoe (Cherokee), Sarah Liese (Navajo / Turtle Mountain Chippewa), Candi Carter Olson, Cristina Azocar (Upper Mattaponi Indian Tribe), Benjamin R. LaPoe II, Bharbi Hazarika (India) and Julia Weber co-authored 'We are not your offensive mascots: Knowledge

O. Ripeka Mercier

Beth Ginondidoy Leonard

Debra Harry

surveys exploring US national coverage and comments about Native people'. They discuss offensive and racist imagery in sports, such as team names, mascots and gestures, as well as racism and name-calling in political rallies, such as when then-President Trump called Senator Warren 'Pocahontas'. But how widespread is that understanding of casual and everyday racism in politics and sports? To find out, the authors designed and conducted a nation-spanning survey of more than 1,000 US participants, as well as duplicate surveys of students at Ohio University and Utah State University. They asked about their general knowledge regarding Native peoples and their level of agreement with statements such as 'The Washington National Football League name [Redskins] is racist'. The Merriam-Webster dictionary defines 'redskins' as being 'used as an insulting and contemptuous term for an American Indian'. Given that even the dictionary cites the term 'redskin' as insulting, the response from participants was sobering. The findings overall highlight not just a lack of general knowledge about Native American peoples, but disturbingly high numbers of respondents who don't know or don't consider overtly racist names as such. University-based survey respondents, however, were better able to identify offensive and racist slurs and to be more critically and politically aware and active.

In 'Missing women news coverage and implications of standpoint theory', Grace James, Victoria LaPoe (Cherokee), Benjamin R. LaPoe II and Alesha Davis explore the content of 250 North America-based news articles from mainstream, Black and Indigenous media. The authors utilised feminist, Indigenous and intersectional standpoint theory in their analysis that uncovered four key themes: missing person, social commentary, family perspective and changes/action taken. The majority of stories examined by the authors include only a brief report of the 'missing person', while social commentary 'focused on comments from public figures, activists, or community members on the issue of missing and murdered Indigenous people'. The family perspective centred on the victim's family and changes/action taken focused on policy or other initiatives addressing missing persons of colour. The authors recommend that media stories provide broader contextual information for MMIWG stories that are 'multi-themed' and that future research include 'multi-language news outlets'.

Margaret Forster (Ngāti Kahungunu, Rongomaiwāhine) and Peter Meihana (Ngāti Kuia, Rangitāne, Ngāti Apa ki Te Rā Tō, Ngāi Tahu), in 'Pouwhenua: Marking and storying the ancestral landscape', describe and explore a revival of the ancient landscape marking technology of pou (posts) in Manawātū, Aotearoa New Zealand. This work is giving new visibility to historic engagements by local Māori with their landscapes and the stories embedded within them. Forster and Meihana describe specific place-based projects that are re-telling Indigenous stories in public places, such as revising interpretive signage, and (re-)instituting traditional forms of communication, such as pou whenua (land-marker posts) and sculpture. Hamuera Kahi (Ngāti Paoa, Tainui), one of the paper's reviewers, notes that the paper gives 'an understanding of how these pouwhenua are more than symbolic markers, storying the land, and adding to the presence of tribal authorities'. These pouwhenua, thus, are a contemporary decolonisation strategy for geographical landscapes that goes beyond symbolism and tokenism.

In 'Tautitotito – Kama'ilio: Talking story – health storytelling between relations', co-authors Ashlea Gillon (Ngāti Awa, Ngāpuhi, Ngāiterangi), Samantha Keaulana-Scott (Kānaka Māoli), Kiri West (Ngāti Marutūāhu) and Mapuana Antonio (Kānaka Māoli) invite us to listen in on their exchange, as Kānaka Maoli from Hawai'i and tāngata Māori from Aotearoa. Their experiences and stories from their work in various Western institutional health settings illustrate pathways they have forged in spite of challenges and constraints of their respective nations' health sectors. The creative ideas they share in their striving towards sovereignty and self-determination highlight the 'importance of stories of strength, resilience, healing, survival and thriving, as well as and opposed to only stories of kaumaha, taumaha, and trauma'. Indeed, reviewer Dr Victoria LaPoe (Cherokee) describes this paper as 'medicine'. This is the first of two contributions whose paper is structured as a conversational discourse between the authors.

In 'Shijyaa haa research: Reflections on positionality, relationality, and commonality', Charleen Fisher (Gwich'in, Dena'ina, Tl'eeyegge Hʉt'aane) and Nina Nikola Doering (German) discuss the challenges and opportunities for relationship-building between Indigenous and non-Indigenous researchers, allies and advocates. They broach this territory through use of storywork and conversational methodologies through a 'Two-Eyed Seeing' framework, building on Shawn Wilson's relationality model. In partnership with Charleen, Nina was confronted by the ethics of engaging Indigenous knowledges in Arctic research by Western academia. Nina came to realise her academic journey had uprooted ethical structures, which made her question the systems of research and teaching 'unsettled by my PhD experience and realised that I had come to a point at which I either needed to re-learn how to work in academia or leave research behind.' Reviewer Ashlea Gillon (Ngāti Awa, Ngāpuhi, Ngāiterangi) calls attention to significant questions raised by Charleen Fisher within this paper: 'Why do I have to change the Western world when I can actively contribute to 10,000 years of knowledge transmission within my own community? Are colonists or settlers having discussions and committing lifetimes of work to ensure that their knowledge is included in Gwich'in decision-making or governance or do they make the assumption that their knowledge replaces it?' In the engaging dialogue to which we are invited Charleen and Nina work through these issues and more.

In 'Traversing Indigenous communication landscapes: Translation, Uptake, and Impact (TUI) of Māori research', co-authors Tanya Allport (Te Āti Awa o Te Waka A Māui), Tom Johnson (Te Ati Haunui-a-Pāpārangi, Mōkai Pātea Nui Tonu) and Meretini Bennett-Huxtable

O. Ripeka Mercier

Beth Ginondidoy Leonard

Debra Harry

(Ngāti Whitikaupeka, Tamakōpiri, Hauiti, Ngāi te Ohuake) describe a unique reshaping of the research landscape in Aotearoa New Zealand. Whakauae Research is a Māori-led research institution that, in the TUI project, actively seeks to bring communities closer to the research that could positively impact their lives. The TUI framework is unique in that it emerged outside of Western academic settings, through conversations with and engagements within Māori communities. This paper examines practical shifts in Whakauae Research practice that enable translation and uptake of their research to traditionally underserved communities, to enhance the impact of their research. Professor Te Kani Kingi (Ngāti Pūkeko, Ngāti Awa), who reviewed the paper, comments: 'The "Tui" framework is an inspired model/approach/method. ... Like all great frameworks (Te Whare Tapa Wha for example) its genius is derived from its simplicity and the idea that it is dynamic enough to be adapted, or nuanced to operate within a number of environments or research settings.'

Peter Lucas-Jones (Te Aupōuri, Ngāi Takoto, Ngāti Kahu, Te Rarawa), Keoni Mahelona (Kanaka Maoli), Suzanne Duncan (Te Rarawa, Te Aupōuri, Ngāi Takoto) and Gianna Leoni (Ngāti Kurī, Ngāi Takoto, Te Aupōuri) work for Te Hiku Media, a tribal radio station that has generated audio content dating back to 1992. The content captures significant events from the past three decades, in English and te reo Māori, as well as noting important aspects of iwi (tribal) living. Their paper 'Ngā taonga tuku iho: Intergenerational transmission using archives' describes the strategic determinations and decisions made by the five iwi of Te Hiku o te Ika (far North of New Zealand), as well their processes and decisions regarding digitisation to preserve and, therefore, enhance Indigenous sovereignty over the heritage data, knowledge and language their radio broadcast has generated. They describe the archive as 'a tangible resource for the community from which the kaumātua come [which] holds great spiritual value in creating space for people to connect with their linguistic and cultural identity'. Guardianship and preservation protocols align with elder aspirations and local tikanga (Māori values). This contribution also describes the importance of archivists working on the project being Indigenous but also of local iwi, who can thus best understand and interpret tribal specificities like local dialect. Reviewer Paul Meredith (Ngāti Maniapoto, Pākehā), deputy chief executive (Māori) of Ngā Taonga: Sound and Vision, the New Zealand government's repository for audio-visual media, writes: 'The authors are widely recognised as being at the vanguard of the indigenisation of digital devices in the language space. It is right that they themselves tell their own story in written scholarship rather than leave it to others.'

The same authors also contributed 'Kia tangata whenua: Artificial intelligence that grows from the land and people', describing their experience with AI in the form of NLP (natural language processing) tools on te reo Māori recordings from their radio archives. In doing so they not only explore 'ethical space for indigenous peoples in a predominantly Western communication landscape' but navigate an ethical and existential minefield, using Indigenous values for guidance. Software engineer and reviewer Kevin Shedlock (Ngāpuhi, Ngāti Porou, Whakatōhea) notes the novelty of Indigenous AI enfolding natural language processing, as well as the uniqueness of the team's technical infrastructure: 'Given the level of indigenous resources required to model, interpret and report on such large amounts of unstructured data in this paper ... the article provides a lifecycle exemplar of Indigenous AI to navigate bias in a manner that can be culturally safe.' Extending on the theme of cultural safety, Kevin writes that Te Hiku Media bring a 'decolonised framework to shape ethical AI practice by valuing expert knowledge. This is an important aspect of the paper that announces an ethical NLP toolkit for speech recognition, speech synthesis and assessing speech pronunciation using a tribal team of Indigenous experts'. Professor Te Taka Keegan (Waikato-Maniapoto, Ngāti Porou and Ngāti Whakaue), reviewer and technology expert, also notes the practical legacy Te Hiku Media's work leaves: 'The examples described are completely relevant and serve as important examples should other Indigenous groups be in a position to undergo similar work.'

In her paper 'Future visions for te taiao', Ellen Tapsell (Te Arawa) reports on a community film competition she co-organised, called *Future Visions for te Taiao* (the environment). This festival 'provides an alternative avenue for political communication on environmental governance that centres an Indigenous communication and environmental ethic'. Ten films were crafted, submitted and exhibited by a range of participants from taiohi (youth) and rangatahi (young adult) to pakeke (adult), Māori and non-Indigenous. Tapsell notes four themes emerging from the film stories: change in the face of environmental threats is hampered by apathy and shortcomings in current approaches; the need to shift to collective, intergenerational and hands-on approaches; importance of human connection to nature and the more-than-human; and joy and fun while caring for the environment. These chart aspirations for an ethical approach to natural landscape underpinned by an Indigenous standpoint and facilitation. Associate Professor of Future Environments and reviewer Amanda Yates (Te Arawa) noted that 'The subject is timely and relevant as it addresses how extant colonial governance and policy structures are unable to meet and redress current ecological crises. The paper reveals a strategy for Indigenous communication ethics founded in Aotearoa's storytelling practices, affirmed as foundational to Māori epistemologies. A short film competition becomes an activation tool that builds engagement with a wide range of publics, including Rangatahi / Taiohi, enabling their voice.'

And finally, in their contribution 'Examining how *Reservation dogs* and *Rutherford Falls* critically craft community narratives: Indigenous storytellers celebrate non-stereotypical designs', Benjamin R. LaPoe II, Victoria L. LaPoe (Cherokee), Sarah Liese (Navajo/Chippewa/Cree), Hannah Ötting and Julia Weber examine Indigenous authorship and representation in these 'cultural stories'. The authors contextualise their discussion by looking at the historical and contemporary under-

O. Ripeka Mercier

Beth Ginondidoy Leonard

Debra Harry

representation of Indigenous peoples in television storytelling. For example, their research includes data from the 2020 'Hollywood diversity report' showing 'only 1.1 per cent of film leads and 0.6 per cent of overall roles included Indigenous peoples, with no US film directors represented'. In their analysis, the authors engage with mediatisation and Indigenous standpoint theory, drawing out common themes including 'humour, family, community and honesty'. The paper recommends future research topics include an exploration of 'ethical professional standards' for Indigenous-led productions, and surveys of non-Indigenous peoples that gauge the impact of these stories in decreasing the stereotypes of Indigenous peoples.

This collection, focused as it is on contributors' homelands of Alaska, Aotearoa, Hawai'i and North America, is just one window into Indigenous communication ethics. The diversity represented here reveals a rich, intersecting and complex set of issues and opportunities that respond well to the practicality of Indigenous approaches. Indigenous communication landscapes are local, language-based, heritage-facing, relational, intergenerational, contemporary, ethical and value-laden and as such shine light onto the deficiencies evident in Western systems, where Indigenous peoples work with sometimes incompatible and hostile media. As we call across spaces to each other, from our local places and through the forum that is this *Ethical Space*, we retell and enliven the stories, strengthening our identities as Indigenous peoples of vibrant, contemporary yet deeply rooted landscapes of communication.

PAPER

Melissa Greene-Blye

Speaking into the silences: American Indian representation and negotiation in news media

Non-Native news media too often fail to offer authentic representations of Indigenous identities, issues and individuals. Sometimes this occurs through a simple failure to cover important issues facing Native communities; at other times it results from a tendency to rely on culturally programmed, default narratives regarding those communities and issues. The very nature of the news-gathering process and subsequent narrative conventions of storytelling place journalists in a central role, as their work shapes broader understandings about individuals and groups represented in the final news product. Relying on historical context and examples culled from contemporary news accounts, this paper argues for the need to reconsider our definitions of history and communication through a critical examination of the ways in which narrative formulas and journalistic conventions have been used to silence Native voices and perpetuate misrepresentations. It also offers thoughts on what can be done to offer a more authentic representation of Indigenous persons in history and journalism.

Key words: Native American, Indigenous identity, stereotypes, American Indian, representation

Introduction
Preeminent Native scholar Vine Deloria Jr. writes: 'The more we try to be ourselves the more we are forced to defend what we have never been. The American public feels most comfortable with the mythical Indians of stereotype-land who were always THERE. ... To be an Indian in modern American society is in a very real sense to be unreal and ahistorical.' Deloria Jr., a renowned activist and author, penned these words in 1969 as part of his groundbreaking treatise, *Custer died for your sins: An Indian manifesto* (Deloria Jr. 1969: 1). Sadly, this statement still rings true five decades after it was originally penned. American news media

Melissa Greene-Blye

too often fail to offer authentic, accurate representations of Native American communities and individuals, sometimes through a simple failure to cover important issues facing Native nations and individuals, at other times through a tendency to rely on culturally programmed, default narratives regarding those nations and individuals. Media portrayals of Native Americans are often based on old stereotypes at worst and, at best, inadvertently perpetuate those stereotypes, in part, because Native people are not given voice in their own stories. Naming and labeling also play an important part in the way that news media often fail to accurately represent Native individuals and communities.[1]

Historian and the founding director of the National Museum of the American Indian, W. Richard West, argues for the importance of hearing directly from Native people: '... we hold that it is only when a people assume authority over their stereotypes that they can truly begin to dispel them' (West 2007: xiv). This paper explores the myriad ways Native voices have been, and continue to be, marginalised in the narrative-building process that informs the stories we tell ourselves about who we are as individuals and how we fit into the larger story of America's past, present and future; it seeks to examine how those stories inform our perceptions of individuals, groups and issues that fall outside the limited bounds of our lived experiences and the ways in which journalism shapes those narratives. In order to facilitate the process of allowing Native individuals and communities to 'assume authority over their stereotypes', with the goal of discrediting those stereotypes, we must first have an understanding of how mediated words and images contribute to the misinformation that are the building blocks of misrepresentation and, ultimately, marginalisation.

The very nature of the news-gathering process and subsequent narrative conventions of storytelling necessarily place journalists in a central role, as their work shapes broader understandings about the individuals and groups represented in the final product; newsroom decisions determine who is seen and heard and, ultimately, whether those images and voices are helpful or hurtful. Journalist and media critic Walter Lippmann recognised early on the power of media messaging as a substitute for first-hand knowledge: 'Inevitably our opinions cover a bigger space, a longer reach of time, a greater number of things, than we can directly observe. They have, therefore, to be pieced together out of what others have reported and what we can imagine' (Lippmann 1965 [1922]: 53). This 'piecing together' is aided by the use of stereotypes which, Lippmann argues, offer a comfortable way of knowing, while ultimately reinforcing the perceptions that we need to believe in order to justify our own attitudes and circumstances. According to Lippmann, journalists can be considered master quilt-makers, for it is they who stitch together disparate events and issues into a semblance of cohesive normality and, just as one quilter recognises another's work by its unique styling, so too do journalists bring their unique perspective to the finished product: 'A report is the joint product of the knower and the known, in which the role of the observer is always selective and usually creative. The facts we see depend on where we are placed, and the habits of our eyes' (ibid: 63-64).

Rethinking our history and our journalism

With this understanding, it becomes imperative that we 'examine newspapers and other media not just for what they are, but for what they do and how they fit into a larger cultural framework' (Hamilton 1987: 78-85). Such an examination highlights the necessity of reconsidering our definitions of history and communication in order to allow a critical examination of the ways in which narrative formulas and journalistic conventions have been factored into the stories used to define and explain American history, specifically as it relates to our understanding of American Indian nations and individuals (see Gramsci 2011 [1947]).

But history is more than politics or economics and while these factors certainly play an important role in shaping history, we miss out on important elements of individual and community agency if we rely solely on government documents or financial trends and data to understand the past. It is the nuanced aspects of the story that, more often than not, provide the answers that help us answer the 'why' questions, broadening our understanding of how history unfolded. Historian Jacques Barzun aptly points out that much of what we think of as factual history is the result of the limitations imposed by the convention of naming and characterising (Barzun 1973: 387-402). If we accept that meaning can be found in a culture's language and systems of representation, we can find the necessary freedom to pursue what James Carey describes as a 'cultural history of journalism'. A move away from the traditional 'great man' narratives and toward scholarship that critically examines the process of reporting and positions journalism as a text with the power to shape social consciousness (Carey 2011: 22-27). Carey's call is seconded by the concept of cultural materialism as put forth by Raymond Williams which states that a study of media is a credible way to understand and evaluate power dynamics historically and in the current moment. In examining the origin of the word 'mediated', Williams explains that when the term is associated with 'media' or 'mass media' it typically has a negative connotation wherein 'certain social agencies are seen as deliberately interposed between reality and social consciousness to prevent an understanding of reality' (Williams 2015: 153). Expanding on this point, Williams relies on Gramsci's notion of cultural hegemony to argue that a study of cultural artefacts serves to inform how the dominant group at any given time period seeks to maintain its power and control over groups that fall outside of the dominant ideology.

Media messaging contributes to this process in important ways, specifically by moulding public opinion for or against certain policies or persons and also by contributing constructions of group identity and consensus. The press historically served as a major instrument of nation-building by defining 'American', by default defining who belonged and, more importantly, who did not. Benedict Anderson posits that mass media contribute to the notion of 'nation' through the creation of 'imagined communities'. Media, through the use of stereotypes, contribute to an individual's construction of who they are (or are not), their sense of identity, offering a sense of 'belonging', often in opposition to a defined construction of the 'other' (Anderson 2016 [2006]: 46). Nineteenth-century newspaper representations of American Indians as a 'problem' that needed to go away or as people who needed to be civilised through assimilation taught newspaper readers that to be 'American' meant supporting policies which furthered American progress; that support meant either turning a blind eye toward the government's mistreatment of Indian nations or a willingness to justify that mistreatment by adopting an 'end justifies the means' mindset. Both viewpoints were employed in the history of America's journalism, often in tandem with major shifts in government Indian policy.

Speaking into the silences

In addition to broadening our definition of the fields of history and communication to include a more critical perspective, we must also rethink how we approach and examine archival materials, particularly in scholarship about Indigenous peoples. In both traditional history and media history that means making room for research that speaks into the silences, closely examining spaces where we do not readily, nor easily, hear the voices or find the words of Native Americans. Archaeologist Ann Laura Stoler (2009) stresses the necessity of reading along the archival grain as an avenue to understanding what the content, organisation and structure of an archive reveals about the dominantly represented groups that created and continue to maintain those archives. It is in the process of reading archives oppositionally, essentially exploring the margins and absences, that we are able to find the too-often overlooked voices. Historian Stewart Rafert (1982) furthers this point specifically as it relates to the lack of Indian narratives in established archives: 'Historians have had to talk to the Indians themselves to understand their viewpoint and the powerful understanding of their own history. Much Indian history is still passed on from generation to generation, and therefore is not contained in any documents' (Rafert 1982: vii).

An effective tool for analysing the ways in which historic and journalistic texts reproduce power-based inequalities is critical discourse analysis. This method of close reading analysis, combined with an understanding of the frame of reference in which a text was produced, allows us to assess the significance of particular ideas or meaning in historical documents or in the journalism of a given period and offers insight into the ways problematic representations continue to manifest. As discussed, these misrepresentations often rely on the use of stereotypes, a key component in what Gerbner labelled 'symbolic annihilation', a process that relies on stereotyping, misrepresentation, or underrepresentation to maintain the status quo by failing to give authentic voice to marginalised groups

(Gerbner and Gross nd). Tuchman saw the same process working by means of omission, trivialisation and condemnation (Tuchman et al. 1978). All of these means have been used, sometimes subconsciously, at other times with determined deliberation, to silence Native voices in the telling of United States history and in news coverage of American Indian issues and identity.

Journalism historian John Coward, in his seminal work on representations of Native Americans in the nineteenth-century press, argues that even in the moments when the tone of news coverage was not negative, it still fell short: 'Nineteenth-century journalists could be sympathetic to Indians from time to time, but they could not render Native Americans as fully realised individuals from cultures as valuable and as important as their own' (Coward 1999: 7). Coward also notes that even in moments when Native leaders or citizens were heard from in their own words, they did not have control over the presentation or editing of those words.

At its most basic level, it is a problem of sourcing. Journalists are trained to seek out the best source for the information necessary to tell the various sides of any story yet, typically, when it comes to stories about Native issues and individuals, journalists end up talking about Native people when they should be in conversation with them. Too often, the conventions of a given field mean Native voices are, once again, silenced, but there are simple, effective ways we can move toward a more authentic representation of American Indians in our history and our journalism.

In our historical scholarship we must take a more interdisciplinary approach in the examination of Native issues, individuals and identity. This requires us to be open to including non-traditional source materials including but not limited to tribal archives and oral histories. As historian Philip J. Deloria explains: 'Indian history – as it is and has been preserved, narrated, and owned by native people – is absolutely central to any thinking about American Indian pasts' (Deloria 2004: 1). It is a call to seek out and cite the research and writings of Indigenous scholars. Lastly, we should not leave history in the past. The problematic representations found in the historical press continue to manifest today; we must connect the past with the present to offer a more thorough and authentic representation. If we as historians do research about, or as journalists report on, Native peoples but fail to be in dialogue with Native scholars and sources, we are complicit in sustaining the systemic processes that have silenced Native voices. Overlooking, or failing to offer, the Native perspective perpetuates power as a weapon in the production of any history or practice, including journalism.

Complexities of naming and labelling

It is also important to acknowledge that issues of American Indian identity are complex and often controversial. As Lakota scholar

Melissa
Greene-Blye

Hilary Weaver argues: 'There is little agreement on precisely what constitutes an Indigenous identity, how to measure it, and who truly has it' (Weaver 2010: 28). The constitution of that identity is further complicated by a lack of consensus on correct terminology; do we use Indian, American Indian, Native American, Indigenous or indigenous? These issues of naming and labelling are problematic within individual tribal communities as well as within the broader Native community, so it is perhaps understandable that non-Native scholars and journalists struggle in this regard. It is more difficult to understand why they repeatedly fail to reach out to sources that can point them in the right direction. One of the easiest sources for information about covering Native issues is the Native American Journalists Association (NAJA). The NAJA website (najanewsroom.com) offers multiple resources to assist both Native and non-Native journalists with their coverage of newsworthy issues affecting Native communities. One of NAJA's long-standing resources is 'BINGO: Reporting in Indian Country edition' which aims to help reporters and editors recognise when they are relying on 'clichéd storytelling' or 'stereotypes'.

Image of 'BINGO: Reporting in Indian Country edition' (courtesy of the Native American Journalists Association)

NAJA also offers an Associated Press (AP) style guide to educate journalists about use of the terms 'Indigenous', 'Tribe', and 'Indian', among others, noting that best practices mean it is always preferable, when possible and appropriate, to use a specific tribal nation name in lieu of blanket labels such as 'Native American' or 'American Indian'.

In once again considering Barzun's discussion around the limitations imposed by the need to name and characterise, it is worth considering whether journalists, who are trained to write clearly and concisely, feel uncomfortable using language they find to be awkward or uncomfortable or that they consider to be difficult or confusing for their audience. Indigenous journalist Jenni Monet points out that often when a specific nation is named, it is because it carries a sense of familiarity for the intended audience, names such as the Lakota, Navajo or Cherokee: 'It is not a mistake that these tribes are among the most popular in the mainstream because the mainstream goes towards the familiar' (Monet 2019). It is also important to note that 'Dine' is the name preferred in place of Navajo, as Lakota is the proper name for the nation once popularly referred to as Sioux. Also worth noting is that 'Sioux' was a blanket term for many autonomous tribes and bands with similar, yet distinct dialects. But it is important to ask since some generations still use the older names to identify themselves and their broader communities. It is this type of detail, when overlooked, that fuels criticism of non-Native coverage of Indian issues and identity.

Challenges within and without

There seems to be an unwritten assumption in the broader media industry that ongoing coverage of Indian Country is the sole purview of tribal news outlets and Native journalists; this assumption is problematic for multiple reasons. Too often, stories about Native communities and individuals that capture the attention of major national news outlets are not 'news' to the communities and individuals affected, meaning the issues and challenges receiving attention have been ongoing for years, if not generations. When a Native-centric story makes national headlines, it is typically because it is part of a larger non-Native narrative. The coverage often perpetuates negative stereotypes, furthers ongoing coverage gaps and solidifies the existing distrust Native communities often feel toward outsiders (Alvarez 2019).

Dr Sandy Grande, director of the Center for Critical Study of Race and Ethnicity at Connecticut College, examined this dynamic at work in non-Native press coverage of the protests surrounding the Dakota Access Pipeline (DAPL) in 2016. Grande explains how the mediated 'spectacularised' version of 'the Indian' employs hyper-visibility as a means of perpetuating Indigenous invisibility, ultimately elevating Indigenous performance 'at the expense of *actual* Indigenous voices and histories' (Grande 2019: 1022). Citing analysis from Fairness and Accuracy in Reporting (FAIR), an organisation that advocates for diverse viewpoints in news reporting, Grande points out how the '#NoDAPL warrior' representation overshadowed the Lakota peoples and Indigenous water protectors as major news outlets focused on the story as a 'clash' between protestors and various law enforcement agencies: 'Water protectors were consistently misrepresented as protestors (not protectors), agitators, and trespassers engaged in a "clash" with Morton County officials and Energy Transfer Partners; such false equivalences between unarmed peaceful protectors and heavily armed officers and their billionaire corporate backers can only be drawn through erasures of history and power' (ibid).

Courtesy of honorearth.org, an organisation dedicated to raising awareness of, and money for, Indigenous struggles for environmental justice

A 'conflict' focus in news content also serves to frame the story as a 'negative' versus a 'positive', highlighting oppositional elements instead of proactive ones, 'emphasizing the objection to the pipeline rather than the goal of saving the region's water supply'. Mendoza and Reese contextualise the events at Standing Rock as part of the ongoing struggle by Indigenous peoples to protect their sovereignty and vital resources, arguing that 'the Standing Rock resistance was especially effective at interrupting stereotypes and mistaken ideas about Indigenous peoples that have infected the minds of non-Native people since the 1400s' (cited in Dunbar-Ortiz 2019: 212). While there are differing opinions regarding the efficacy of media representations at Standing Rock, there is agreement that there is still much work to be done to provide authentic, accurate representations which are appropriately situated within the larger historical narrative as it relates to the lived experiences of Native individuals.

NAJA's 2020 *Media spotlight report* reinforces the need to seek out appropriate sourcing when covering Indigenous peoples and communities. In a qualitative thematic analysis of news coverage by five national news outlets in the United States, NAJA researchers concluded: 'A lot of the stories we reviewed included placing people in the past and official-heavy interviewing versus talking to those impacted in communities. Sadly, there were *not* a lot of Indigenous journalists reporting on Indigenous issues within this sample; we feel had there been more Indigenous authors, these stories would have included more inclusive community sources' (NAJA 2020).

Findings such as these reinforce the belief that non-Native media outlets are not equipped to accurately cover stories in Indian Country (Dunbar-

Ortiz 2019). A frequently cited example of this resulted from news coverage of a 2016 case involving a six-year-old Choctaw girl who had been placed with a White foster family. The story made national news, but there was a stark contrast in the tone of the coverage based on who was telling the story. KGO-TV, the ABC affiliate in San Francisco, California, headlined its coverage on 20 March 2016: 'Indian Child Welfare Act separates foster daughter from Santa Clarita family', going on to tell readers on its website: 'In photos, they are a happy family – but Sunday could be the worst day for the lives of Rusty and Summer Page and their 6-year-old foster daughter, Lexi.' The story notes that Lexi is 1.5 per cent Choctaw. 'Because of that, her case fell under the Indian Child Welfare Act (ICWA), a federal law passed in the 1970s that aims to protect the best interests of Native American children and promote stability of tribal families' (Powell 2016). That same week in a news report dated 22 March 2016, indianz.com ran a story headlined: 'Anti-Indian Child Welfare Act attorney takes on another dispute.' This article offers a more detailed explanation of the facts of the case, explaining that it has been ongoing for at least two years, that the foster family knew for some time that 'Alexandria P.', the child they called 'Lexi', fell under the guidelines of the ICWA and that the father had been pursuing his parental rights for several years leading up to 'Lexi's' removal from the Page home (Indianz 2016).

Before the passage of the ICWA, generations of Native children had been taken from their communities, first by missionaries and government officials and, later, by social workers, all representatives of a government that believed assimilation into the dominant society through adoption, foster care or education in off-reservation boarding schools was in the long-term best interests of those children. These policies of placing Indian children in non-Indian homes and families serves to perpetuate the assimilationist policies of the nineteenth and twentieth centuries which resulted in 'a de facto ethnocide of values, attitudes, and customs' (Westermeyer 1977: 48). Native children were forced to substitute Euro-American values, language and dress for their traditional ones.

Anthropologist Pauline Turner Strong, in drawing a comparison between modern day legal cases challenging ICWA and colonial-era captivity narratives made popular in early-American books and newspapers, points once again to the importance of connecting the past with the present in any news coverage of Native issues, noting the problematic coverage that results when non-Native media outlets fail to understand and 'appreciate the strength of these historical memories' (Strong 2013). The need to provide this critical historical context is an important way news media could include the Native perspective in coverage of issues affecting Native communities.

While finding credible and appropriate Native sources is clearly crucial to improving reporting on the issues facing Native communities, we must also consider that an emphasis on demanding that it must be a Native journalist covering Native issues may have unintended consequences for those journalists. Many Native scholars, artists and professionals feel a responsibility to give back to or advocate for their respective communities. Doing so is certainly an important and oft-needed use of their time and talents, but when a Native person excels in their chosen field without making their work explicitly about their lived experience, we must consider how we choose to identify that individual. Must they always identify as Native American before identifying with their chosen field, i.e. a 'Cherokee doctor' versus a doctor who happens to be Cherokee? The danger being that work done by Native journalists on topics other than those directly affecting Native communities could be overlooked, resulting in a 'professional pigeonholing' of that journalist. Failing to recognise that Native journalists are journalists first, meaning they share the same training and skill-set as a non-Native journalist and are equipped to report any story, is ultimately another way of silencing them, particularly when Native individuals are disproportionately missing in the employment stats of most newsrooms.[2]

Another problematic issue resulting from the emphasis on Native journalists covering Native issues brings us back to the need to acknowledge once again that the terms 'Native American' and 'American Indian' are generic. There are almost 600 federally-recognised tribal nations (alongside other nations who are not federally recognised) living within the borders of the United States; to assume a journalist, simply because they are 'Native' can be the voice for all 'Native' issues nullifies the unique histories and experiences of individual Indigenous communities while simultaneously reinforcing the generic 'Indian' stereotype.

Conclusions

For many Native journalists it is an ongoing struggle to find a balance: recognising the need to tell stories from an Indigenous perspective that are relevant to specific tribal communities, while also fighting to have non-Native news outlets recognise the news value in those same stories. Many Native journalists see the coverage of DAPL as a hopeful starting point. According to Jenni Monet, an award-winning independent journalist who is a member of the Laguna Pueblo tribe: 'Standing Rock is going to continue to be a case study for us when we look at the power of Indigenous media' (Monet 2017: Section 3). For Monet, 'the goal is an intentional integration of Indigenous perspective into the dominant narrative' (Monet 2019: Section 2). For that to come to fruition there are some challenges that must be addressed.

Economics certainly factor into the picture. Newsroom budgets are shrinking nationwide which means staff numbers are down and ultimately there are fewer journalists to cover the plethora of stories in any given news cycle. In that environment the 'easy grab' stories that affect the broadest segment of the news audience are going to receive more attention. As bleak as the budget outlook is for mainstream media outlets, economic sustainability has always been a challenge for Native news outlets. Independent outlets struggle to survive and, while some outlets benefit from tribal funding, that also sometimes means tribal journalists feel pressured to appease tribal leadership. That can influence which stories are covered and how they are covered and, in extreme cases, can prompt outright censorship (Woods 2020) This contributes to a credibility challenge for Native media outlets under the auspices of journalistic objectivity; this same issue also contributes to another challenge to integrating Native journalists into the larger journalistic narrative. Many times, contributors providing content for Native outlets are agenda-based, coming from an activist or advocacy background rather than a journalistic one and may decrease the likelihood of those stories being used in non-Native outlets. The conversation necessary to address these challenges to tribal and Indigenous news outlets and journalists is beyond the scope of this paper, but it must be acknowledged as part of the larger conversation around the silencing of Native voices in the broader journalism discourse.

The challenges outlined in this paper serve as a clarion call on the absolute necessity of placing Native people in the centre of their own narrative, enabling them to 'assume authority over their stereotypes' as so aptly stated by West. To make that come to fruition we must be willing to reconsider and redefine what we think we know about what it means to be Native American, starting with the labels we choose in describing individuals who are citizens of Native nations. It requires us to reevaluate the history we know and the stories we tell ourselves about the people and events that led us to where we are today. It will also require adjustments and improvements in the way we train journalists, with an eye toward telling more inclusive, more authentic stories in the future. An important way to meet this goal is to ensure the viability of Indigenous media outlets and through including those outlets, and the journalists who work for them, in the broader discourse of journalism as it is practised in the United States.

Notes

[1] The issue of preferred 'naming' or 'labelling' can prove to be challenging for both scholar and journalist alike. Historian Malinda Maynor Lowery (a member of the Lumbee Tribe of North Carolina) contends that labels such as 'Indian' or 'Native American' are insufficient and confusing because their meanings and use are dependent on context and varied cultural perspectives. Lowery suggests prioritising the words that people use to describe themselves while also being aware of the context and audience. In the United States, most Native individuals will use the term 'Indian' when they are talking amongst themselves. These same individuals might use 'American Indian', 'Native American' or simply 'Native' or 'Indigenous' when speaking in a multi-tribal or international context. The author follows this precedent for purposes of this article. For more on this discussion see: Lowery, Malinda Maynor (2010) Introduction to *Lumbee Indians in the Jim Crow south: Race, identity, & the making of a nation*, Chapel Hill, University of North Carolina Press p. xxv

[2] For an examination of trends in minority hiring over time see: Becker, Lee B., Lauf, Edmund and Lowrey, Wilson (1999) Differential employment rates in the journalism and mass communication labor force based on gender, race, and ethnicity: Exploring the impact of affirmative action, *Journalism & Mass Communication Quarterly*, Vol. 76,

No. 4 pp 631–645. Available online at https://doi.org/10.1177/107769909907600402. For an analysis of current statistics see: Tameez, Hanaa' (2020) Two new studies about media and diversity can help newsrooms through their reckoning with racism, Nieman Lab, 26 June. Available online at https://www.niemanlab.org/2020/06/two-new-studies-about-media-and-diversity-can-help-newsrooms-through-their-reckoning-with-racism/. The same information is also available online at https://pewrsr.ch/3dBuMsK

References

Alvarez, Destiny (2019) 7 tips for non-native journalists covering indigenous communities, *International Journalists' Network*. Available online at https://ijnet.org/en/story/7-tips-non-native-journalists-covering-indigenous-communities

Anderson, Benedict (2016 [2006]) *Imagined communities: Reflections on the origin and spread of nationalism*, New York, Verso

Barzun, Jacques (1973) Cultural history as a synthesis, Stern, Fritz (ed.) *The varieties of history from Voltaire to the present*, New York, Vintage pp 387–402

Carey, James (2011) The problem of journalism history, Brennan, Bonnie and Hardt, Hanno (eds) *The American journalism history reader*, New York, Routledge pp 22–27

Coward, John (1999) *The newspaper Indian: Native American identity in the press, 1820-90*, Chicago, University of Illinois Press

Deloria, Philip J. (2004) Introduction, Deloria, Phillip J. and Salisbury, Neal (eds) *A companion guide to American Indian history*, Malden, Blackwell Publishing

Deloria Jr., Vine (1969) *Custer died for your sins: An Indian manifesto*, Norman, University of Oklahoma Press

Dunbar-Ortiz, Roxanne (2019) *An Indigenous peoples' history of the United States for young people*, adapted by Jean Mendoza and Debbie Reese, Boston, Beacon

Gerbner, George and Gross, Larry (nd) *Cultural indicators: The social reality of television drama*, unpublished manuscript, Annenberg School of Communications, Pennsylvania, University of Pennsylvania

Gramsci, Antonio (2011 [1947]) *Prison notebooks: Volumes I-III*, New York, Columbia University Press

Grande, Sandy (2019) Refusing the settler society of the spectacle, McKinley, Elizabeth Ann and Tuhiwai Smith, Linda (eds) *Handbook of Indigenous education*, New York, Springer pp 1013–1029

Hamilton, James F (1987) Newspapers, migration, and small town culture, *Journalism History*, Vol. 14, No. 2 pp 78–85. Available online at https://doi.org/10.1080/00947679.1987.2066647

Indianz (2016) Anti-Indian Child Welfare Act attorney takes on another dispute, 22 March. Available online at https://www.indianz.com/News/2016/020764.asp

Lippmann, Walter (1965 [1922]) *Public opinion*, New York, The Free Press

Monet, Jenni (2017) Native American journalists break free of mainstream media, RFI, 30 October. Available online at https://www.rfi.fr/en/americas/20171029-native-american-media. For more about Jenni Monet's work see https://www.jennimonet.com

Monet, Jenni (2019) The crisis in covering Indian country, *Columbia Journalism Review*, 29 March. Available online at https://www.cjr.org/opinion/indigenous-journalism-erasure.php

Native American Journalists Association (2020) *Media spotlight report*. Available online at https://najanewsroom.com/wp-content/uploads/2020/02/2020-2-5-Media-Spotlight.pdf

Powell, Amy (2016) Indian Child Welfare Act separates foster daughter from Santa Clarita family, ABC7, 21 March. Available online at http://abc7news.com/news/indian-child-welfare-act-separates-foster-daughter-from-santa-clarita-family/1254346/

Rafert, Stewart (1982) The hidden community: The Miami Indians of Indiana, 1846-1940, PhD dissertation, University of Delaware

Stoler, Ann Laura (2009) *Along the archival grain: Epistemic anxieties and colonial common sense*, Princeton, Princeton University Press

Strong, Pauline Turner (2013) *American Indians and the American imaginary: Cultural representation across the centuries,* New York, Routledge

Tuchman, Gaye, Daniels, Arlene Kaplan and Bénét, James (eds) (1978) *Hearth and home: Images of women in the mass media,* New York, Oxford University Press

Weaver, Hilary N. (2010) Indigenous identity: What is it, and who really has it? Lobo, Susan, Talbot, Steve and Morris, Traci (eds) *Native voices,* Boston, Prentice Hall pp 28–35

West, W. Richard (2007) Introduction, Barrows, Sally (ed.) *Do all Indians live in tipis? Questions and answers from the National Museum of the American Indian,* New York, HarperCollins

Westermeyer, Joseph (1977) The ravage of Indian families in crisis, Unger, Steven (ed.) *The destruction of American Indian families,* New York, Association of American Indian Affairs pp 47–56

Williams, Raymond (2015) *Keywords: A vocabulary of culture and society,* New York, Oxford University Press

Woods, Alden (2020) Our *New York Times*: Premier tribal news outlet relaunches, still faces old hurdles, *AzCentral*, 13 June. Available online at https://www.azcentral.com/story/news/local/arizona-best-reads/2018/06/13/indian-country-today-revived-after-closure-aims-cover-tribal-news-mark-trahant/677380002/

Note on the contributor

Melissa Greene-Blye is an enrolled citizen of the Miami Tribe of Oklahoma. Her research examines journalistic representations and negotiations of American Indian identity past and present. Most recently, her work has been published in *Journalism History* and *American Journalism*. She has presented research at the American Journalism Historians Association annual conference as well as the Joint Journalism Conference held in New York City each year. Melissa worked as an anchor and reporter during 20 years in the news business. She enjoys using her knowledge and experience to educate the newest generation of journalists.

Conflict of Interest

The author did not receive any funding for this research or publication.

PAPER

Victoria LaPoe
Sarah Liese
Candi Carter Olson
Cristina Azocar
Benjamin R. LaPoe II
Bharbi Hazarika
Julia Weber

We are not your offensive mascots: Knowledge surveys exploring US national coverage and comments about Native people

The harmful effects that Indigenous-themed mascots have created for Indigenous communities have prompted some US educational institutions and national sports teams to rethink and discard their mascots. In 2018, a year after then-US President Donald J. Trump took office, a national baseball team retired their racist mascot. That same year, we developed and administered a national survey, as well as a student survey, about media use, political engagement, censorship and Indigenous communities. Using priming, researchers shared factual reports to see if respondents' views changed on mascot imagery as well as politically-charged federal events and if respondents later understood their views as unethical. We discovered low levels of general knowledge about Indigenous communities. We found student respondents more likely than the general population to be able to identify racist names and imagery. We also found that respondents overall were far more likely to identify and call out racism in political situations than in sporting spheres.

Key words: Indigenous, politics, sports, knowledge surveys, mascots

Introduction

The relationship between Indian Country and the United States is built on a constant fight for politics, power and policy. Perhaps the most visible space for Indigenous people's battles to control their identities and representations in popular culture has been in athletics, where school-age to professional teams have co-opted Indigenous images for their mascots. These co-opted images have exaggerated, caricatured features coupled with belittling, cartoonish names, such as the memorably offensive 'Chief Noc-a-Homa' and 'Chief Wahoo'. The result of that imagery has prompted ongoing protests, as illustrated by activity on social media and in US Indigenous communities.

While Atlanta discontinued 'Chief Noc-a-Homa' in 1985, Major League Baseball (MLB) did not ban the demonic-looking Cleveland 'Chief Wahoo', with its garish red face and triangle-shaped eyes, until 2018. The National Football League's (NFL) Washington DC team recently changed its name from 'Redskins' to 'Commanders' after growing protests against the racist name (Homler 2021). Graham Brewer (Cherokee Nation) (2021) notes that changing the name does not end the harm that racialised images of Native Americans have inflicted on Indigenous people. Our research here examines the use of social media during the 2018 election season to examine Americans' views on athletic teams that use mascots reflecting US Indigenous stereotypes.

Imagery injustice and Indian Country

When the act of cultural appropriation occurs, 'there is always a power imbalance that is being exploited' (Keane 2016: 56). Imagery injustice is cultural appropriation, often evident in mockery, erasure and disparagement of cultures and people.

In the US, the most televised broadcast in 2020 was the Super Bowl LIV (Pucci 2020). It pitted NFL teams Kansas City Chiefs against San Francisco 49ers, two teams whose 'names, iconographies and fan cultures play off of and in some cases trivialise real history and real suffering that has occurred and continues to occur to real people' (Rozsa 2020: para 34). Kansas City's name, Chiefs, has been contentious because of its appropriation of stereotypical Indigenous imagery including fans painting their faces, performing a gesture known as the Arrowhead Tomahawk Chop, and showcasing a horse named 'War Paint'.[1] Rhonda LeValdo (Acoma Pueblo) (2021), an instructor at Haskell Indian Nations University in Kansas, wrote in *Vox* that teaching people about why Native mascot names are inappropriate is important because they are a reminder of 'massacres, racism, and genocide carried out against the people Indigenous to this country. It is also getting exhausting' (para 8). Granted, the debate over sports mascots did not begin nor end with one Super Bowl game. Suzan Shown Harjo (Cheyenne and Hodulgee Muscogee) has actively fought for Indigenous rights and against mascots for more than 60 years (Little and Little 2017). Political symbolism in sports is deeply rooted in America's fabric, from

Victoria LaPoe

Sarah Liese

Candi Carter Olson

Cristina Azocar

Benjamin R. LaPoe II

Bharbi Hazarika

Julia Weber

presidents throwing the first pitch on opening day of MLB games to Colin Kaepernick protesting racial inequality by kneeling during the national anthem before NFL games (Rozsa 2020). The politics of selling race-based imagery and negativity is not just prevalent in sports. Former US President Donald Trump used the name 'Pocahontas', a past living Indigenous woman, as a racial slur, referring to Massachusetts senator Elizabeth Warren. During an event meant to honour the Navajo Code Talkers, Trump used the same racial insult when referencing his political rival, Elizabeth Warren. He also met with the code talkers in front of a picture of Andrew Jackson, a former president who signed the 1830 Indian Removal Act, which acted as a catalyst for displacing thousands of Indigenous people in America (Taylor 2017).

Literature review

Non-Indigenous journalists continue to misrepresent Indigenous narratives across the US. For example, the reduction of land in the Bears Ears National Monument in Utah left Indigenous sacred sites open to desecration through mining operations. The most well-known examples globally are perhaps protests against the Dakota Access pipeline. The topic made international headlines and brought thousands of people from around the world to where the pipeline would cross the Missouri River close to the Standing Rock Indian Reservation in North Dakota. Related pipeline protests also appeared in international news publications, such as the Keystone XL pipeline that impacted on multiple Indigenous nations in both the United States and Canada. News narratives repeated government framing of the protesters as 'extremists and violent criminals', and that same government framing 'warned of potential "terrorism", according to recently released records' (Parrish and Levin 2018: para 3).

Representation in media

Representations of Indigenous people by US non-Indigenous media have traditionally attempted to erase Indigenous people with stories that misrepresent the reality of Indigenous lives. A special report by student investigative reporters for the University of Montana's *Montana Journalism Review* found that 'partisan narratives on social media overtook old-fashioned reporting methods' for reporters who were working on the Standing Rock protests (Stone et al. 2016: para 6). The students found that:

> Traditional media outlets were frequently criticized for neglecting the story, while a Google News search in late November 2016 yielded 1.6 million results for 'Standing Rock'. Demonstrators blamed professional journalists for focusing on violence, but even on social channels, interest spiked whenever violence occurred. The vast majority of people at the Standing Rock camps said they learned about the movement from social media, not traditional media, yet social media repeatedly spread misinformation about developments on the ground (Stone et al. 2016: para 10).

Primarily local news organisations covered the protests in the early days, and it was not until the Standing Rock Sioux Tribe filed a lawsuit with the Army Corps of Engineers on 4 August 2016 that the mainstream US media took more widespread notice of the story.

Erasure and annihilation

There is a kind of violence to these narratives that plays into what Gaye Tuchman (1978) theorised as symbolic annihilation. If people form images of reality based on what they see in mass media, Tuchman posited that when mainstream news does not represent people and ideas it may annihilate those same people and ideas from overall public consciousness, rendering them completely unimportant or invisible. The idea of annihilation is violent. If a person or thing is annihilated, there is no recovery. They are obliterated fully and cannot come back to life. If a person's voice is highlighted and foregrounded, however, the moment is empowering and helps to amplify the stories of those who have been previously silenced. Kim TallBear (Sisseton Wahpeton Oyate) (2019) argues that Indigenous people have been consistently annihilated from mainstream narratives so that an ideal of a homogenised United States can exist.

Caricatures and unsound narratives, like stereotypes, can mislead and cause harm. Take for example depictions of Pocahontas, a member of the Pamunkey tribe in the 17th century. The image of Pocahontas in 19th century North American colonial imagery has represented her as both sacrificial virgin and seductress (Mayer 2015). The Disney movie, *Pocahontas* (1995), grossed more than $14 million at the box office (Tapia 2021) while presenting a harmfully inaccurate depiction of her story (Schilling 2017). About two decades after the release of the movie, former President Donald Trump criticised Senator Elizabeth Warren of Massachusetts for identifying as a Native American by calling her 'Pocahontas'. Artists, the team at Disney, and the former president distorted and stretched this Pamunkey woman's image to belittle, mystify and sexualise. The ironic part is that, while the Disney franchise was profiting from a false narrative, the tribe Pocahontas belonged to still was not federally recognised. The Pamunkey tribe did not receive federal recognition until 2016, after fighting for it for 34 years (Stoddard 2016).

Shifting perspectives through knowledge

For almost 20 years, the American Psychological Association (2011) has said 'the continued use of American Indian mascots, symbols, images and personalities' is harmful to Indigenous and non-Indigenous people (para. 3). The organisation called for an end to practices that promoted negative stereotypes and undermined real-life education experiences. Indigenous researcher Stephanie Fryberg (Tulalip Tribe) is quoted in the APA report: 'American Indian mascots are harmful not only because they are often negative, but because they remind American Indians

Victoria LaPoe

Sarah Liese

Candi Carter Olson

Cristina Azocar

Benjamin R. LaPoe II

Bharbi Hazarika

Julia Weber

of the limited ways in which others see them. This in turn restricts the number of ways American Indians can see themselves' (para. 6). Fryberg and her research team on *The reclaiming Native truth* project later found that, 'after hearing accurate history, a majority of Americans – spanning major racial and ethnic groups, ages, and education levels – believe more should be done to help Native Americans' (First Nations 2018: 13). Organisations such as the Native American Journalists Association (2021) have provided resources to disrupt inaccurate news coverage. However, even the power of Indigenous presses to intervene in mainstream narratives is questioned by contact theory, which argues that two different groups can develop tolerant and positive attitudes about one another if they are exposed to one another under circumstances where both groups are given equal status (Zuma 2014).

Research questions

To understand attitudes toward mascots as well as other national US incidents involving Indigenous people, this research asks the following research questions:

>RQ1: What were national respondents' perceptions of US Indigenous communities?

>RQ2: What were national respondents' connections to US Indigenous communities?

>RQ3: When providing national respondents knowledge-based information, did perspectives change about US Indigenous communities?

>RQ4: How did younger respondents in locations with regional sports teams differ from the national and additional youth?

>RQ5: How did younger respondents who note they lived near US Indigenous communities differ in opinion from national US respondents?

>RQ6: How did this overall data speak about understanding of minority communities?

Method

We designed this study considering how priming sheds light on contextual associations for research participants (Gorham 2010; Sullivan and Arbuthnot 2009).

The online survey we designed went out the same day in January 2018 that Cleveland, Ohio's baseball team, announced that they would no longer use 'Chief Wahoo', a stereotypical red-faced cartoon-looking mascot (Creamer 2018). At the same time in Utah, the Bears Ears National Monument was still in the headlines, as President Trump worked to roll back protected boundaries to profit from natural resources there (LaPoe et al. 2018). The survey company Qualtrics administered a national survey until they received a robust enough response. In this case, the sample size ended up being N=1,070. The authors then replicated and administered this survey at two universities – Ohio and Utah State – for a combined total of 206 students, mostly Ohio University students (N=183).

Priming to challenge default perspectives
In a study of Indigenous press coverage, LaPoe and LaPoe (2018) researched the grassroots organisation, Native Lives Matter, during the Dakota Pipeline protests and attitude change based on whether the protestor in the story appeared to be a man or woman, had lighter or darker skin by altering the photo's ambience, or if the story was from the Indigenous or non-Indigenous press. They found that if the story was from an Indigenous news source or if the photo was darker, the mainly White respondents did not believe it was as credible. Since priming had a significant effect, in terms of gender and skin colour, in the LaPoe and LaPoe study, we decided to adapt our analysis in this current study to what they defined as 'knowledge-based priming'.

On a seven-point Likert scale, the survey asked respondents for their level of agreement to the following statements:

- Invoking the name of Pocahontas in a 'name-calling' manner is racist.
- 'Honouring' the Navajo Code Talkers in front of a picture of Andrew Jackson, who signed the Indian Removal Act, is racist. *(Priming effect given here by adding the fact that this president forced Indigenous people to leave their homes and stole their land.)*
- Images such as Cleveland's 'Chief Wahoo' mascot are offensive.
- The Washington NFL team name is racist.
- When you turn people/communities into products to be sold, you take away their human rights. *(Priming effect here: trying to connect thoughts about people and human rights, following Indian Removal Act mentioned above.)*
- Please indicate your agreement on the following: all American Indian mascots, symbols, images, and personalities should be changed. *(Priming effect given here by linking to the memo by the American Psychological Association study that notes the psychological effects of mascots on youth.)*
- Washington's NFL team logo should be changed.

Additional knowledge questions
Two more knowledge-based questions followed these statements, so we could understand our respondents' level of general knowledge. The first question: 'How many federally recognised tribes are there in the

Victoria LaPoe

Sarah Liese

Candi Carter Olson

Cristina Azocar

Benjamin R. LaPoe II

Bharbi Hazarika

Julia Weber

United States?'[2] Choices included less than 100, 100-200, 200-300, 300-400, 400-500 or 500 or more. After this question, we had an open-ended question asking for respondents to try to add context to their answers; it asked for participants to 'respond in detail your knowledge of Native American communities. Please list any news sources (Native/non-Native) and/or any other areas where you have gained information or had meaningful interaction with Native American communities'.

We also asked about participants' level of activism connected to current US issues, using a seven-point agreement scale. Response for engagement and activism are much lower in the national survey (Table 1) than the student surveys (Table 2).

Engagement and activism

Table 1. *National survey respondents' level of activism in connection with current issues in US*

Activism activity	Strongly Agree %	Agree %	Somewhat Agree %	Neutral %	Somewhat Disagree %	Disagree %	Strongly Disagree %
I protested	8.1	6.8	7.0	22.8	6.0	18.2	31.3
I helped organise a protest	6.2	3.9	4.4	21.4	6.6	19.3	38.2
I posted/shared content	13.7	13.3	14.1	21.6	5.6	12.6	19.1
I discussed with friends/peers	20.9	20.5	19.1	17.4	3.9	6.6	11.8
I debated online/ through social media	10.2	12.3	12.2	19.9	5.4	14.9	24.5
I donated money to an organisation I am passionate about	11.2	11.6	7.7	19.9	6.8	13.3	29.5
Other	11.4	7.4	3.4	38.3	3.4	11.4	24.8

Table 2. *Student survey respondents' level of activism in connection with current issues in US*

Activism activity	Strongly Agree %	Agree %	Neutral %	Disagree %	Strongly Disagree %
I protested	19.7	14.3	23.2	23.12	19.7
I helped organise a protest	14.9	4.0	23.8	33.2	24.3
I posted/shared content	26.6	24.6	23.7	14.3	10.8
I discussed with friends/ peers	37.6	30.2	19.8	6.9	5.5
I debated online/ through social media	20.2	16.8	24.7	24.1	14.3
I donated money to an organisation I am passionate about	20.2	12.8	22.7	26.6	17.7
Other	22.9	3.0	53.0	7.8	13.3

Demographics

In the national survey sample, the biggest age group was 65 or above (16 per cent); the rest of the age groups varied from 7 to 15 per cent. Most of the respondents were female (60 per cent), heterosexual (88.2 per cent), White (67 per cent), 'Christian' (38 per cent) or 'Catholic' (18 per cent). More people were educated to high school graduate (27 per cent) and bachelor degree levels (20 per cent) than to other levels. The largest region was the South (37 per cent), followed by Midwest (23 per cent); other regions (North, East and West) ranged between 12 and 14 per cent. The majority of respondents lived in the suburbs (43 per cent), followed by urban (29 per cent) and rural (24 per cent) areas.

In the student sample, the largest groups within the sample were aged 18-24 (99 per cent), female (73 per cent), heterosexual (89 per cent), White (76 per cent). Among other ethnicities were Black (9 per cent), Asian (3 per cent), American Indian/Alaska Native (2 per cent) and Hispanic (1.36 per cent). The largest religious affiliations were 'Christian' (32 per cent) and 'Catholic' (20 per cent). Most came from the Midwest (55 per cent). Other regions were represented as follows: North (17 per cent), East (16 per cent), West (8 per cent) and South (4 per cent). Students were largely from suburban areas (62 per cent), followed by rural (30 per cent) and urban (8 per cent).

Findings and discussion

We analysed the results of the national and student surveys first together and then separately. We have presented the research by each research question, highlighting salient perceptions found within the survey as well as overall beliefs about media use, political engagement, censorship and Indigenous communities. We compared different demographics to highlight differing perspectives. For example, one subsample we analysed included respondents who said they were Indigenous, had Indigenous family members or friends, were familiar with Indigenous reservations (lived in, worked in or visited Indigenous communities frequently) and/or were actively or recently engaged in Indigenous research or news. We compared that subset to participants who had no interactions or knowledge pertaining to Indigenous people and communities.

RQ1: What were national respondents' perceptions of US Native communities?

The survey revealed respondents had low general knowledge about Native peoples. Fourteen per cent of respondents were aware that there are more than 500 recognised tribes in the United States. A majority of respondents had limited to no knowledge on Native communities nor sought out information connected to Indigenous people. Many had never interacted with any Native communities. However, those who had information gained it from friends, family, news channels or social media. For instance, one respondent wrote, 'most information that I've

Victoria LaPoe

Sarah Liese

Candi Carter Olson

Cristina Azocar

Benjamin R. LaPoe II

Bharbi Hazarika

Julia Weber

seen about Native Americans I got from Twitter. I don't really know much about their communities except stereotypes like they gamble a lot'.

Overall, a majority of respondents expressed a neutral view on whether a mascot or name-calling is racist, some adding: 'I don't know.' However, there was an apparent divide between people's understanding of what counts as racist. Although more than 21 per cent strongly agreed that 'when you turn people/communities into products to be sold, you take away their human rights', only 9 per cent felt that 'all American Indian mascots, symbols, images, and personalities should be changed'. Twenty-two per cent of the respondents strongly disagreed that mascots and other American Indian imagery used in professional sports were racist at all. Instead, these respondents justified it as an honorary practice or, as one survey participant put it, 'just a name'.

There were large differences for two attitude statements: 'Invoking the name of Pocahontas in a "name-calling" manner is racist' and 'The Washington NFL name is racist'. While almost 37 per cent of the students believed that name-calling, using terms such as 'Pocahontas', was racist, approximately 22 per cent of the national survey participants strongly disagreed that the Washington NFL name, 'Redskin', was racist.

In most answers to the open-ended question of whether name-calling 'Pocahontas' is racist, participants mentioned Senator Warren most of the time, which suggests that they directly associated the term with the Massachusetts senator. Those who disagreed with the statement that 'invoking the name of Pocahontas in a "name-calling" manner is racist' tended to justify the usage by saying it was 'just inappropriate and stupid' but 'not racist'. Those participants who felt that 'name-calling' was a racist act expressed strong sentiments claiming it to be 'offensive' and 'careless'.

In contrast, only 10 to 11 per cent strongly agreed that the former Washington NFL team and logo should be changed. Similarly, the statement that 'images such as Cleveland's "Chief Wahoo" mascot are offensive' met with disagreement, with 19 per cent feeling strongly that such mascots were not offensive. Respondents justified the usage by explaining it as a 'cartoon' or 'only a fictional comic character'. Survey results also revealed that more than 15 per cent strongly agreed with the statement '"Honouring" the Navajo Code Talkers in front of a picture of Andrew Jackson, who signed the Indian Removal Act, is racist.'

The results of the survey clearly show the stark difference in US national respondents' perceptions of what is racist. For the most part, respondents did not perceive American Indian imagery in sports to be racist. However, usage of Indigenous references in political and social scenarios was met with a relatively negative attitude. Still, a majority of the respondents held a neutral view towards the issues, which suggests that their attitudes toward US Indigenous communities are indifferent or they are not knowledgeable enough to understand the issues.

RQ2: What were national respondents' connections to US Indigenous communities?

In the national survey, participants were asked an open-ended question on their connection, or lack thereof, to Native American communities. We categorised the responses in 10 sections: no knowledge, unsure of their knowledge, minimal knowledge, locational knowledge, is Indigenous or has Indigenous family members, has Indigenous friends, receives information about US Indigenous communities through news, receives information about Indigenous communities through the internet or social media, receives information about Indigenous communities through school or research, and has worked for tribal Nations or on a reservation. In multiple cases, some of the responses overlapped and thus certain categories were combined to maintain accuracy.

Fifty-seven per cent of respondents said they were unsure or had no knowledge pertaining to US Indigenous communities. When asked: 'How many federally recognised tribes are there in the United States,' 15 per cent answered with the correct answer '500 or more'. Only 2 per cent of participants stated that their understanding of US Indigenous communities was established in school or by conducting their own research, which would explain the small percentage of respondents who knew the accurate number of federally recognised tribes in the United States. Additionally, 6 per cent had family members or friends who were Indigenous while 0.38 per cent said they worked on a reservation or for a tribal Nation. In total, 3 per cent identified as American Indian or Alaska Native.

Among some of the responses were comments such as: 'The Indian reservations are self-governed, and they have a lot of alcohol problems … and rape problem(s)' suggesting the participant had negligible knowledge – as evident in the described stereotypes – and they were classified in the minimal knowledge category with those who simply responded that they had 'little to no' or 'barely any' knowledge. In total, 16 per cent of respondents made up the minimal knowledge category. Those who had entirely inaccurate knowledge were put into the 'no knowledge' category.

Location was also a factor of identifying the surveyed participants' level of awareness, evidenced by the fact that 5 per cent of participants noted they had some connection with or lived near US Indigenous communities. These participants listed specific areas where Native communities could be found, either by specifying the state, the reservation or both.

Out of those who sought information regarding US Indigenous communities, 5 per cent acquired information through social media

Victoria LaPoe

Sarah Liese

Candi Carter Olson

Cristina Azocar

Benjamin R. LaPoe II

Bharbi Hazarika

Julia Weber

or the internet. Most respondents provided obscure answers, such as 'Facebook' or 'Google'. Out of the total respondents, only 8 per cent said they turned to the news media to learn about Indigenous communities, with many (8 per cent) relying on mainstream news outlets such as CBS, CNN, Fox News and *The New York Times*, while a minority sought out Native news outlets.

RQ3: When providing national respondents knowledge-based information, did perspectives change about US Indigenous communities?

In the national sample, we asked participants to select how strongly they agreed or disagreed with eight statements related to Native Americans, including symbols and situations that participants could view as racist. The results did not show that there was a notable shift in their agreement with these statements, particularly after respondents were made aware of an APA study that noted the psychological effects of mascots on both Indigenous and non-Indigenous people, specifically youth. In fact, most of the respondents expressed neutral attitudes towards the changing of the Washington NFL team name and logo, with the second highest percentage saying they strongly disagreed with these two ideas (24 per cent strongly disagreed with the changing of the Washington NFL team name and 22 per cent strongly disagreed with the changing of the Washington NFL team logo).

RQ4: How did student survey respondents in locations with regional sports teams differ from respondents in the national survey?

More than half of the Utah State University (USU) student respondents (52 per cent) and 43 per cent of the Ohio University (OU) students agreed or strongly agreed with the statement that 'Images such as Cleveland's "Chief Wahoo" mascot are offensive'. One student responder said that 'racist mascots/icons, while a beloved icon in certain circles, are long overdue to be retired'. However, 41 per cent of the national survey respondents felt that such imagery was not offensive. For example, one national respondent said: 'No, they are no worse than cartoon images of whites, blacks, orientals, or any other race.' Others who disagreed expressed it as either a matter of freedom of speech, 'just a cartoon', or chose not to elaborate on their opinion. As we know, 'freedom of speech' can be used as a cloak for speech that incites violence or harm and which damages the building of a sustainable global community.

In contrast, when the respondents were asked if they felt 'the Washington NFL name is racist', there was an overall disagreement with the statement. Fifty-five per cent of the OU student respondents, 52 per cent of the USU student respondents and 48 per cent of the national survey-takers felt that the Washington NFL name was not racist. We note that 27 per cent of the national respondents maintained a neutral stand in response to the statement. Respondents who disagreed with the statement waved it off as a name that was 'never meant to be racist'. One responder said that 'the word racist implies hateful. I don't think "Redskins" is hateful, therefore not racist'. Yet, even the Merriam-Webster dictionary classifies the term 'Redskins' as 'insulting and contemptuous'.

When asked if 'the Washington NFL team should change its name', 59 per cent of the OU student respondents and 46 per cent of the national respondents disagreed with the statement. Several of the respondents felt the name was more a gesture of honour than offence. Additionally, 27 per cent of the national respondents had no opinion or were neutral on this issue. One respondent said that 'it was never meant to be racist, and how is naming your organisation after a group of people offensive – I think it is more honouring them – in the end much ado about nothing!' On the other hand, 61 per cent of the USU student respondents agreed that the Washington NFL team name should change. One USU student respondent felt the name was not 'respectful'.

Similarly, regarding the statement, 'Washington's NFL team logo should be changed', 55 per cent of the OU student respondents and 44 per cent of the national respondents disagreed. Of the national respondents, approximately 27 per cent held a neutral stance in response to the statement. One of the respondents who disagreed said: 'Now once again, it's just an Indian head. There's nothing racist about thinking that they're strong enough to help the team win.'

In contrast to OU and national respondents, just over half of the USU student respondents (57 per cent) felt the Washington NFL team logo should be changed. Those who agreed with the statement felt the Washington NFL team logo was 'racist' and needed to be changed. None of the participants thoroughly explained their negative opinions regarding the logo. Perhaps the majority of USU student respondents were more receptive to the idea that the name and logo of Washington NFL team are offensive because of the location of USU's campus. Utah is home to multiple tribes while the USU campus is closer to the state of Washington than Ohio University is.

RQ5: How did younger respondents who noted living near US Indigenous communities differ in opinion from national US respondents?

When comparing three groups among those surveyed – OU students, USU students and respondents in the national sample – significant differences emerged. A majority of both OU students and USU students agreed or strongly agreed with all of the nine statements listed in the survey, while the majority of respondents in the national sample expressed neutrality for seven statements. The statement in which the majority of national participants did not remain neutral was: 'Invoking the name of "Pocahontas" in a "name-calling" manner is racist' as the majority (24 per cent of all respondents) strongly agreed this act was racist. Almost half of the USU survey participants strongly agreed with the statement: 'When you turn people / communities into products to

Victoria LaPoe

Sarah Liese

Candi Carter Olson

Cristina Azocar

Benjamin R. LaPoe II

Bharbi Hazarika

Julia Weber

be sold, you take away their human rights' compared to 26 per cent of OU participants who strongly agreed.

In the national survey, 34 per cent of respondents, who resided in or had resided near US Indigenous reservations and/or who said they were more knowledgeable about Indigenous issues, strongly disagreed with the statement regarding turning people/communities into products to be sold. However, the majority of this same group of national respondents, 31 per cent, strongly disagreed that the Washington NFL team should change its name, with one respondent stating that 'people are overreacting'.

Those who said they resided near US Indigenous communities and/or were knowledgeable about these communities were examined separately. Those included in this sub-sample consisted of respondents who said they were Indigenous, had Indigenous family members or friends, were familiar with Indigenous reservations (lived in, worked in or visited Indigenous communities frequently) and/or were actively or recently engaged in Indigenous research or news. Among those in this additional sample, most had opposing views from those of the other demographics. For example, the majority of this 'more knowledgeable' sample strongly disagreed with over half of the statements that asked if certain scenarios regarding Native American logos, mascots and situations were offensive. Twenty-four per cent of the sample strongly disagreed that images such as Cleveland's 'Chief Wahoo' were offensive, 25 per cent strongly disagreed that the Washington NFL name was racist, 31 per cent strongly disagreed that the Washington NFL team should change their name and 30 per cent strongly disagreed that Washington's NFL team logo should be changed. All of those percentages listed were the highest percentages compared to the other rating scale percentages. The findings in this section were unexpected and raised questions about how to gauge knowledge about Indigenous communities and whether our sample was an accurate reflection of knowledgeable participants. It should be noted that the respondents' level of understanding could not be completely measured, rather it was trusted that their response was forthright, based on their current comprehension of Native American issues.

One respondent who claimed they had 'several friends who are Native American' strongly disagreed with most of the statements, as this respondent saw the act of using the name 'Pocahontas' to describe Elizabeth Warren as 'just a term for a senator' and that 'a large percentage of Native Americans feel differently' from the idea that the Washington NFL name was racist. Another respondent who said that their 'best friend is Native' strongly disagreed with most of the seven statements. However, not all of the respondents in this sample who said their main or only connection to US Indigenous communities was from a friendship with an Indigenous individual disagreed or strongly disagreed with these statements. For example, one respondent said they had 'Indian friends' from the military and that they 'like that term no matter what others think'. This same respondent strongly agreed that all of the scenarios included in the statements were racist. Additionally, another respondent who said they had a 'best friend' who was Native Apache and 'grew up on a reservation in Oklahoma' agreed with most of the statements – varying from somewhat agree to strongly agree – and was indifferent to the remaining two statements about whether the honouring of the Navajo Code Talkers in front of a picture of Andrew Jackson and the Washington NFL name were racist. Therefore, no concrete conclusion can be drawn that there is a correlation between the alleged identified contact with Indigenous people and viewing the use of Indigenous mascots and symbols as racist.

Regarding the respondents who reported geographical known closeness to US Indigenous communities through location (working on or frequenting Indigenous reservations, or living near US Indigenous communities), 38 per cent strongly disagreed that honouring the Navajo Code talkers in front of a picture of Andrew Jackson, who signed the Indian Removal Act, was racist. This was the case for five other statements inquiring about the level of racism they inferred. The majority of those who said their connection to US Indigenous communities was due to living nearby strongly disagreed that the 'Chief Wahoo' mascot was offensive as well as the Washington NFL name. Out of the total, 43 per cent of those within this group strongly disagreed that both the Washington NFL team should change its name and logo. The only statement this demographic strongly agreed with was concerning the act of name-calling Elizabeth Warren, as 39 per cent concurred this was racist.

RQ6: How did this overall data speak about understanding of minority communities?

The data overall pointed to a disagreement among the survey takers on what constitutes racism. For example, while some believed that the 'Chief Wahoo' symbol was 'racist' and 'offensive', others felt that the imagery was 'fictional' and therefore 'should not be taken too seriously'. The same can be seen in the quantitative data collected. In the national sample, almost 32 per cent agreed that the 'Chief Wahoo' imagery was racist, 40 per cent disagreed and 27 per cent were neutral. Moreover, the latter highlights a trend witnessed throughout the national sample responses: a larger portion of the national respondents tended to be neutral compared to the student responses throughout the data set.

A majority of the participants agreed with the statement that 'invoking the name "Pocahontas" in a name-calling manner is racist', with only 12 per cent of national respondents and 3 per cent of student respondents strongly disagreeing. Similarly, in response to the statement, '"honoring" the Navajo Code Talkers in front of a picture showcasing Andrew Jackson', only 13 per cent of the national respondents and 9 per cent of student respondents strongly disagreed that the event was racist. Respondents were more likely to condemn certain situations that

Victoria LaPoe

Sarah Liese

Candi Carter Olson

Cristina Azocar

Benjamin R. LaPoe II

Bharbi Hazarika

Julia Weber

involved Indigenous individuals rather than offensive mascots employed by sports teams. In the case of the former Washington NFL name, 26 per cent of national respondents and 44 per cent of the student respondents agreed that the name was racist. The majority in both the cases disagreed that the Washington NFL name was racist; participants felt it was more of an honorary symbol than a bigoted name. Thus, we can conclude that there was a palpable discrepancy between people's perceptions of which Indigenous imagery or name is racist.

Moreover, the data revealed that there was an overwhelming lack of knowledge among the survey-takers on US Indigenous communities. As evidenced, 57 per cent of the national respondents and 53 per cent of the student respondents said they were unsure or had no knowledge regarding Indigenous communities. When asked: 'How many federally recognised tribes are there in the United States,' 86 per cent did not offer the correct answer. Most of the national and student respondents said they had 'no knowledge'. Those who claimed to have some knowledge cited mainstream news outlets, the internet and Indigenous friends or relatives as their information sources. Only two participants cited Indigenous news outlets such as *Indian Country Today* as an information source.

The data revealed that national and student respondents were largely unaware of information and issues relating to Indigenous communities. Moreover, there was not a clear trend on any of the attitude statements. However, it was apparent that imagery relating to sports was perceived more positively compared to those involved in political or social rhetoric such as 'Pocahontas' or '"Honoring" Navajo Code Talkers'.

Conclusion

Though sporting events have had a long history involving politicians and presidents throwing the first pitch on opening day, respondents were more opposed to politicians using racist rhetoric than sporting teams using racist imagery. Our data showed that participants allowed sport teams more latitude to utilise inaccurate Indigenous portrayals by writing it off as a trivial issue or glorified acknowledgement.

Despite our inclusion of text boxes for participants to expand on their perceptions, participants did not always elaborate on their reasoning. Therefore, there was no way to reliably identify why all respondents agreed or disagreed with the statements provided. Certain answers written in the text boxes were also left up to interpretation, which could have caused participants to be grouped in a subset that did not fully pertain to the individual. Additionally, it could have been beneficial to ask participants to define 'racist' to clarify their reasoning and overall understanding of the term and potential repercussions of racist choices. The same could also be true about defining the term 'protesting,' especially when respondents were asked about their involvement in protests.

The data offered insight into the lack of general knowledge and understanding about Indigenous communities, which could offer an explanation why participants thought Indigenous imagery in sports was acceptable, as well as racist situations involving politicians. It should be noted that those in our student data sample appeared to be more empathetic overall and tended to express opposition toward sports teams' decisions to utilise Native American mascots or team names. Yet overall, participants had a difficult time recognising the harmful rhetoric and imagery discussed in the survey, even when given information from unbiased sources prior to asking the question. Future research should continue to probe newsrooms and audiences through surveys, interviews, education and exposure to see how to promote important messages that are representative of communities.

Limitations for this study include not having a diverse enough sample. It would be useful to partner with Indigenous and other diverse organisations to have more global perspectives. While we do have some Indigenous self-identified individuals, the numbers are small compared to the number of unique tribes in the US, which is why we are thankful for the *Reclaiming Native truth* project. If we accepted our small sample as speaking for Indigenous communities, it would be unethical and problematic. Future studies should consider a more globally diverse mixed-method data set with robust Indigenous as well as other diverse communities..

Notes

[1] Reporter Jourdan Bennett-Begaye covered the Super Bowl LIV for *Indian Country Today* and noted the irony of a significant Indigenous presence at the event, which featured a team with a racist mascot and traditions, the Kansas City Chiefs (Bennett-Begaye 2023). The article featured telling tweets of Indigenous people protesting over the mascot and non-Indigenous people ignorant to the racism

[2] There are 574 federally recognised tribes in the US, according to the National Congress of American Indians

References

American Psychological Association (APA) (2011) *Summary of the APA resolution recommending retirement of American Indian Mascots*, January. Available online at https://www.apa.org/pi/oema/resources/indian-mascots, accessed on 19 August 2022

Bennett-Begaye, Jourdan (2023) The irony of Kansas City winning Super Bowl LVII – ICT News, *Indian Country Today*, 13 February. Available online at https://ictnews.org/news/the-irony-of-kansas-city-winning-super-bowl-lvii, accessed on 3 April 2023

Brewer, Graham Lee (2021) Cleveland's Guardians' name change isn't the end of the fight against racist symbols in sports, *NBC News*, 30 July. Available online at https://www.nbcnews.com/news/us-news/cleveland-guardians-name-change-isn-t-end-fight-against-racist-n1275509, accessed on 18 August 2022

Creamer, Chris (2018) Cleveland Indians, MLB announce Chief Wahoo is gone after 2018, *Sportslogos.net*, 29 January. Available online at https://news.sportslogos.net/2018/01/29/chief-wahoo-gone-after-2018/baseball/, accessed on 18 August 2022

First Nations Development Institute (2018) *Reclaiming Native truth: Compilation of all research from the* Reclaiming Native truth *project*. Available online at https://www.firstnations.org/publications/compilation-of-all-research-from-the-reclaiming-native-truth-project/, accessed on 18 August 2022

Victoria LaPoe

Sarah Liese

Candi Carter Olson

Cristina Azocar

Benjamin R. LaPoe II

Bharbi Hazarika

Julia Weber

Gorham, Bradley W. (2010) Considerations of media effects: The social psychology of stereotypes: Implications for media audiences, Houston, Akil (ed.) *Beyond blackface: Africana images in US media*, Dubuque, Iowa, Kendall Hunt Publishing, third edition pp 93–101.

Homler, Ryan (2020) A timeline of Washington football team's name change saga, *NBC Sports*, 3 June. Available online at https://www.nbcsports.com/washington/football-team/timeline-washington-football-teams-name-change-saga, accessed on 19 August 2022

Keane, Adrienne (2016) Engaging Indigeneity and avoiding appropriation: An interview with Adrienne Keane, *The English Journal*, Vol. 106, No. 1 pp 55–57. Available online at http://www.jstor.org/stable/26359320

LaPoe, Benjamin R. and LaPoe, Victoria L. (2018) Online momentum: Priming in the Native American press, LaPoe, Victoria L., Carter Olson, Candi S. and LaPoe, Benjamin R. (eds) *Underserved communities and digital discourse*, New York, Lexington Books pp 171–184

LaPoe, Victoria L., Tallent, R. J., Ahtone, Tristan and LaPoe, Benjamin R. (2018) Ethics and reporting on native communities: Going beyond the parachute story, LaPoe, Victoria L., Carter Olson, Candi S. and LaPoe Benjamin R. (eds) *Underserved communities and digital discourse*, New York, Lexington Books pp 185–203

LeValdo, Rhonda (2021) The Kansas City Chiefs' racist 'Arrowhead Chop' chant isn't a tribute to people like me. It's racist, *Vox*, February 6. Available online at https://www.vox.com/first-person/2020/2/1/21115858/super-bowl-2020-chiefs-kansas-city, accessed on 19 August 2022

Little, John and Little, Kenn (2017) *More than a word* [video], Kanopy. Available online at https://www.kanopy.com/product/more-word, accessed on 19 August 2022

Mayer, Sophie (2015) Pocahontas no more: Indigenous women standing up for each other in twenty-first century cinema, *Alphaville: Journal of Film and Screen Media*, Vol. 10 pp 113–128. Available online at https://doi.org/10.33178/alpha.10.07

Native American Journalists Association (NAJA) (2021) 2021 NAJA media spotlight report, *NAJAnewsroom*, 2 August. Available online at https://najanewsroom.com/2021-naja-media-spotlight-report/, accessed on 19 August 2022

Parrish, Will and Levin, Sam (2018) 'Treating protest as terrorism': US plans crackdown on Keystone XL activists, *Guardian*, September. Available online at https://www.theguardian.com/environment/2018/sep/20/keystone-pipeline-protest-activism-crackdown-standing-rock, accessed on 19 August 2022

Pucci, D. (2020) Sunday final ratings: 'The masked singer' third season premiere on Fox generates second-largest total audience and adults 18-49 delivery for a Super Bowl lead-out in five years, *Programming Insider*, 11 February. Available online at https://programminginsider.com/sunday-final-ratings-the-masked-singer-third-season-premiere-on-fox-generates-second-largest-total-audience-and-adults-18-49-delivery-for-a-super--bowl-lead-out-in-five-years/, accessed on 28 March 2023

Rozsa, Matthew (2020) Both Super Bowl LIV team names are pretty racist – Kansas City Chiefs and San Francisco 49ers, *Salon*, 2 February. Available online at https://www.salon.com/2020/02/02/both-super-bowl-liv-team-names-are-pretty-racist--kansas-city-chiefs-and-san-francisco-49ers/, accessed on 19 August 2022

Schilling, Vincent (2017) The true story of Pocahontas: Historical myths versus sad reality, *Indian Country Today*, 8 September. Available online at https://ictnews.org/archive/true-story-pocahontas-historical-myths-versus-sad-reality, accessed on 3 April 2023

Serwer, Adam (2019) The President's pursuit of white power, *The Atlantic*, 14 January. Available online at https://www.theatlantic.com/politics/archive/2019/01/trump-embraces-white-supremacy/579745/, accessed on 19 August 2022

Stoddard, Christine (2016) The uphill battle for native federal recognition, *Bustle*, 4 March. Available online at https://www.bustle.com/articles/142421-even-the-native-american-tribe-famous-for-pocahontas-only-just-won-federal-recognition-heres-why, accessed on 19 August 2022

Stone, Kathleen, Roberts, Matt, Vanni, Olivia, Vercruyssen, Kira, Koostra, Zoie Begay, Jason, Irvine, Tailyr, Upham, Lailani, Crews, Taylor, Hockett, Corey, Reid, Anna and Vincent, Maddie (2016) Framing a movement: The media at Standing Rock, *Montana Journalism Review.* Available online at https://features.mjr.jour.umt.edu/2016/11/27/framing-a-movement/, accessed on 19 August 2022

Sullivan, Jas M. and Arbuthnot, Keena N. (2009) The effects of Black identity on candidate evaluations: An exploratory study, *Journal of Black Studies,* Vol. 40, No. 2 pp 215–237

TallBear, Kim (2019) Elizabeth Warren's claim to Cherokee ancestry is a form of violence, *High Country News,* 17 January. Available online at https://www.hcn.org/issues/51.2/tribal-affairs-elizabeth-warrens-claim-to-cherokee-ancestry-is-a-form-of-violence, accessed on 19 August 2022

Tapia, A. (2021) The most popular Disney Princess movies, according to Rotten Tomatoes, *Newsweek,* September 22. Available online at https://www.newsweek.com/most-popular-disney-princess-movies-rotten-tomatoes-1630722, accessed on 28 March 2023

Taylor, Jessica (2017) Trump brings up 'Pocahontas' at event honoring Navajo Code Talkers, *NPR,* 27 November. Available online at https://www.npr.org/2017/11/27/566783261/trump-brings-up-pocahontas-at-event-honoring-navajo-code-talkers, accessed on 19 August 2022

Tribal Nations & the United States: An introduction (2020) NCAI, February. Available online at https://ncai.org/about-tribes, accessed on 3 April 2023

Tuchman, Gaye (1978) Introduction: The symbolic annihilation of women by the mass media, Tuchman, Gaye, Daniels, Kaplan, Arlene and Benét, James (eds) *Hearth and home: Images of women in the mass media* Oxford, Oxford University Press pp 3–38

Zuma, Buhle (2014) Contact theory and the concept of prejudice: Metaphysical and moral explorations and an epistemological question, *Theory & Psychology,* Vol. 24, No. 1 pp 40-57. Available online at https://doi.org/10.1177/0959354313517023

Notes on the contributors

Victoria L. LaPoe, PhD (Cherokee) is an associate professor in Ohio University's E. W. Scripps School of Journalism and Director of Journalism in the Honor Tutorial College, where she teaches both news and information and strategic communication courses. LaPoe served as vice-president and education chair of the Native American Journalists Association. She continues to serve on NAJA's education committee and is a lifetime NAJA member as well as Indigenous issues editor for the national Media Diversity Forum. She is co-author of *Indian Country: Telling a story in a digital age.*

Sarah Liese, MSc (Navajo/Turtle Mountain Chippewa) is a 2022 Indigenous Non-Fiction Sundance Institute Fellow, researcher and mitigation video specialist. She completed her Master of Science degree in Journalism at Ohio University in July 2022. While pursuing her Master's degree, she served as a Full Circle Fellow at the Sundance Institute, Native American Journalism Fellow and Mentor-In-Training at the Native American Journalist Association, as well as a research assistant and teaching assistant at Ohio University. Her previous work focused on social media management, content creation and broadcast journalism.

Candi Carter Olson, PhD is an associate professor of media and society at Utah State University in Journalism and affiliate faculty in American Studies. She has an MA from Boston University, an MSc from Carnegie Mellon University and a PhD from the University of Pittsburgh. Her research focuses on the history of women's press clubs and newswomen more generally and she also researches the ways that social media communities are used for support and activism. Her writing has been published in *Journalism History, Pennsylvania History* and *Feminist Media Studies,* among others.

Dr Cristina L. Azocar is a citizen of the Upper Mattaponi Indian Tribe and a Professor of Journalism at San Francisco State University. She is the author of *News media and the Indigenous fight for federal recognition.* Her research focuses on the intersection of race and journalistic practice, particularly in the area of news coverage of Indigenous people. Azocar earned her doctorate in Communication Studies at the University of Michigan.

Victoria LaPoe

Sarah Liese

Candi Carter Olson

Cristina Azocar

Benjamin R. LaPoe II

Bharbi Hazarika

Julia Weber

She holds a Master's degree in Ethnic Studies and a Bachelor's degree in Journalism, both from San Francisco State University.

Benjamin R. LaPoe, II, PhD is an Assistant Professor and Political Communication Certificate Director at Ohio University. He received his MSc in Journalism from West Virginia University and his PhD in Political Communication from the Manship School at Louisiana State University. His research focuses on the intersections of racism, sexism, political communication and media. LaPoe is co-author of *Resistance advocacy as news: Digital Black press covers the Tea Party* and *Indian Country: Telling a story in a digital age*, where he wrote about the history of media and minority press.

Bharbi Hazarika, MSc, is from Assam, India, and she is currently a Journalism Master's student at New York University. She is an Ohio University alumna. During her time at OU, she received an award for 'outstanding Master's student' and worked for CNN international as a writer/producer. She has also worked at a variety of outlets as a reporting intern, including the *Los Angeles Times* and the *Hindu*. She was also a part of *The New York Times* Journalism Institute's 2021 class. Apart from English, Hazarika is proficient in Hindi and Assamese.

Julia Weber is a second-year undergraduate student in the Ohio University Honors Tutorial College where she is working toward a Bachelor of Science in Journalism with a minor in Art History. She is the features editor for Ohio University's All Campus Radio Network, a student-run station. She has also worked in editorial, research and strategic communication settings and her main areas of interest include reporting and audience engagement. After graduation, her goal is to work in a newsroom setting as a reporter primarily covering music, art and culture.

All authors contributed equally.

Conflict of interest
Authors do not have any known conflict of interests.

Funding statement
Funding from Ohio University purchased a panel of respondents in the US national survey from Qualtrics.

PAPER

Grace James
Victoria LaPoe
Benjamin R. LaPoe II
Alesha Davis

Missing women news coverage and implications of standpoint theory

Missing women are not a new story. However, the disparity between who tells the story of missing women, in what way and with what context, is one not fully documented across presses. Utilising standpoint theories, this research examines more than 250 North American-based news articles detailing the coverage of missing women. Multiple themes emerge within the data set: the overall missing person story, social commentary, family perspective and changes/action taken. The study finds that both Indigenous and Black presses tell a more contextually complete story about missing women, with more thematic news coverage, along with greater calls for changes and action. Indigenous media, specifically, has more multi-thematic stories. This research highlights the need for more frequent coverage of missing women of colour and for news organisations to commit to coverage by providing not just event or episodic news, but contextual stories covered across time.

Key words: missing women, Indigenous, standpoint theory, news, Black press

Introduction

When a young woman went missing while travelling cross-country with her fiancé, much of the United States was hooked as the gruesome case unfolded throughout the course of several months (Pitts 2021). The story began with 22-year-old Gabby Petito, an internet vlogger who documented her travels on her Instagram and YouTube accounts, giving a behind-the-scenes look into 'van life' with her fiancé, Brian Laundrie (Weitzman and Naravaez 2021). They began their journey

Grace James
Victoria LaPoe
Benjamin R. LaPoe II
Alesha Davis

in July 2021 for a four-month, cross-country road trip. After several altercations between the couple during which bystanders called the police, Petito's family reported her missing on 11 September (Maxouris 2022). Officials found her remains on 19 September in Grand Teton National Park, a remote area of northern Wyoming (Pruitt-Young 2021).

In the weeks following, a rigorous manhunt ended at the Carlton Reserve in Florida for the fiancé turned murder suspect (NBC 2011). Here officials found his skeletal remains and a notebook, where a Federal Bureau of Investigation report states, Laundrie wrote he killed Petito; a Florida Medical Examiner found Laundrie then shot himself in the head. Media covered the story, even attracting the attention of celebrities such as Dog the Bounty Hunter, who became involved in the search (NBC 2021).

Within a seven-day period during the Petito investigation, multiple news outlets mentioned her name: 398 times on Fox News, 346 times on CNN and 100 times on MSNBC (Barr 2021). Along with this coverage, however, came the re-emergence of a phrase coined by Gwen Ifill at the 2004 conference for Journalists of Colour: the 'Missing White Woman Syndrome' (C-SPAN 2004). The term represents the argument that missing White women and girls receive disproportionate news coverage (Sommers 2016).

The *Columbia Journalism Review* worked with an agency to research missing people across all forms of media, reviewing around 3,600 articles. To bring awareness to this issue, they created a tool to calculate a user's 'press value' if they went missing that they could openly share, highlighting the bias in the calculation toward gender, race, age and location of where a person lives (see Franklin 2022).

The statistics are flipped for Black versus White reported missing women and girls in the US. When considering those missing versus actual population numbers, Black missing women and girls are proportionately a lot higher than White reported missing women and girls. In 2020, the US National Crime Information Center reported more than 260,000 women and girls missing in the United States. A third of these women were Black. During the same time period, three out of every twenty women were Black in the US. In comparison, missing White women made up more than half of the data set and in terms of the overall population, three out of every four people were female in the US (Katz 2021).

Sommers (2016) tested the argument of Missing White Woman Syndrome (MWWS) and looked at national and local data from the FBI and four online news sources. Results found empirical evidence for MWWS at all age levels, both regarding the intensity of news coverage and whether there was any news coverage at all. This phenomenon is apparent in the Petito case, as officials found Petito's remains in Wyoming, a state where more than 400 Indigenous women and girls went missing between 2011 and the fall of 2020. Only 18 per cent of these women received news coverage, compared to 51 per cent of White women who went missing in the state (Katz 2021).

There are several concepts behind MWWS. First, storytellers portray White women as damsels in distress in need of protection. These stories of young, beautiful women gone missing symbolise the loss of innocence or death of purity. As professor and true crime scholar Jean Murley notes: 'It's not a surprise that we still have this symbol of the missing White woman. It has a deep history — it's fraught with a lot of meaning for the American imaginary' (Rosner 2021: para 8). These stories also often resonate more deeply with media organisations with mostly White reporters and assignment editors, resulting in greater coverage (Robertson 2021).

On the other hand, women of colour are often subject to tropes such as the 'angry' Black woman or the 'strong' Hispanic woman, neither of whom are seen as innocent or in need of protection (Ardrey 2021). Furthermore, women of colour often deal with the stereotype of blame for their own misfortune (List 2021). A report from the Urban Indian Health Institute finds that 38 per cent of media articles about the disappearances and murders of Indigenous women and girls make references to drugs and alcohol (Lucchesi and Echo-Hawk 2018).

This paper discusses a qualitative thematic analysis to understand news coverage about people gone missing, specifically missing Indigenous women and girls, and Black women and girls, to see if news coverage differs. We collected three types of media: mainstream media, Black media, and Indigenous media. For Black and Indigenous media, we included outlets dedicated to providing content for each community, as well as mainstream outlets that have dedicated desks for news such as Indigenous affairs. We classified articles into four main themes: missing person story;

- social commentary;
- family perspective, and
- changes/action taken.

If a story used more than one theme, we counted separately for each theme included. This study also considers both feminist and Indigenous standpoint theory which detail how different communities can use their unique perspective to influence and shape the collection of knowledge, understanding and morality (Foley 2003).

Literature review
Feminist standpoint theory

While the definition of a standpoint is wide-ranging, it often refers to a perspective or a socially situated subject of knowledge; this includes ideas, theories and/or methodologies (Moreton-Robinson

Grace James

Victoria LaPoe

Benjamin R. LaPoe II

Alesha Davis

2013). Within a feminist context, however, a standpoint comprises a perspective on social reality as well as a moral or political commitment (Rolin 2009). These two factors – epistemology and political action – are intrinsically linked at the heart of feminist standpoints (Hartsock 1998). From this perspective, feminist standpoint theory challenges the conventional scientific practices that previously excluded women from the construction and benefits of knowledge (Gurung 2020).

Hekman (1997) contends that feminist standpoint grew from Marxism and adopts two central epistemological tenets: first, knowledge is situated and perspectival; second, knowledge is produced by multiple standpoints. Because of these principles, a feminist perspective is integral to understanding social reality. For example, Martin et al. (2002) argue that women are more conscious of the realities of gender inequality because of their devalued gender status and subsequent negative experiences. As a result of this inequality, modern epistemologies revolve around dominant patriarchal paradigms and male standpoints. Feminist standpoint theory challenges these paradigms, such as the notion that to maintain integrity during scientific experimentation researchers need to forget personal knowledge (Moreton-Robinson 2013). In addition to scientific fields, Martin et al. (2002) argue that feminist standpoint can also have implications for legal institutions.

Standpoint theory and race

As with feminist standpoint theory, scholars use standpoint theory to examine epistemological approaches of different racial groups. Hill Collins (1997) examines the epistemology of Black women and argues that Black women have a 'unique angle of vision' on the social world repressed by White, patriarchal forms of knowledge. Harnois (2010) analyses data from the National Black Feminist Study (2004-2005) to test Hill Collins's perspective on the standpoint of Black women and finds that this standpoint represents an intersectional understanding of oppression and the legacy of struggle against this oppression. However, the study also concludes that gender is not a significant predictor of this standpoint, as both Black men and Black women embrace these ideas.

Standpoint theory is used to examine perspectives of Black/African Americans on multiple social issues, from gender to collegiate sports (Walker and Melton 2015). For example, Davis et al. (2022) analyse racial differences in perspectives of benevolent sexism entailing positive attitudes toward women that are layered with undertones of stereotypes and paternalism. The study finds that Black men and women have a higher endorsement of benevolent sexism. While gender is not differentiated between Black men and women, there is a gender difference between White participants, as White men have a higher endorsement of benevolent sexism than White women. For Black women, their perspectives are influenced by cultural factors such as religion or racial identity.

Intersectional standpoint theory: Gender, race and sexual minorities standpoints

Walker and Melton (2015) examine standpoint theory from an intersectional lens in terms of gender, race and sexual minorities' standpoints (LGBTQ+). These scholars recognise that the groups researched are often those 'othered' in research; an intersectional standpoint theory approach instead places these individuals and their voices at the centre of the discussion.

Indigenous standpoint theory

Standpoint theory privileges a unique perspective from and by Indigenous peoples. Nakata (2007) contends that Indigenous standpoint theory (IST) is informed by family and collective consciousness, politics and history. It is a method of inquiry that leads to objective knowledge. Foley argues that IST is emancipatory and unique from other forms of discourse, as well as 'flexible and applicable for numerous Indigenous if not all Indigenous nations' (2003: 50). Foley (ibid) also asserts that feminist standpoint theory is the evolutionary basis for IST and that an Indigenous standpoint is flexible in nature, with three interacting worlds. First, the physical world (land, living organisms, etc); second, the human world (individuals, families, etc); and third, the sacred world. The sacred world is not entirely metaphysical in nature, as it also comprises elements such as healing and the law.

Other characteristics of IST include an emphasis on social, political and historical contexts that shape the lives of Indigenous communities and provide an outlet for Indigenous voices (Martin and Mirraboopa 2003). IST also helps Indigenous scholars define research, methodologies and results in a culturally relevant way – therefore, Indigenous scholars become active participants in research rather than relegated to passive subjects (Rigney 1997; Yunkaporta and Shillingsworth 2020). Ardill (2013) employs IST to advocate for the sovereignty of First Peoples and the recognition of this sovereignty by non-Indigenous scholars. Choy and Woodlock (2007) use the theory to highlight the importance of improving vocational education and training for Indigenous Australians and Foley (2003) investigates the need for Indigenous epistemological approaches to scientific Indigenous research in Australia.

IST is an effective tool in media research as it allows scholars to investigate the differences between goals and methods of Indigenous and non-Native (mainstream) journalism (Azocar et al. 2021). Indigenous media plays an important role in communities because it empowers Indigenous voices to discuss their perspectives and concerns (Sunuwar 2019). Carter Olson et al. (2022) use IST to examine the role of gender during Indigenous news coverage in the early days of the Covid-19 pandemic. Women's voices act as a guide toward community solutions and healing and stories are community focused. IST also is used to analyse Covid-19 news coverage about economic loss faced by Indigenous communities, particularly in the gaming industry.

Grace James
Victoria LaPoe
Benjamin R. LaPoe II
Alesha Davis

Mainstream media often publish stereotypical reporting on this issue, due in part to economic misunderstandings and misunderstandings of Indigenous gaming operations (Azocar et al. 2021). LaPoe et al. (2021) evaluate differences in health reporting among Indigenous and non-Indigenous news sources and find that Indigenous media provides 14 times more health stories than mainstream media — these stories provide depth and specificity, and they emphasise unequal power. On the other hand, non-Indigenous news often focuses on lack of resources and the struggle of Indigenous communities.

Missing and murdered Indigenous women and girls (MMIWG)

Within the United States officials do not know the true number of missing and murdered Indigenous women. This is due to several issues such as reporting problems, distrust of law enforcement and jurisdictional issues (Associated Press 2022). However, the statistics available paint a grim picture. In 2016 there were 5,712 noted cases of MMIGW, with only 116 logged in the Department of Justice database (Lucchesi and Echo-Hawk 2018). Furthermore, more than 80 per cent of Indigenous women have experienced violence and American Indian/Alaska Native people experience higher rates of violence than any other group (Associated Press 2022; Joseph 2021). US Indigenous women make up 40 per cent of all women sex trafficked in the US; sadly, this trafficking has existed since the time of Christopher Columbus (Hunt 2021). Lucchesi and Echo-Hawk (2018) investigated cases of MMIWG in specifically urban areas and found 501 cases across 71 cities, with victims from less than one year old to 83 years old. More than 95 per cent of the cases analysed were not covered by the media (Lucchesi and Echo-Hawk 2018).[1] However, for the ones who were, nearly a third of media outlets surveyed use violent language in their stories — including references to drugs or alcohol, victim-blaming, racial misclassification, etc.

Joseph (2021) argues that due to the sheer volume of cases, the MMIWG crisis is a modern form of genocide. The study, which analyses data from the National Missing and Unidentified Persons System, National Crime Information Center and the Urban Indian Health Institute, investigates the root causes of MMIWG and located cities in the US with the highest rates of MMIWG. There are 23 hotspots, many with increased instances of fracking, often bringing in large groups of non-residents to areas. The crisis is exacerbated by systemic racism in the US justice system. Scholars also examined this crisis on a local and state level. Hunt (2021) analyses cases of MMIWG among the Lumbee Tribe of North Carolina and the Associated Press (2022) investigates cases on the West coast, from San Francisco to the Oregon border. The Lumbee tribe, the largest tribe in North Carolina, is located mainly in Robeson County in the southern part of the state. Robeson County had the highest violent crime rate in North Carolina in 2020 according to a report from the North Carolina State Bureau of Investigation and is included in the 2016 top 30 'murder capitals' of the US (Horne 2021; Tribune Media

Wire 2016). Mallonee (2021) examines instances of MMIWG in Alaska, noting factors that facilitated the crisis such as Alaska's vast landscape, confusing jurisdiction and history of systemic racism. The study then advocates for solutions grounded in a recognition of colonial history, empowerment of local voices and increased cultural competency in law enforcement.

The crisis of MMIWG is not unique to the United States. Bailey and Shayan (2016) examine the role that technology plays in First Nation MMIWG cases in Canada. They argue that technology facilitates acts such as stalking, intimate partner violence, human trafficking, pornography, child abuse images, online hate and harassment. Canada began a National Inquiry in 2016 into cases of MMIWG, with a body of five Indigenous commissioners and a budget of $53.8 million. The inquiry found that the Aboriginal rating of police officers was a mere 2.8 out of 10 (Walsh 2017). Additionally, Razack (2016) argues that inquiries may only reproduce colonial truths and focus more on Indigenous dysfunction instead of colonial violence and dispossession.

Given the national spotlight placed on the story of Gabby Petito, the differences between her case and the epidemic of MMIWG are noticeable. More than a dozen states launched task forces or other resources to help (Haynie 2021). These efforts have mixed results among communities — some argue that they have already seen positive results, while others argue that task forces are public relations stunts led by too many law enforcement officials instead of Indigenous advocates and affected families (Haynie 2021). On 31 March 2022, Washington governor Jay Inslee (D) signed House Bill 1725 into law, which created the nation's first statewide alert system for missing Indigenous people. The alert system broadcasts information about missing Indigenous people on electronic highway signs, social media and radio messages. The state, in addition, sends out press releases to alert local and regional media (Aadland 2022). The US federal government has also made efforts to address the crisis. Interior secretary Deb Haaland (D), who is a member of the Laguna Pueblo tribe, announced the formation of a Missing and Murdered Unit within the Bureau of Indian Affairs Office of Justice Services to use resources at the federal level to help investigate cases (US Department of the Interior 2021). Additionally, President Biden signed legislation to set up guidelines between the federal government and tribal police to help solve and prevent crimes against Indigenous people (Associated Press 2022).

Missing Black women and girls

Sadly, missing women and girls spread across multiple communities. The National Crime Information Center reported more than 90,000 Black women and girls missing in 2020 — this number increased to 100,000 in 2021 (CBS News 2022). Furthermore, Black women account for more than one-third of missing women but comprise less than 15 per cent of the US population (Kelly 2022). There are several factors that contribute

Grace James

Victoria LaPoe

Benjamin R. LaPoe II

Alesha Davis

to this disparity. First, there are racial disparities in mainstream media depictions of Black Americans as criminals and White Americans as victims, even though Black Americans account for 22.7 per cent of victimisations in the US (Moss 2019). The Congressional Caucus on Black Women and Girls (CCBWG) discussed this issue, including voices from law enforcement, social workers, educators and community leaders. Users on Twitter also attempted to bring awareness by using the hashtag #MissingBlackGirls (Mayo 2017).

Cases of missing or murdered Black women occur across the US, and local leaders and activists have raised their voices to speak for the victims and their families. Chicago Mayor Lori Lightfoot states:

> … In Chicago we just have to be honest and say we don't have a good track record when it comes to finding missing Black women and girls, supporting families and survivors, solving homicides relating to Black women. We absolutely must do better (CBS News 2022).

Alexandria Onuoha, director of political advocacy for the community organisation Black Boston, spoke out after two police officers were suspended over their handling of the case of Lauren Smith-Fields, who was found dead in her apartment. Onuoha notes the discrepancies in data collection and legislative action, as well as negative stereotypes that prevent them from receiving appropriate help and care. She advocates for legislative action, arguing: 'This is not a one-person issue. This is a collective issue' (Tauber 2022). Moss (2019) also advocates for the creation of legislation at the state and local level to help remedy the unequal treatment of missing Black women and girls. The study gives the example of the RILYA alert system, which is used in Florida to expand the AMBER alert, a child abduction emergency alert system, to address missing people of colour.

Patton and Ward (2016) use critical race framework (CRF) to analyse media coverage of missing Black undergraduate women and find that these cases typically receive limited or no media coverage. Digital or social media sites are the most likely media outlets to cover these cases. Stories that do get covered are often negative in connotation, as media and law enforcement narratives of Black women are often framed around crime, mental illness and other issues that suggest that the victims are responsible for what happens to them. Additionally, law enforcement is typically portrayed in a positive light with regards to their involvement with the cases. The study also finds that if the cases of missing or murdered Black women are gruesome, they are more likely to receive media attention.

An online media source dedicated to telling the stories of missing or murdered Black women, called Our Black Girls, was launched in 2018 by journalist and activist Erika Marie Rivers. Each post first explains the details of a case, then expands into the fuller story of who the victim is and provides a voice for her family members or friends to speak about her (Pruitt-Young 2021). In addition, the four-part HBO documentary series titled 'Black and Missing' tells the story of Natalie and Derrica Wilson, co-founders of the Black and Missing Foundation (Nawaz and Reynolds 2021). Several podcasts bring this issue to light as well, including Crime noir, Black girl gone, and Black girl missing (Pruitt-Young 2021).

Based on past research, the following research questions, which examine different presses as well as frequency of content, guide this study: RQ1: What themes emerge in media coverage of missing individuals across mainstream, Black, and Indigenous news sources? And RQ2: What is the frequency of episodic compared to thematic stories published within these presses?

Method

The total number of news articles included in our qualitative thematic analysis is N=274. Articles are categorised by mainstream media, Black media, and Indigenous media. We collected 132 articles from mainstream media published between 1 September 2021 and 24 October 2021; 81 articles from Black media sources published between 1 September 2021 and 21 April 2022; and 61 articles from Indigenous media sources published between 14 April 2021 and 9 April 2022. Articles are also broken down within each category by media organisation (See Tables 1-3). We searched for articles on Google and on news sites using search terms such as 'missing', 'murdered', 'missing and murdered Indigenous women', and 'missing person'.

Table 1: Mainstream media sources and relevant articles collected 1 September 2021-24 October 2022

Total number of articles	132
ABC7/KABC, Los Angeles, California	2
CNN, National Network News	10
The *Guardian*	1
The New York Times	4
The *Daily Record*	1
Buzzfeed	5
NBC News, National Network News	19
Today, National Network News	2
MSNBC, National Network News	1
AP News, National News Wire Service	9
19 News/WOIO-CBS, Cleveland, Ohio	43
FOX 40/KTXL, Sacramento, California	10
FOX News	25

Grace James
Victoria LaPoe
Benjamin R. LaPoe II
Alesha Davis

Table 2: Black media sources and relevant articles collected 1 September 2021-21 April 2022

Total number of articles	81
Blavity	38
Essence	8
Black and Missing Foundation	3
Our Black Girls	18
The Root	5
AFRO News	5
The Miami Times	1
The Atlanta Voice	1
TheGrio	2

Table 3: Indigenous media sources and relevant articles collected 14 April 2021-9 April 2022

Total number of articles	61
Indian Country Today	10
Native News Online	16
High Country News (includes an Indigenous affairs desk)	2
Indianz	6
KOSU Radio Oklahoma State University/ Stillwater, OK (includes an Indigenous affairs desk)	5
NBC News (includes an Indigenous news team)	2
Yellowstone Public Radio	7
Navajo-Hopi Observer	5
Osage News	1
Cherokee Phoenix	1
Navajo Times	6

We organised information for each article in an Excel spreadsheet – information noted for each story included the media outlet, publication date, URL, author, and headline – and sorted the stories according to several themes. We also categorised articles as either episodic or thematic, two frames that influence how an audience attributes responsibility for social issues (Iyengar 1991). An episodic frame focuses on an individual case study, whereas a thematic frame focuses on trends throughout time and highlights contexts and environments. In other words, an episodic frame paints a story like a portrait, highlighting a more central image, while a thematic frame paints a landscape that shows a broader picture (Benjamin 2007). We replicate studies by LaPoe et al. (2021) where themes emerge when common narratives are repeated. Once we saw repetitions in the packaging of the news content, we noted it as a theme, which we describe in our results.

Results

Data collected from 272 news stories across the mainstream, Black and Indigenous presses show noticeable differences in how each press covers and frames the crisis of missing people. The four themes that emerge from our data include the overall missing person story, social commentary, family perspective and changes/action taken.

- Theme 1: *Missing person* (Story). Articles categorised by this theme centre on the case of a missing person(s). This includes a breaking news story, an update that provides additional details to an existing case or the conclusion of a case.

- Theme 2: *Social commentary*. This theme encompasses stories that focus on comments from public figures, activists or community members on the issue of missing and murdered Indigenous people. Additionally, the social commentary theme includes stories about events or protests that relate to missing peoples.

- Theme 3: *Family perspective*. These articles place the viewpoint of a victim's family member at the heart of the story.

- Theme 4: *Changes/action taken*. The final theme focuses on stories about legislative changes, or new initiatives to tackle the crisis of missing people of colour. These changes are at the local, state or national level. The frequency of each theme in mainstream, Black and Indigenous media sources is calculated, as well as whether stories from certain media categories focusing on more than one theme.

RQ1: What themes emerge in media coverage of missing individuals across mainstream, Black and Indigenous news sources?

For the first theme of missing person stories, the mainstream press has the highest rate of articles that fit into this category — 90 per cent of articles collected. Articles are typically brief and state information about the missing person, such as their demographics (race, gender, age, etc.), the last place they were seen, or how long they have been missing. For example, the headline of an article published within this category reads, 'FBI joins search for Maya Marcano, who has been missing in Florida for nearly a week' (CNN 2021). Similarly, another headline reads, 'Authorities search for girl unaccounted for since February' (AP News 2021). The Black press has the second highest rate, at 74 per cent and last was Indigenous media, where only 25 per cent of stories fit into the missing person theme.

The second theme is social commentary which describes stories that focus on the issue of missing peoples as a whole and highlights systemic issues within the crises of MMIWG, or missing Black women and girls.

Grace James

Victoria LaPoe

Benjamin R. LaPoe II

Alesha Davis

The Indigenous press focuses most heavily on social commentary, with 56 per cent of stories falling into this category. Headlines within this category include: 'Help us bring attention to our missing and murdered Indigenous relatives' (*Osage News* 2021) and 'MMIWG: Known and not forgotten' (*Indian Country Today* 2021). The Black press is second in this category (23 per cent) and mainstream press is third (12 per cent).

Thirdly, the Family Perspective theme notes articles that place the perspective of a victim's family members at the centre of the story. This includes mentioning comments from the victim's family in the headline or making a family member's comments the main focus of the story. All three presses had very close percentages on this theme – stories from Black media outlets has the highest rate (18 per cent), followed by Indigenous media (15 per cent) and mainstream media (10 per cent). One article from *Blavity News*, an organisation defined on its website as 'the community for Black creativity and news', is published using the headline: 'Family of Indigenous trans woman, Aubrey Dameron, missing for two years, believe she's hate crime victim' (*Blavity News* 2021). Similar headlines are found in mainstream articles, such as an article from CNN: '"He didn't deserve this." Jelani Day's mother criticises efforts to find son' (CNN 2021).

The final theme used for analysis is changes/action taken which refers to stories that entail action taken to address or combat the crisis of missing people. This includes demonstrations, vigils, legislative actions or other public safety measures. The Indigenous press has the highest rate of these stories (38 per cent), while the Black press is second (6 per cent) and mainstream media a distant third (.7 per cent). The number of stories in each theme is shown in Table 4. We note a story more than once if it falls into more than one theme.

Table 4: Story theme categorisation for mainstream, Black and Indigenous presses

Type of press	Missing person	Social commentary	Family perspective	Changes/ action taken
Mainstream	118 stories (90%)	16 stories (12%)	13 stories (10%)	1 story (.7%)
Black	59 stories (74%)	18 stories (23%)	14 stories (18%)	5 stories (6%)
Indigenous	15 stories (25%)	34 stories (56%)	9 stories (15%)	23 stories (38%)

RQ2: What is the frequency of episodic compared to thematic stories published within these presses?

Next, we analyse each story as episodic (a story that focuses only on one incident in particular) or thematic (gives a broader perspective on a topic or issue). All three media organisations have a higher rate of episodic stories compared to thematic stories. However, there are noticeable differences for each type of press. The mainstream media has the highest percentage of episodic stories (85 per cent), with only 15 per cent of stories classified as thematic. Black media sources have a slightly lower percentage of episodic stories, at 73 per cent, with thematic stories making up 27 per cent of the total. Finally, the Indigenous press has the most balanced ratio of episodic to thematic stories – 56 per cent episodic and 44 per cent thematic. Table 5 lays out results for episodic/thematic coverage for each press group.

Table 5: Episodic/thematic coverage for mainstream, Black, and Indigenous presses

Type of press	Number of episodic stories	Number of thematic stories
Mainstream	112 (85%)	20 (15%)
Black	59 (73%)	22 (27%)
Indigenous	34 (56%)	27 (44%)

Stories with more than one of the four major themes (missing person, social commentary, family perspective and changes/action taken) are additionally noted. Stories from Indigenous media outlets have the highest percentage of multi-themed stories (30 per cent). *Indianz* published an example of an Indigenous multi-themed story with the title: 'Native community comes together to honor missing and murdered relatives.' The article fit into both the social commentary and family perspective categories, as it begins with the story of one woman, Renee Sans Souci (Umonhon), whose uncle was murdered, then pivots to her efforts to help others who have lost loved ones and bring awareness to the MMIWG crisis. Black media outlets have the second highest percentage of multi-themed stories at 20 per cent and the mainstream press has the lowest rate (13 per cent). Figures for each outlet are shown in Table 6.

Table 6: multi-thematic news present in coverage

Type of press	Articles and percentage
Mainstream	17 (13%)
Black	16 (20%)
Indigenous	18 (30%)

This research study has limitations. Only a small sample of news articles were collected and analysed, and there is room to add articles from different news sites, or different publication timeframes.

Conclusion

This study began with the idea to investigate how different media organisations cover the issue of missing persons after the media frenzy that followed the Gabby Petito case. There is a documented crisis of missing and murdered Indigenous women and girls, as well as Black

Grace James

Victoria LaPoe

Benjamin R. LaPoe II

Alesha Davis

women, and this study analyses news stories from mainstream, Black and Indigenous news outlets. The MMIWG crisis is exacerbated in part by issues in reporting, law enforcement and jurisdiction, which lead to disproportionate numbers of Indigenous women that go missing or die under suspicious circumstances (Associated Press 2022). However, a majority of these cases are not covered by the media (Lucchesi and Echo-Hawk 2018). We wanted to see how the cases that did receive media attention are reported and examined each article through a series of story themes.

Our research utilises standpoint theory, which defines a standpoint as a socially situated subject of knowledge (Moreton-Robinson 2013). Previous scholarship focuses on feminist standpoint theory, which revolves around a feminist perspective that is integral to understanding social reality (Hekman 1997). Additionally, the standpoint of Black women provides a unique point of view previously oppressed by other epistemological viewpoints (Hill Collins 1997). Indigenous standpoint theory, which is flexible in nature like feminist standpoint theory and is informed by family, collective consciousness, politics and history, is also utilised in our study (Foley 2003; Nakata 2007).

From our insights on how different media groups report on the crisis of missing or murdered individuals, there are many ways in which the media can improve ethical coverage of this crisis. First, there is a clear need for an increase in multi-themed stories that offer a more comprehensive perspective on the MMIWG crisis and other crises involving missing and murdered peoples. This goes hand in hand with the need to increase the number of thematic stories that give context to a story instead of zeroing in on a specific incident. Media coverage of the Gabby Petito case does not focus solely on the details of her disappearance and death; it paints a picture of a young woman's life – her friends, her family, her career and her relationship. Countless articles and TV news segments revealed her story bit by bit, leading to a captivated audience of millions, many of whom personally tried to solve the mystery of what happened to Petito. When it comes to the disappearance of other missing persons, particularly missing people of colour, this same intensity of coverage is not replicated in the mainstream news. While it is important to avoid sensationalising the news, perhaps a more thorough and humanising approach to the topic of missing women of colour in the mainstream media can lead to an increased awareness of the crisis and direct attention to families and communities that call for help. Future studies should also consider broadening the sample, including multi-language news outlets such as Spanish-language media.

References

Aadland, Chris (2022) State approves 1st alert system for missing Indigenous people, *Indian Country Today*, 31 March. Available online at https://indiancountrytoday.com/news/state-approves-1st-alert-system-for-missing-indigenous-people, accessed on 13

April 2022

Ardill, Allan (2013) Australian sovereignty, indigenous standpoint theory, and feminist standpoint theory, *Griffith Law Review*, Vol. 22, No. 2 pp 315–343. Available online at https://doi.org/10.1080/10383441.2013.10854778

Ardrey, Taylor (2021) Experts say the 'missing white woman syndrome' leaves girls of color disproportionately out of news coverage, *Insider*, 28 September. Available online at https://www.insider.com/experts-missing-women-of-color-are-not-centered-news-coverage-2021-9, accessed on 17 February 2022

Associated Press (2022) Tribe grapples with crisis of women disappearing between San Francisco and Oregon border, *Oregon Live*, 22 February. Available online at https://www.oregonlive.com/crime/2022/02/tribe-grapples-with-missing-women-crisis-between-san-francisco-and-oregon-border.html, accessed on 9 March 2022

Associated Press (2021) Gabby Petito was strangled 3 to 4 weeks before her body was found in Wyoming, *NPR*, 12 October. Available online at https://www.npr.org/2021/10/12/1045344198/gabby-petito-was-strangled, accessed on 18 February 2022

Azocar, Cristina L., LaPoe, Victoria, Carter Olson, Candi S., LaPoe, Benjamin and Hazarika, Bharbi (2021) Indigenous communities and Covid-19: Reporting on resources and resilience, *Howard Journal of Communications*, Vol. 32, No. 5 pp 440–455. Available online at https://doi.org/10.1080/10646175.2021.1892552

Bailey, Jane and Shayan, Sara (2016) Missing and murdered Indigenous women crisis: Technological dimensions, *Canadian Journal of Women and the Law*, Vol. 28, No. 2 pp 321–34172. Available online at https://doi.org/10.3138/cjwl.28.2.321

Barr, Jeremy (2021) Even within the media, some question the amount of Gabby Petito coverage, *Washington Post*, 23 September. Available online at https://www.washingtonpost.com/media/2021/09/23/gabby-petito-media-coverage-missing-white-black/, accessed on 18 February 2022

Benjamin, Diane (2007) Episodic vs thematic stories, FrameWorks Institute, December. Available online at https://www.frameworksinstitute.org/article/episodic-vs-thematic-stories/, accessed 14 April 2022

C-SPAN (2004) Gwen Ifill coins the term 'missing white woman syndrome', 5 August. Available online at https://www.c-span.org/video/?c4666788%2Fuser-clip-gwen-ifill-coins-term-missing-white-woman-syndrome, accessed on 17 February 2022

CBS News (2022) Lightfoot says Chicago 'must do better' finding missing Black women and girls, whose cases are disproportionately ignored, 6 February. Available online at https://www.cbsnews.com/chicago/news/missing-black-women-girls-chicago-lightfoot/, accessed on 26 August 2022

Carter Olson, Candi S., LaPoe, Benjamin, LaPoe, Victoria, Azocar, Cristina L. and Hazarika, Bharbi (2022) 'Mothers are medicine': US indigenous media emphasizing indigenous women's roles in covid-19 coverage, *Journal of Communication Inquiry*, Vol. 46, No. 3 pp 289–310. Available online at https://doi.org/10.1177/01968599221083239

Choy, S. and Woodlock, J. (2007) Implementing indigenous standpoint theory: Challenges for a TAFE trainer, *International Journal of Training Research*, Vol. 5, No. 1 pp 39–54. Available online at https://doi.org/10.5172/ijtr.5.1.39

Columbia Journalism Review (n.d.) Are you press worthy? Available online at https://areyoupressworthy.com/, accessed on 19 December 2022

Davis, Tangier M., Settles, Isis H. and Jones, Martinique K. (2022) Standpoints and situatedness: Examining the perception of benevolent sexism in black and white undergraduate women and men, *Psychology of Women Quarterly*, Vol. 46, No. 1 pp 8–26. Available online at https://doi.org/10.1177/03616843211043108

Foley, Dennis (2003) Indigenous epistemology and Indigenous standpoint theory, *Social Alternatives*, Vol. 22, No. 1 pp 44–52

Franklin, Jonathan (2022) Racial bias affects media coverage of missing people. A new tool illustrates how, NPR, 5 December. Available online at https://www.npr.org/2022/12/05/1137193397/missing-persons-of-color-news-coverage-disparities, accessed on 19 December 2022

Grace James

Victoria LaPoe

Benjamin R. LaPoe II

Alesha Davis

Gurung, Lina (2020) Feminist standpoint theory: Conceptualisation and utility, *Dhaulagiri Journal of Sociology and Anthropology*, Vol. 14 pp 106–115. Available online at https://doi.org/10.3126/dsaj.v14i0.27357

Harnois, Catherine E. (2010) Race, gender, and the Black women's standpoint, *Sociological Forum*, Vol. 25, No. 1 pp 68–85. Available online at https://doi.org/10.1111/j.1573-7861.2009.01157.x

Hartsock, Nancy C. M. (1998) *The feminist standpoint revisited and other essays*, Boulder, CO, Westview Press

Haynie, Devon (2021) How states are addressing violence against Indigenous women, *US News and World Report*, 1 November. Available online at https://www.usnews.com/news/best-states/articles/2021-11-01/how-states-are-addressing-the-missing-indigenous-women-crisis, accessed on 26 August 2022

Hekman, Susan (1997) Truth and method: Feminist standpoint theory revisited, *Signs: Journal of Women in Culture and Society*, Vol. 22, No. 2 pp 341–365. Available online at https://doi.org/10.1086/495159

Hill Collins, Patricia (1997) Comment on Hekman's 'Truth and method: Feminist standpoint theory revisited': Where's the power?, *Signs: Journal of Women in Culture and Society*, Vol. 22, No. 2 pp 375–381. Available online at https://doi.org/10.1086/495162

Horne, Jessica (2021) Robeson County again top in violent crime rates across the state, *Robesonian*, 28 December. Available online at https://www.robesonian.com/news/152804/robeson-county-again-top-in-violent-crime-rates-across-the-state#:~:text=Robeson%20County%20had%20the%20highest,rape%2C%20robbery%20and%20aggravated%20assault, accessed on 16 July 2022

Hunt, Brittany (2021) Ain't no sunshine when she's gone: Missing and murdered Indigenous women and girls in North Carolina, *North Carolina Medical Journal*, Vol. 82, No. 6 pp 417–419. Available online at https://doi.org/10.18043/ncm.82.6.417

Iyengar, Shanto (1991) *Is anyone responsible?: How television frames political issues*, Chicago, University of Chicago Press

Joseph, A. Skylar (2021) A modern trail of tears: The missing and murdered indigenous women (MMIW) crisis in the US, *Journal of Forensic and Legal Medicine*, Vol. 79. Available online at https://doi.org/10.1016/j.jflm.2021.102136

Katz, Joette (2021) 'Missing white girl syndrome' continues to plague US government, public sector – United States, *Mondaq*, 5 November. Available online at https://www.mondaq.com/unitedstates/indigenous-peoples/1128128/missing-white-girl-syndrome39-continues-to-plague-us#:~:text=According%20to%20the%20National%20Crime,of%20the%20overall%20female%20population, accessed on 16 February 2022

Kelly, Robin (2022) Crisis of missing Black women and girls deserves more public attention, *Chicago Sun Times*, 10 March. Available online at https://chicago.suntimes.com/2022/3/10/22969776/missing-black-women-girls-abuse-sex-trafficking-house-subcommittee-representative-robin-kelly-op-ed, accessed on 11 March 2022

LaPoe, Victoria L., Carter Olson, Candi S., Azocar, Cristina L., LaPoe, Benjamin R., Hazarika, Bharbi and Jain, Parul (2021) A comparative analysis of health news in Indigenous and mainstream media, *Health Communication*, Vol. 37, No. 9 pp 1192–1203. Available online at https://doi.org/10.1080/10410236.2021.1945179

List, Monica (2021) Counting women of color: Being angry about 'missing white woman syndrome' is not enough, *MSU Bioethics*, 9 November. Available online at https://msubioethics.com/2021/10/25/counting-women-of-color-missing-white-woman-syndrome-list/, accessed on 17 February 2022

Lucchesi, Annita and Echo-Hawk, Abigail (2018) Missing and murdered indigenous women and girls report. Available online at http://www.uihi.org/wp-content/uploads/2018/11/Missing-and-Murdered-Indigenous-Women-and-Girls-Report.pdf, accessed on 17 February 2022

Mallonee, Megan (2021) Selective justice: A crisis of missing and murdered Alaska Native women, *Alaska Law Review*, Vol. 38, No. 1 pp 93–120. Available online at https://scholarship.law.duke.edu/cgi/viewcontent.cgi?article=1593andcontext=alr, accessed on 26 August 2022

Martin, K. and Mirraboopa, B. (2003) Ways of knowing, ways of being and ways of doing: A theoretical framework and methods for Indigenous re-search and Indigenist research, *Journal of Australian Studies*, Vol. 76, No. 203 pp 203–214

Martin, Patricia Y., Reynolds, John R. and Keith, Shelley (2002) Gender bias and feminist consciousness among judges and attorneys: A standpoint theory analysis, *Signs: Journal of Women in Culture and Society*, Vol. 27, No. 3 pp 665–701. Available online at https://doi.org/10.1086/337941

Maxouris, Christina (2022) A timeline of 22-year-old Gabby Petito's case, *CNN*, 21 January. Available online at https://www.cnn.com/2021/09/16/us/gabby-petito-timeline-missing-case/index.html, accessed on 15 February 2022

Mayo, N. (2017) Our girls: More than a hashtag: The Congressional Caucus on Black Women and Girls brings issue of missing Black girls to forefront, *Crisis*, Vol. 124, No. 2 pp 5-6

Moreton-Robinson, Aileen (2013) Towards an Australian Indigenous women's standpoint theory, *Australian Feminist Studies*, Vol. 28, No. 78 pp 331–347. Available online at https://doi.org/10.1080/08164649.2013.876664

Moss, Jada L. (2019) The forgotten victims of the missing white woman syndrome: An examination of legal measures that contribute to the lack of search and recovery of missing Black girls and women, *William and Mary Journal of Race, Gender, and Social Justice*, Vol. 25, No. 3 pp 737–764

NBC New York (2021) Dog the bounty hunter shares evidence possibly linked to Brian Laundrie disappearance, 6 October. Available online at https://www.nbcnewyork.com/news/local/dog-the-bounty-hunter-shares-evidence-possibly-linked-to-brian-laundrie-disappearance/3309038/, accessed on 18 February 2022

Nakata, Martin (2007) *Disciplining the savages: Savaging the disciplines*, Canberra, Aboriginal Studies Press

Nawaz, Amna and Reynolds, Talesha (2021) New documentary highlights plight of missing Black women and why their cases go ignored, *PBS*, 23 November. Available online at https://www.pbs.org/newshour/show/new-documentary-highlights-plight-of-missing-black-women-and-why-their-cases-go-ignored, accessed on 11 March 2022

Patton, Lori D. and Ward, LaWanda W. (2016) Missing black undergraduate women and the politics of disposability: A critical race feminist perspective, *The Journal of Negro Education*, Vol. 85, No. 3 pp 330–349. Available online at https://doi.org/10.7709/jnegroeducation.85.3.0330

Pitts, Rachel (2021) Gabby Petito case timeline, 94.7 WCSX, 20 September. Available online at https://wcsx.com/listicle/gabby-petito-case-timeline/, accessed on 17 February 2022

Pruitt-Young, Sharon (2021) Tens of thousands of Black women vanish each year. This website tells their stories, *NPR*, 24 September. Available online at https://www.npr.org/2021/09/24/1040048967/missing-black-women-girls-left-out-media-ignored, accessed on 12 March 2022

Razack, Sherene H. (2016) Sexualized violence and colonialism: Reflections on the inquiry into missing and murdered indigenous women, *Canadian Journal of Women and the Law*, Vol. 28, No. 2 pp i–iv. Available online at https://doi.org/10.3138/cjwl.28.2.i

Rigney, Lester I. (1997) Internalisation of an Indigenous anti-colonial cultural critique of research methodologies: A guide to Indigenous research methodologies and its principles, *Journal of American Studies*, Vol. 14, No. 2 pp 109–122

Robertson, Katie (2021) News media can't shake 'missing white woman syndrome', critics say, *New York Times*, 22 September. Available behind a paywall online at https://www.nytimes.com/2021/09/22/business/media/gabby-petito-missing-white-woman-syndrome.html, accessed on 19 February 2022

Rolin, Kristina (2009) Standpoint theory as a methodology for the study of power relations, *Hypatia*, Vol. 24, No. 4 pp 218–226. Available online at https://www.jstor.org/stable/20618192

Grace James

Victoria LaPoe

Benjamin R. LaPoe II

Alesha Davis

Rosner, Helen (2021) The long American history of 'missing white woman syndrome', *New Yorker*, 8 October. Available online at https://www.newyorker.com/news/q-and-a/the-long-american-history-of-missing-white-woman-syndrome, accessed on 16 February 2022

Semali, Ladislaus M. and Kincheloe, Joe L. (eds) (1999), *What is Indigenous knowledge?*, New York, Falmer Press

Sommers, Zach (2016) Missing white woman syndrome: An empirical analysis of race and gender disparities in online news coverage of missing persons, *Journal of Criminal Law and Criminology*, Vol. 106, No. 2 pp 275–314. Available online at https://scholarlycommons.law.northwestern.edu/cgi/viewcontent.cgi?article=7586andcontext=jclc, accessed on 26 August 2022

Tauber, Rebecca (2022) Local activist calls for state action on missing black women and girls, GBH News, 1 February. Available online at https://www.wgbh.org/news/local-news/2022/02/01/local-activist-calls-for-state-action-on-missing-black-women-and-girls, accessed on 12 March 2022

Tribune Media Wire (2016) 3 NC counties make list of top 30 'murder capitals' in the US, FOX8 WGHP, 29 February. Available online at https://myfox8.com/news/the-30-murder-capitals-in-the-u-s/, accessed on 16 July 2022

Sunuwar, Dev Kumar (2019) Indigenous media caucus amplifies indigenous voices globally, *Cultural Survival*, 19 September. Available online at https://www.culturalsurvival.org/news/indigenous-media-caucus-amplifies-indigenous-voices-globally, accessed on 26 August 2022

US Department of the Interior (2021) Secretary Haaland creates new missing and murdered unit to pursue justice for missing or murdered American Indians and Alaska natives, *DOI News*, 1 April. Available online at https://www.doi.gov/news/secretary-haaland-creates-new-missing-murdered-unit-pursue-justice-missing-or-murdered-american, accessed on 16 July 2022

Walker, Nefertiti A. and Melton, E. Nicole (2015) The tipping point: The intersection of race, gender, and sexual orientation in intercollegiate sports, *Journal of Sport Management*, Vol. 29, No. 3 pp 257–271. Available online at https://doi.org/10.1123/jsm.2013-0079

Walsh, Jenna (2017) The national inquiry into the missing and murdered Indigenous women and girls of Canada: A probe in peril, *Indigenous Law Bulletin*, Vol. 8, No. 30 pp 6–10

Weitzman, Tamara and Naravaez, Chelsea (2021) Gabby Petito case: A timeline of her disappearance and homicide, *CBS News*, 21 October. Available online at https://www.cbsnews.com/news/gabby-petito-brian-laundrie-timeline/, accessed on 17 February 2022

Yunkaporta, Tyson and Shillingsworth, Doris (2020) Relationally responsive standpoint, *Journal of Indigenous Research*, Vol. 8. Available online at https://doi.org/10.26077/ky71-qt27

Note on the contributors

Grace James is a graduate student in the dual-degree programme at Ohio University (MSc, Journalism) and Universität Leipzig (MA, Global Mass Communication). She received her undergraduate degree in Communication at the University of Dayton in 2020, where she worked as a reporter and news editor for the student-run newspaper, *Flyer News*. She has also worked for Dayton Public Radio, the *Dayton Business Journal* and Ohio University as a research assistant. After graduation, she hopes to work in the publishing industry as a book editor or publicist.

Victoria L. LaPoe, PhD (Cherokee) is an Associate Professor in Ohio University's E. W. School of Journalism and Director of Journalism in the Honor Tutorial College, where she teaches both news and information and strategic communication courses. LaPoe served as vice-president and education chair of the Native American Journalists Association. She continues to serve on NAJA's education committee and is a lifetime NAJA member as well as Indigenous Issues editor for the national Media Diversity Forum. She is co-author of *Indian Country: Telling a story in a digital age*.

Benjamin R. LaPoe, II, PhD, is an Assistant Professor and Political Communication Certificate Director at Ohio University. He received his MSc in Journalism from West Virginia University and his PhD in Political Communication from the Manship School at Louisiana State University. His research focuses on the intersections or racism, sexism, political communication and media. LaPoe is co-author of *Resistance advocacy as news: Digital Black press covers the Tea Party* and *Indian Country: Telling a story in a digital age*, where he wrote about the history of media and minority press.

Alesha Davis is a third-year student at Ohio University, where she is pursuing a dual degree in Journalism and English in the Honors Tutorial College. She works as the equality director at the local student publication, the *Post*, inside the university's Division of Diversity and Inclusion, and risk management department of the university's Office of Global Opportunities. She is dedicated to issues involving race, gender and sexuality, and hopes to advocate for minority groups in academia. After graduation, Alesha hopes to work in the publishing industry and additional research pursuits.

All the authors contributed equally.

Conflict of Interest

The authors did not receive funding to conduct this research.

PAPER

Margaret Forster
Peter Meihana

Pouwhenua: Marking and storying the ancestral landscape

Colonisation stifled our storytelling traditions, disrupting the Indigenous communications landscape by silencing Māori voices and removing the tangible markers of our authority, histories, relationships and connections. Yet, Māori have a long legacy of resisting erasure of our memories and authority derived from the tribal territory. This paper explores a series of contemporary strategies to restore and share our stories and knowledge of Te Tapuwae Tahi a Rangitāne-nui-a-Rangi (the single footprint of great Rangitāne of the heavens); the tribal territory once occupied and controlled by the descendants of the ancestor Rangitāne. As part of He Tātai Whenua, a project to develop a Māori landscape classification system, we explore contemporary practices of mapping and marking the tribal territory and systems for assembling our knowledge of the environment. We describe here contemporary physical expressions and associated rituals in the tribal area of the Rangitāne people (i.e., Wairau area and along the Manawatū River) of the tradition of pouwhenua (posts used to mark tribal authority over an area or resource). We argue that this practice is a form of Indigenous and ethical mapping that seeks to disrupt mapping traditions that colonise and silence Indigeneity. Māori therefore are building on old traditions for naming and visualising the cultural landscape to continue our storytelling traditions, decolonise the landscape and connect with the communication landscapes of our ancestors.

Key words: storytelling, Indigeneity, sovereignty, Indigenous mapping

Introduction
Storytelling is an integral part of te ao Māori (the Māori world) expressed in a variety of ways – through our histories, narratives, carvings, artworks and performance such as song, dance and theatre. Stories carry our

cultural world, ideals and dreams and connect us to the gods, ancestors and tribal territory, providing a foundation for Indigenous identity and sense of belonging (Davis et. al. 1990a, 1990b; Harmsworth 1997; Harmsworth et. al. 2005; Hauiti 2011; Walker 1990).

Colonisation stifled our storytelling traditions, disrupting the Indigenous communications landscape by silencing Māori voices and removing the tangible markers of our authority, histories, relationships and connections (see, for example, Smith 1999; Walker 1990). Our pā or fortified villages are replaced by towns and cities. Our food gathering sites are felled or drained and replaced by farms. Our rivers are altered and straightened, turned into drains or areas for flood protection. This substantive transformation of the landscape (see, for example, Pawson and Brooking 2011; Young 2004) alters tribal connections with the environment and culminates in what Pawson and Brooking (2011) refer to as the 'Empires of Grass' with an emphasis on productivism.[1] Yet, Māori have a long legacy of resisting erasure of our memories and authority derived from the tribal territory. Although the visibility of Māori knowledge in public spaces is low, its ability to shape identity and sense of belonging of present and future generations remains. Building on this legacy this paper explores how continuity and connection is maintained with the communication landscapes of our ancestors. We argue that Indigenising public spaces is one initiative and a powerful ethical device to connect with culture, continue our storytelling traditions and decolonise the landscape.

This research was completed as part of He Tātai Whenua — a project to develop a Māori landscape classification system. A team of Indigenous environmental specialists and scientists explored contemporary practices of mapping and marking the tribal territory to synthesise a landscape classification system that can reveal, convey and express Māori environmental knowledge. By rendering visible this information bicultural spatial governance becomes a reality and Māori authority and Māori knowledge have a greater influence on environmental management.

Whakapapa is the underlying methodology of this research. Whakapapa is a Māori intellectual tradition that is often translated as genealogy or to place, in layers. As a methodology a whakapapa approach generates contemporary explanations for origin, relationships and expressions of phenomena (Royal 1998; Sadler 2007). It draws on Māori knowledge and ways of knowing to construct a critique that is cognisant of Māori understandings and key Māori political agendas such as rights and tribal sovereignty resulting in an evolving commentary of Māori identity and belonging (Royal 1998; Sadler 2007). Whakapapa methodology is used to explore a range of topics from tribal origins (see for example Te Rito 2007), social issues (see, for example, Graham 2009; Sadler 2007) through to histories (see, for example, Forster 2019; Mahuika 2019). In this paper, a whakapapa methodology is used to critique physical markers (i.e., carvings, signs, recreational areas) of Māori culture in public spaces. Key questions posed include: why and how certain

Margaret Forster

Peter Meihana

Māori practices such as taunahanaha (a process of naming of places) and pouwhenua are expressed today, and how do these expressions decolonise public spaces and reaffirm tribal authority?

This paper explores how Rangitāne in the Wairau and Manawatū regions tap into the ancestral communications landscape to assert their tribal authority and share that territory, their history and knowledge with others. As part of a national commemoration project Rangitāne ki Wairau unveiled a tau iho (canoe prow) that talks to ancestors and tribal relations and authority in the area. Peter Meihana narrates this story. Along the Manawatū River the local iwi collaborates in a community river framework that through storytelling recognises significant tribal sites and facilitates connectivity between people and the river. Several pouwhenua, posts used to mark tribal authority, are found along the Manawatū River. Margaret Forster narrates this story. Together we argue that these practices are a form of Indigenous and ethical mapping that seeks to disrupt mapping traditions that colonise and silence Indigeneity.

Ethical mapping: Disrupting the insidious effects of mapping

There are some aspects of the past that are best left behind such as mapping traditions that colonise and silence Indigeneity. While maps are complicit in the colonising project there is huge potential to repurpose to support a decolonising agenda; to create more ethical and equitable spaces for Indigeneity by reconsidering naming conventions and capturing Indigenous environmental knowledge (see Chambers 2006; Pearce and Louis 2008; Syme 2020). For example, increasingly Geographical Information Systems (GIS) and new spatial technologies are used to visualise the tribal landscape by recording Indigenous knowledge and oral histories in culturally appropriate ways. These new methodologies and tools are then used to support tribal land – and water-scape development – and perform environmental modelling and planning to contribute to meaningful self-management (Proctor and Harmsworth 2021). Access to this type of information also facilitates participation in land claims, contemporary resource management and local government planning processes supporting a shift towards bicultural spatial governance.

Another dimension that is quickly lost in a mapping environment is the lived experiences and links between people, communities (i.e. the human components) and place. Davis et al. refer to this as signposts that remind us that 'place has a human dimension' (1990b: 5). So, maps excel at capturing geophysical aspects but not at representing thoughts, aspirations, histories, or broader socio-political interests. In the remainder of this paper, we explore contemporary expressions of Māori place naming and mapping traditions that mark territory and convey human presence and ancestral connections to the tribal territory.

Te Tapuwae Tahi a Rangitāne-nui-a-Rangi: Mapping the tribal territory

Naming the land is an important practice common to all peoples and cultures. Since the arrival of the first Polynesian explorers Māori named the places they discovered and later settled. The process of naming – taunahanaha – embedded tribal authority, sacredness, spirit and tribal knowledge in the landscape; moreover, it was a means of mapping and claiming authority over newly discovered lands (Davis et. al. 1990a, 1990b).

Te Tapuwae Tahi o Rangitāne-nui-a-Rangi – the single footprint of great Rangitāne of the heavens – is a whakataukī (saying) that references the extent of the territory once occupied and controlled by the descendants of Rangitāne. This area was originally demarcated by Whātonga, the grandfather of Rangitāne (McEwen 1990). Traditions refer to the arrival of the Kurahaupō waka (ocean-going vessel) at Nukutaurua, on the Mahia peninsula. From here Whātonga and his family moved south where they built a meeting house, giving it the name *Heretaunga*. Following a domestic dispute with his wife, Hotuwaipara, Whātonga took leave, sailing south along the Wairarapa coast. He entered Raukawakawa Moana (Cook Strait) and crossed to the northern South Island where he stopped briefly before sailing north up the Kāpiti coast until he reached the Manawatū River. From here he sailed upstream arriving at Te Taperenui o Whātonga (Forty Mile Bush). The descendants of Whātonga over generations populated the area encircled by their ancestor (Meihana and Morris 2020). Successive generations walked the land, named it, occupied it and utilised its resources until European explorers arrived and imposed their own names on the landscape as a precursor to colonisation, settlement and the eventual taking of the land. By 1870, Rangitāne in both North and South Islands were divested of nearly all their traditional lands, save some small reserves (NZ Government 2010, 2015). The impact of land loss was devastating, not only in lost economic opportunities, but also in terms of lost mātauranga (knowledge) (NZ Government 2010, 2015).

Today the descendants of Whātonga make up four distinct but connected contingents in the Manawatū, Tamaki-nui-a-rua, Wairarapa and Wairau. Each contingent has engaged in activities including processes that investigate unethical alienation of tribal territory and cultural revitalisation projects to reaffirm authority over the tribal territory. This paper explores how descendants of Whātonga in the Manawatū and Wairau areas are disrupting colonial narratives by centring and retelling their stories to make explicit the continuity and connections with communication landscapes of the ancestors.

Ethical storytelling in the Wairau region

On 24 January 2020, Rangitāne ki Wairau unveiled Te Tauihu o te Waka a Māui, a large canoe prow made of bronze and steel on land owned by Rangitāne (Figure 1). Te Tauihu o te Waka a Māui is the result of a tremendous amount of work by numerous people, throughout an

Margaret Forster

Peter Meihana

extended period of time. This project acknowledges the authority of mana whenua (local tribal groups) and raises the visibility of Māori histories and tribal relations in the Wairau area. In this regard it is a decolonising project creating an ethical and equitable space for Indigenous voices. It is also a physical symbol of bicultural relations across the Wairau community. In years to come the significance of the Tauihu will become even more apparent.

Figure 1: Te Tauihi o te Waka a Māui, a carved canoe prow located in Blenheim that symbolises Rangitāne ki Wairau authority and local history in the area. Credit: Peter Meihana

Te Tauihu o te Waka a Māui

Before commenting on the Tauihu itself some background to its construction is warranted. This background speaks to the ways in which Māori contest existing narratives in an attempt at creating space for tribal-centred narratives. In 2019, as part of the Tuia 250 commemorations, Rangitāne, Ngāti Kuia and Ngāti Apa welcomed a flotilla of vessels into Meretoto – Ships Cove. Tuia 250 was a national commemoration of initial contact in 1769-70 between Māori and Pākehā (non-Māori) (Manatū Taonga, 2019). It celebrates the dual heritage of this country, in particular our shared histories and voyaging and navigation traditions.

The Tuia 250 flotilla included two waka hourua (double hulled canoes) and a replica of the Endeavour (Manatū Taonga 2019). All three tribes trace their descent from the Kurahaupō waka and ancestors that began migrating south from the North Island beginning in the fifteenth and sixteenth centuries. Ngāi Tara crossed over first, then Ngāti Māmoe and Ngāti Tumatakokiri, who were later joined by Rangitāne and Ngāti Apa. Ngāti Kuri and other Ngāi Tahu hapū (subtribes) followed in quick succession (Phillipson 1995).

The Marlborough Sounds was a staging post for southern migrations. Often the movement of early migrants was recorded in the landscape. Ngāti Tumatakokiri, for instance, are remembered in the names of certain islands and mountains in the Marlborough Sounds and a lake on Rangitoto Island. Ngāti Mamoe is also remembered, particularly in the names of hills to the north of the Wairau Valley and the bays and inlets of Te Koko o Kupe (Cloudy Bay). Among the many ancestors who are immortalised in the landscape, Kupe is the most conspicuous. According to local oral tradition, Kupe did not settle in Aotearoa; rather he and Ngahue led an exploratory expedition, gathering information for later Polynesian settlers. Kupe's granddaughter, Waipuna, married Tautoki and they begat Rangitāne. Their descendants were among the Kurahaupō waka people who migrated to the northern South Island. It is noted that Kurahaupō peoples did not enter an empty land; archaeological research now suggests that Te Pokohiwi o Kupe (Wairau Bar) was first occupied in the 13th century (Walter et al. 2017).

When James Cook arrived in Tōtaranui (Queen Charlotte Sound) in 1770 he learnt from the Kurahaupō community, no doubt with the assistance of the Tahitian, Tupaia, that there were two islands that made up the country – Ea Hei no Mauwe and Toai Poonamoo. These names are as recorded on Cook's map. From that time the oral map constructed by Māori was gradually erased. Tōtaranui was supplanted by Queen Charlotte Sound, Meretoto became Ship's Cove and Punaruawhiti is now more commonly known as Endeavour Inlet. Some names did survive, albeit in a corrupted form. Arapāoa (island), a reference to the downward blow of Kupe's toki (Adze) that killed Te Wheke a Muturangi, was for a long time rendered as 'Arapawa'. That name, and others, were recently corrected as part of the Te Tauihu o Te Waka a Māui Treaty of Waitangi settlement (Rangitāne Settlement).

Tuia 250 drew controversy and condemnation from some Māori communities around Aotearoa as the initial brief was focused on a discovery narrative that privileged British colonial history and downplayed the oppression and trauma experienced by Māori communities (Forster and Belgrave 2022). In the Wairau area the killing of Te Maro, a chief of Ngāti Oneone, is not forgotten by his descendants (Dewes 2018). In the northern South Island the commemorations were also looked on with suspicion. However, what was a celebration of Cook (the first English navigator to land in Aotearoa New Zealand) ended up a celebration of Māori history and knowledge and the connections made with Tupaia, the Tahitian navigator who accompanied Cook on his first expedition. As part of Tuia 250 Ngāti Kuia and Ngāti Apa ki te Ratō built carved waka, providing a catalyst for the revival of waka culture within the tribes. Rangitāne approached this aspect of Tuia 250 in a slightly different way to their Kurahaupō relatives, deciding instead to build a large canoe prow on land owned by the tribe in Blenheim (Manatū Taonga 2019).

Te Rūnanga a Rangitāne, the entity tasked with managing tribal assets, always championed the preservation and retelling of tribal narratives.

Margaret Forster

Peter Meihana

Te Tauihu o te Waka a Māui is not the first work to be commissioned by Rangitāne. Today, pouwhenua representing the ancestors Te Huataki, Kupe, Te Hau, Ihaia Kaikōura and most recently, a pouwhenua dedicated to ancestors credited with the construction of the 22km of hand-dug canals that feed into Waikaripi (Wairau Lagoons), are erected. Although led by Rangitāne, Te Tauihu was a community initiative that brought together a number of groups with an interest in art, culture and heritage.

Te Tauihu is a physical representation of whakapapa (genealogy). It connects ancestors to descendants and people with the physical environment. At one end of the Tauihu stands Māui, the hero figure whose exploits are well known throughout Polynesia. He acquired fire for humanity, slowed down the sun and fished up islands (Orbell 1995). In the present context Maui also embodies navigational achievement and his exploits are clear to see in the nomenclature of the North and South Islands – Te Ika a Māui and Te Waka a Māui. Moreover, Māui ultimately reminds us that we live on a Pacific island and as such share with others in the Pacific a common future.

Standing opposite Māui is Tukauae, a significant figure in the consolidation of Kurahaupō whakapapa in the northern South Island. His name is remembered in a low pass connecting the Wairau Valley and the Para wetlands – Te Whiringa-a-Tukauae. The name is a reference to the lashing together of flax and raupo that was once harvested from the wetland. It also acknowledges Tukauae's marriages to Hinepango, Hinerewha and Ruamate, all of whom are represented on Te Tauihu. Another significant ancestress is Te Heiwi; her marriage to Ngāti Apa migrant, Tarakaipa, produced numerous descendants, many of whom married Tukauae's children and grandchildren. Today these lines of descent flow into the Rangitāne, Ngāti Kuia and Ngāti Apa.

Lastly, Te Tauihu also acknowledges the physical environment. Running through the centre of the middle section, linking Māui and Tukauae, is Nga-Wairau-o-Ruatere (Wairau River) and Paepaetangata (the ranges dividing Wairau and Whakatū-Nelson). Both were fundamental to human occupation. Nga-Wairau-o-Ruatere comprises not only the main river, but the valley's springs and wetlands also. Paepaetangata was a source of pakohe (metasomatised mudstone or argillite) which was exploited by the first Polynesian settlers. Large adzes made of pakohe were often interred with the dead indicating its importance. Some individuals were also buried with perforated moa eggs (Meihana and Bradley 2018).

The aforementioned ancestors were recorded in tribal whakapapa manuscripts during the nineteenth century. On 2 September 1863, Meihana Kereopa, an early Kurahaupō scribe, met with Rangitāne elders at Wairau. Among those present was Ihaia Kaikōura (*Meihana Manuscript, n.d.*). Ihaia was the only Kurahaupō rangatira to sign Te Tiriti o Waitangi and was a signatory to the 1856 Rangitāne receipt of payment (Te Tau Ihu o Te Waka a Māui 2008). The whakapapa provided by Ihaia was to accompany monies collected from Rangitāne and Ngāti Kuia elders to support 'Te Kereme', the Ngāti Māmoe and Ngāi Tahu claim (*Meihana Manuscript, n.d.*). It was this particular whakapapa that underpins the construction of Te Tauihu, providing another layer of interpretation that might well have been confined to the archives.

Prior to the physical construction of Te Tauihu certain protocols were observed. Whatu mauri – stones imbued or invested with a life force – were buried beneath where Te Tauihu would eventually stand. On this occasion whatu were collected from the summit of maunga Tapuae-o-Uenuku and Te Pokohiwi-o-Kupe were chosen. Also buried with the whatu was the pito (umbilical cord nearest to the baby's body) of a child thus establishing a connection with the land. Once Te Tauihu was erected, a dawn ceremony was conducted. At this time Te Tauihu itself was imbued with mauri, binding it to the mauri implanted in the stones that lay beneath it. Dawn is the appropriate time for such ceremonies because karakia (incantations) are at their most potent and the breaking of dawn allowed the welcoming of Te Tauihu immediately into the world of light.

Te Tauihu is a modern pouwhenua, a marker of tribal authority and a communicative device that carries whakapapa, relations and history and most importantly, connects the present and the future to the past. A characteristic of Indigenous resistance is the ability to invert colonising practices and create spaces where Indigenous ways of story telling are privileged. Tuia 250 was a highly contested moment; nevertheless, it was the context in which Te Tauihu was realised. The whakapapa that underpins Te Tauihu was in the first instance recorded for the purpose of land claims. Just as whakapapa is a statement of mana whenua (authority of local tribe over land), so too is Te Tauihu.

Ethical storytelling along the Manawatū River

Along the Manawatū River the continuance of the pouwhenua tradition has been evident for some time, ranging from carvings representing ancestors, tau ihu and more recently whare kōrero also known as educational kiosks. This section of the paper explores how the tribal landscape is storied and mapped in public spaces. As part of the Tātai Whenua project, public signs along the Manawatū River were critiqued to reveal a shift in narration of the river as a public and recreational area to the river as a tribal ancestor and shared space. This shift is facilitated by mana whenua-local government projects to implement the Manawatū River Framework (Palmerston North City Council 2016). These projects and this transition are showcased here.

Signs as indicators of social change

Ethical mapping is evident through a shift in how spaces are publicly narrated. For example, an analysis of signage along the Manawatū River provides a snapshot of Indigenous narrations and the changing meaning and value of the landscape. In part the intent of signage is set by legislation, in particular the Reserves Act 1977 that regulates the 'preservation and management of areas for the public' (s3(1)a) with an emphasis on recreation (s3,(1)i) wildlife (s3,(1)ii), Indigenous flora and fauna (s3,(1)iii), environmental and landscape interests (s3,(1)iv) and the 'natural, scenic, historic, cultural, archaeological, biological, geological, scientific, educational, community, or other special features or value' (s3,(1)v).

These drivers establish three distinct 'styles' of signage. Earlier signs (Figure 1) often feature a map of the area and some basic information about recreational use of the space and safety. These signs are informative, basic and functional, indicating the location of walkways, estimated walking times and areas where caution is required. Use of the Māori language as part of the signage is low and if present, macrons are often missing (for example, Maori not Māori), reflecting a bygone era when very little prominence was given to the Māori language or Māori knowledge of the land.

Many of the maps feature a 'You are here' icon placing an emphasis on the presence and needs of people. This reinforces Western notions of the environment as passive spaces to explore, conquer and consume (see for example, Simmonds 2009). The implication is that the presence of people at a location provides context, meaning and value as opposed to the environment itself taking centre stage, a feature of Māori understandings. The environment is an atua (deity), it is a living entity with its own energies and must therefore be respected as such (see, for example, Forster 2019; Royal 2003; Simmonds 2009). These values and understandings are not reflected within sign structure or text. Indeed, the human dimension, particularly local history – Māori and settler – is often absent, inferring human activity is somehow disconnected from the space. The space is a reserve – set apart from settled spaces where human activity is confined.

Signs created more recently tend to focus on scientific literacy (Figure 2) – providing geographical data and information about local flora and fauna. Māori names of place and native species are often present with correct use of macrons reflecting increased recognition in the public arena of the importance of Māori language and knowledge and the bicultural history of this nation. These spaces are still predominantly considered recreational with the presence of some historical, cultural and social narration. If present, historical information tends to promote the settler experience rather than local Māori history reflecting a privileging of specific types of knowledge and a reminder of the deep-rooted, far-reaching and continued impact of colonisation.

In recent years several projects along the Manawatū River addressing the health and wellbeing of waterscapes were prioritised. These projects are collaborations where Rangitāne (the local iwi) have partnered and codesigned projects with local government. Rangitāne involvement in local planning matters is mandatory. Statutory provisions (see Resource Management Act 1991 and Local Government Act 2002) create space for the pursuit of Māori interests and these are reflected in local plans, policies and strategies. While relations are contentious at times it is common practice now to involve Rangitāne in significant community development projects ensuring that cultural expressions are a feature of projects. The signage accompanying these newer projects (Figure 4) departs significantly from the earlier two styles discussed here (Figures 2 and 3). Four examples are provided here – OURS – the Manawatū River Leaders Accord initiative, Te Apiti (the Manawatū Gorge) Reserve, Tū te Manawa project and He Ara Kotahi network, the Manawatū River walkways and bridges. Each of these examples signifies a shift in the way the tribal landscape is storied and mapped in public spaces.

Figure 2: An example of a map found in a local reserve that is informative and functional and devoid of Indigenous narrative. Credit: Margaret Forster

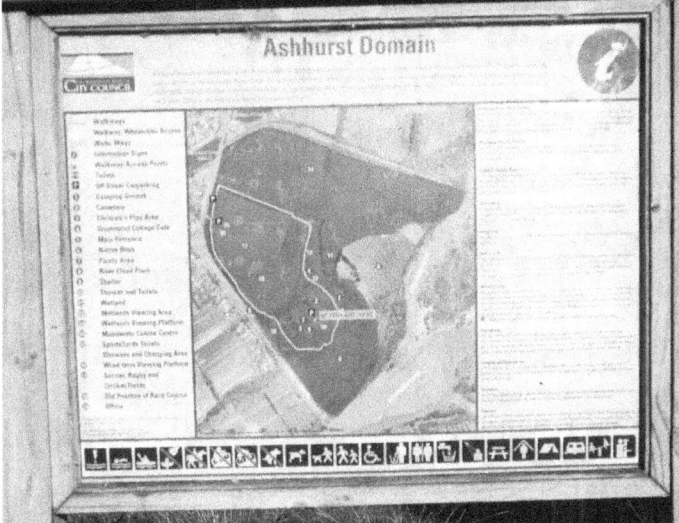

Figure 3: Examples of signs found in a local reserve that emphasise a scientific narration with some references to Indigeneity. Credit: Margaret Forster

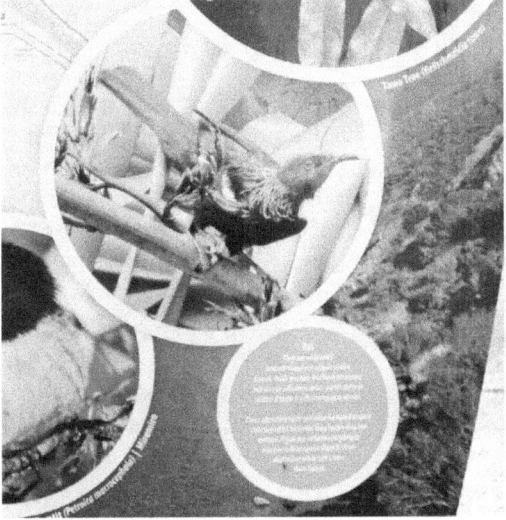

Margaret Forster

Peter Meihana

Figure 4: An example of a sign found in a local reserve that emphasises a protective narrative from both Māori and non-Māori perspectives. Credit: Margaret Forster

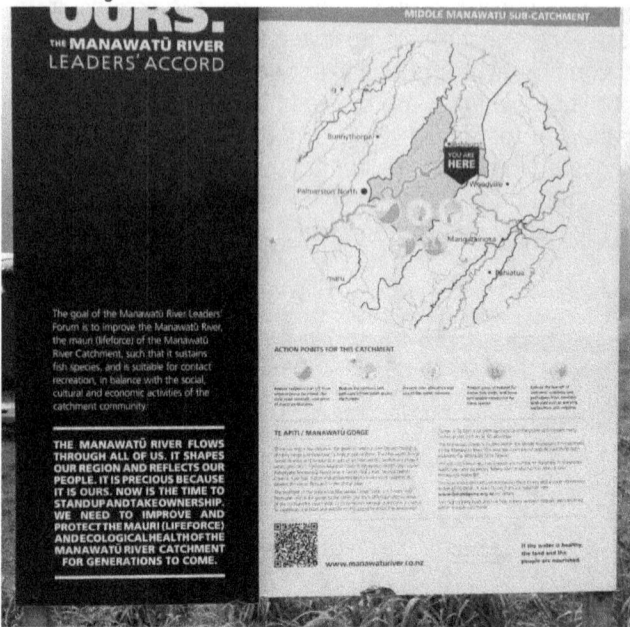

OURS. The Manawatū River leaders' accord

The Manawatū River Leader's Accord brings together a broad range of freshwater stakeholders from the region around a shared goal – to improve the health of the Manawatū River (Manawatū River Leader's Forum 2011). This goal is encapsulated by the following statement:

> The Manawatū River flows through all of us. It shapes our region and reflects our people. It is precious because it is ours. Now is the time to stand up and take ownership. We need to improve and protect the mauri (lifeforce) and ecological health of the Manawatū River catchment for generations to come (OURS. The Manawatū River Leaders' Accord 2011: 47).

This entity is part of a national programme to reform freshwater management in this country that has culminated in the National Policy Statement for Freshwater Management (NPS) (Ministry of Environment 2020). The NPS recognises the fundamental importance of water and the critical need to restore and preserve these resources for the community today and in the future. This policy statement represents a significant shift in freshwater management including substantive roles of tangata whenua (Indigenous people of Aotearoa) in regard to mana whakahaere (involvement in high level decision making), kaitiakitanga (Māori environmental interests and practices) and manaakitanga (the process of demonstrating respect, generosity and care for freshwater and others) (Ministry for Environment 2020).

The Manawatū River Leaders' Accord has devised an action plan to meet the requirements as set out by the NPS (2011). It identifies four goals:

1. The Manawatū River becomes a source of regional pride and mana [authority].
2. Waterways in the Manawatū Catchment are safe, accessible, swimmable, and provide good recreation and food resources.
3. The Manawatū Catchment and waterways are returned to a healthy condition.
4. Sustainable use of the land and water resources of the Manawatū Catchment continues to underpin the economic prosperity of the Region (Manawatū River Leaders' Accord, 2011).

These ideals and the collaborative nature of the Leaders' Forum are reflected in various initiatives and signage along the river. A typical sign communicates the intent of the Accord in its messaging *'Now is the time to stand up and take ownership. We need to improve and protect the mauri (lifeforce) and ecological health'* and through the use of whakatauki: *kei te kōrero wai, kei te kōrero whenua, kei te kōrero tangata (if the water is healthy, the land and the people are nourished)*. Rangitāne interests are also highly visible through the use of Māori place names, brief references to tribal history as narrativised by the tribe (i.e. names and location of pā) and through the kaitiakitanga and stewardship messaging. These types of communications reframe the environment as inclusive spaces where tribal authority and connections are acknowledged and distinctiveness (i.e., Māori and settler histories) is celebrated. The intent of the Manawatū River Leaders' Accord and initiatives that are completed are showcased on a website (https://www.manawaturiver.co.nz/) and through a number of engaging and informative videos (see for example *10 years of the Manawatū River Leaders' Accord* available at this link https://vimeo.com/637244138).

Te Apiti (The Manawatū Gorge)

Signage at the Manawatū Gorge predates the OURS initiative but nonetheless aligns well with the OURS' agenda to reaffirm Indigeneity and make more explicit the stories of the land and its people. A carved tomokanga (gateway) is present at Te Apiti (Manawatū Gorge Scenic Reserve). Tomokanga are often found at the entryway to marae, a cultural complex or meeting area of the local tribe.

The tomokanga was designed and carved by local Rangitāne, Ngāti Apa and Muaūpoko artist Craig Kawana. It evokes a protective karakia (incantation) over all who travel through the gorge. The carvings represent: significant atua associated with the forest; prominent geographical features and cultural markers such as the Ruahine and Tararua ranges; local flora and fauna; connections to local hapū (subtribe), marae (cultural centres) and genealogical connections; common activities associated with the gorge such as travelling between the coasts; and prominent ancestors including Whātonga who named places and waterways in the region, Popoto and Ruatea. This information is provided on a set of signs beside the carving itself.

Inside the carved frame of the tomokanga are a series of signs that provide educational material on geological (formation of the gorge and information about rocks that can be found in the surrounding area), ecological (information about native flora and fauna), historic and cultural information associated with the gorge. Tribal information is given prominence including: the local iwi pepeha (tribal greeting) and the well known (at least locally) whakatauki *Tini whetu ki te Rangi, ko Rangitāne nui ki te whenua* (like the myriad of stars in the sky, so are the people of great Rangitāne on the earth); information about prominent ancestors and local pā; and kōrero tuku iho (tribal narratives) about the creation of the gorge and events from which place names in the region are derived such as Manawatū, Te Ahu a Turanga and Potaehinetewhaiwa. Other information showcased on these signs are: scientific information about the local flora and fauna including the now extinct huia bird; information about a local biodiversity project led by the Department of Conversation and Horizons Regional Council in association with local communities, tangata whenua, local, regional and central government organisations to 'improve the natural, historic and recreational values' (statement found on the sign itself) associated with the gorge; and other cultural information such as settler history and history associated with building the roadways through the gorge.

Tū te Manawa

Tū te Manawa is a project to erect eight whare mātauranga, also known as educational kiosks, along the Manawatū River to 'tell stories of the cultural and historical importance of each of the sites' (OURS. The Manawatū River Leaders' Accord n.d.). The intent is to bring people back to the river and promote an increased appreciation of the area and its resources. Such activities have the potential to establish stronger connections to waterscapes ideally leading to increased emphasis on action around sustainability.

The project is funded by the Ministry for the Environment and is linked to realising the NPS and the objectives of the Manawatū River Leaders' Accord. Each site has a similar design – shaped like a house with two walls where information panels are displayed. There are four types of panels – one containing information about the Tū te Manawa project in the form of a map and other panels containing information about science, culture and community (click on this link https://www.manawaturiver.co.nz/activities/tu-te-manawa/ to find more detailed information and view images of each of the Whare Mātauranga).

The cultural information is selected and narrated by the local hapū. The first whare mātauranga is located at Ngāmoko (Norsewood). It is a carved whare with a koruru (head) at the apex of the roof and carved maihi (outstretched arms). The carvings reference local tribal genealogy and connections. The cultural information provided on the panels expands on the identity and belonging of the local hapū providing narrations about local marae, pepeha, significant local place names, ancestors and pā. The community panel tends to focus on local history particularly associated with settler experiences. The science panels provide information on local protection and enhancement projects and sentinel species. A sentinel species is a native species that provides an indication of the health and wellbeing of the waterways. At the Ngāmoko site there is some additional signage providing information about a native fish habitat restoration project. The restoration project is an OURS initiative. When viewed together this information clearly signals an intent to enhance the river ecosystem and connect communities to whenua as a critical step for achieving shared sustainability goals. This format and objectives are repeated at six more sites along the river with a final whare planned for Te Awahou (Foxton). There are slight variations reflecting the priorities and values of each hapū.

He Ara Kotahi (the Manawatū River network)

In 2018 the Palmerston North City Council released the Manawatū River Plan. A key objective of this plan is to realise the full potential of the river as a significant recreational asset in this region. This plan necessitates close engagement with the local Rangitāne people enabling tribal aspirations and interests to direct the type of activities planned and completed as part of this project.

He Ara Kotahi (A Pathway that Brings People Together) is a centrepiece of the Manawatū River plan. It is a bridge that connects Massey University, the science centres and Linton Army Camp to the city. It also provides access to the various walkways along the river. It is a physical and highly visible marker of Rangitāne authority and identity. From above, the bridge looks like a karaka tree, fallen across the river. The kowhaiwhai designs on the bridge reference the shape made by a native moth, the puriri, when it burrows into the bark of the karaka tree. At night the lights and rail make the bridge look like a waka floating on the river. These design elements acknowledge the importance of the karaka tree that was once a prominent feature and important source of food in this area. The waka metaphor is a reminder that the river was once a major highway connecting Māori communities throughout the region.

Along the bank are a series of educational signs that provide information about the local iwi, historical settlements that were once present alongside the river and the kōrero tuku iho of the creation of the Manawatū River and Te Apiti, the Manawatū Gorge. As is common with recreational reserves there is also information about local flora and fauna. All these narrations have been designed and developed in collaboration with Rangitāne and licensed te reo translators.

The Manawatū River network has several other sites of cultural significance. Key sites include the Ahimate Reserve, the Tini Whetu i te Rangi pathway and the Urban Eels platform. Ahimate was an old pā. In 2020 five pou (carved posts) were erected representing each of the

Margaret Forster

Peter Meihana

five Rangitane hapū. This area is now the site of an annual Matariki fire festival bringing families back to the river. At the entrance to the site is a carved mareikura (female guardian) and whatukura (male guardian) providing a protective presence over the space.

In 2021 the Tini Whetu i te Rangi pathway was opened. This was designed by local Rangitane artist Warren Warbrick and is a physical expression of the whakatauki *Tini whetu i te Rangi, ko Rangitane i te whenua*. The urban eels platform was opened in 2020 and is the fruit of a partnership between Rangitane and local government to restore the habitat and increase the numbers of eels in local waterways. It is a platform that is accessed from He Ara Kotahi where eels can be viewed. The most recent addition is Te Arapiki a Tāne where He Kupu Rangatira, The Proverb Pathway, is located. The pathway represents community unity and the various cultures that now call the Manawatū home. There are 12 signs that appear in the language of origin of the proverb, a Māori language equivalent and an English translation (to access pictures of the pathway and information about the proverbs visit this website: https://www.pncc.govt.nz/Parks-recreation/Walks-and-walkways/Te-Arapiki-a-Tāne.

Each of these sites are visual expressions of rangatiratanga (tribal sovereignty connections) and markers of tribal identity designed specifically to bring people back to the river, to reconnect and to support efforts to enhance the health and wellbeing of the Manawatū River.

Pouwhenua: Marking and storying the ancestral landscape

The examples showcased in this paper are contemporary expressions of tribal authority in the form of physical markers that hold and communicate the lived memories and multi-layered interactions of people and place. This is consistent with the custom of pouwhenua. Pouwhenua are a Māori form of mapping. Mapping the ancestral landscape is an act of rangatiratanga or tribal sovereignty. By naming the landscape and retelling and sharing tribal histories the landscape is living – alive and dynamic. In the past pouwhenua were markers of tribal boundaries or signalled the location of resources under collective protection. Pouwhenua are intricately carved posts as seen marking garden plantations through to natural forms such as a grove of tī kōuka trees or a stack of stones that mark important food gathering sites or settlements. Carved forms were often a focal point for atua evoking their presence and energies to protect an area or resource (Makereti 1938: 193). Carved pouwhenua are also creative representations of tribal connection – telling a story of tribal association with an area or resource.

There is reference to pouwhenua at one of the sites researched for this paper. At the Apiti (Manawatū Gorge Reserve), groves of karaka trees are an indication of settlement sites:

> Located near Te Apiti were a number of significant Rangitāne pā and kāinga (villages). These include Parahaki, Kauhanga, Motuere,

Te Wharau, Kopuanui, Otangaki and Raukawa Pā. The present day locations of these sites are often identified by a grove of karaka trees (text supplied by Rangitāne for sign at Te Āpiti outlining local tribal history).

This point is also reiterated at He Ara Kotahi bridge where there is an entire placard centred on a significant site close to the river called Te Uru Karaka (Karaka Grove). This is one of the few remaining remnants of karaka groves along the river and stands as a monument to the importance of the karaka tree for the survival of Māori communities who resided along the river.

The contemporary examples of pouwhenua discussed in this paper are derived from this tradition. Mana whenua are continuing the practice of marking the landscape and mapping the tribal territory to make visible their interests, to connect to the past, to communicate their stories and celebrate their identity and belonging as shaped by the tribal territory. This includes performing various rituals like dawn ceremonies to activate the space where these markers reside and reawaken connections to the past and to ancestors. This is a decolonising project reasserting Indigenous authority and autonomy. It also develops new relations with others who frequent and reside around these spaces.

Cultural markers or expressions embedded into bridges, walkways, signage and artistic expressions (such as carvings, artworks and written compositions) are all gaining greater prominence and becoming a normalised feature of bicultural spatial governance. These types of expressions are sometimes referred to as tohu whenua 'landmarks associated with whakapapa kōrero [genealogical narratives, ancestral histories] that validated a rohe (region) of a whānau, hapū or iwi, as well as tūrangawaewae [Indigenous homeland]' (Te Atawhai o te Ao 2019: 12). Pouwhenua, therefore, physically transform and decolonise a place. Consequently, Māori knowledge and political agenda (for example Māori language revitalisation and biculturalism) become a normalised feature of the landscape influencing the values and hearts of all who move through that space.

The Tauihu o te Waka a Maui in Wairau and the whare mātauranga, bridge, walkways, pou and other design elements found alongside the Manawatū River are modern versions of pouwhenua. Pouwhenua are part of a new Indigenous communicative landscape that connects the past, present and future. Pouwhenua are clear physical markers of tribal authority and interests. They are designed to connect (or reconnect) people with place and to educate people about place, establishing new connections to Te Tapuwae tahi o Rangitāne-nui-a-Rangi, the territory still occupied and to a certain extent, controlled by the descendants of Rangitāne.

Margaret Forster

Peter Meihana

Glossary

atua	deity
hapū	subtribe
kaitiakitanga	Māori environmental interests and practices
karakia	incantation
kōrero tuku iho	tribal narratives
kōruru	carved head on a carved house
maihi	outstretched 'arms' on a carved house
mana	authority
manaakitanga	generosity, ethic of care
mana whakahaere	involvement in decision-making
mana whenua	tribe with authority over local area
marae	cultural centre
mareikura	carved post representing female guardian
Matariki	Māori new year
mātauranga	knowledge
mauri	lifeforce
pā	fortified villages
Pākehā	non-Māori
pakohe	metasomatised mudstone or argillite
pepeha	tribal greeting of key tribal features
pito	umbilical cord
pou	carved posts
pouwhenua	custom of marking the tribal landscape
rangatiratanga	tribal sovereignty
tangata whenua	indigenous people of Aotearoa
tau iho	canoe prow
taunahanaha	custom, process of naming the tribal territory
Te ao Māori	the Māori world
toki	adze
tomokanga	gateway
tūrangawaewae	place to stand, ancestral authority
Waka/waka hourua	canoe, double hulled canoes
whakapapa	genealogy
whakapapa kōrero	genealogical narratives, tribal histories

whakataukī	sayings
Whānau, hapū, iwi	Māori collectives associated with the extended family, the subtribe and tribe
whare kōrero	school of learning
whare mātauranga	education kiosks
whatukura	carved post representing male guardians
whatu mauri	stones embued with a lifeforce

Note

[1] Maximising the largely economic productivity of the environment. This imperative is premised on an assumption that the environment is a commodity and its value is linked to its economic viability

References

Carter, Lyn (2005) Naming to own: Place names as indicators of human interaction with the environment, *AlterNative* Vol. 1, No. 1 pp 7–24

Chambers, Robert (2006) Participatory mapping and geographical information systems: Whose map? Who is empowered and who disempowered? Who gains and who loses?, *The Electronic Journal on Information Systems in Developing Countries*, Vol. 25, No. 2 pp 1–11. DOI: 10.1002/j.1681-4835.2006.tb00163.x

Davis, Te Aue, O'Regan, Tipene and Wilson, John (1990a) *He kōrero pūrākau mō ngā taunahanahatanga a ngā tūpuna. Place Names of the Ancestors. A Māori oral history atlas*, Wellington, New Zealand Geographic Board

Davis, Te Aue O'Regan, Tipene and Wilson, John (1990b) *Ngā tohu pūmahara: The survey pegs of the past, Understanding Māori place names*, Wellington, New Zealand Geographic Board

Dewes, Te Kura o Te Marama (2018) Ngāti Oneone to re-tell accurate history of Gisborne, *Te Ao Māori News*, 18 August. Available online at https://www.teaomaori.news/ngati-oneone-re-tell-accurate-history-gisborne

Forster, Margaret (2019) He Tātai Whenua: Environmental genealogies, *Genealogy*, Vol. 3, No. 2 pp 1–14. DOI: 10.3390/genealogy3030042

Forster, Margaret and Belgrave, David (2022) Agency and action, McLennan, Sharon, Forster, Margaret Hazou, Rand, Littlewood, David and Neill, Carol (eds) *Tū Rangaranga rights, responsibilities and global citizenship in Aotearoa New Zealand*, Auckland, Massey University Press pp 298–310

Hakopa, Hauiti (2011) The Paepae: Spatial information technologies and the geography of narratives. Unpublished PhD thesis, Dunedin, University of Otago

Harmsworth, Garth (1997) Maori values and GIS, *GIS Asia Pacific: The Geographic Technology Publication for the Asia Pacific Region*, April pp 40–43

Harmsworth, Garth, Park, Mick and Walker, Dean (2005) *Report of the development and use of GIS for iwi and hapū: Motueka Case Study, Aotearoa New Zealand*, Landcare Research New Zealand

McEwen, Jock (1990) *Rangitāne: A tribal history*, Auckland, Raupo Publishing

Mahuika, Nēpia (2019) A brief history of whakapapa: Māori approaches to genealogy, *Genealogy*, Vol. 3, No. 2 Art. 32 pp 1–13. Available online at https://doi.org/10.3390/genealogy3020032

Meihana manuscript (n.d.) Ngāti Kuia Archives, Nelson

Makereti (1938) *The old-time Māori*. London, Victor Gollancz. Available online at http://nzetc.victoria.ac.nz/tm/scholarly/tei-MakOldT.html

Margaret Forster

Peter Meihana

Manatū Taonga/Ministry for Culture and Heritage (2019) *Tuia 250 report*, Wellington, Manatū Taonga. Available online at https://mch.govt.nz/sites/default/files/projects/TUIA_250_Report_English_Digital.pdf

Manawatū Rivers Leaders' Accord (2011) *Action plan*, Palmerston North. Available online at https://www.manawaturiver.co.nz/wp-content/uploads/2018/11/Manawatu-River-Leaders-Accord-Action-Plan-2011-2016.pdf

Meihana, Peter and Bradley, Cecil (2018) Repatriation, reconciliation and the inversion of patriarchy, *Journal of the Polynesian Society*, Vol. 127, No. 3 pp 307–324. DOI: 10.15286/jps.127.3.307-324

Meihana, Peter and Morris, Hone (2020) Tangata Whenua, Tennant, Margaret, Watson, Geoff and Taylor, Kerry (eds) *City at the centre: A history of Palmerston North*, Auckland, Massey University Press pp 28–59

Ministry for the Environment (2020) *National policy statement for freshwater management*, Wellington. Available online at https://environment.govt.nz/assets/Publications/Files/national-policy-statement-for-freshwater-management-2020.pdf

New Zealand Government (2010) *Rangitāne o Wairau deed of settlement*, Wellington, New Zealand Government

New Zealand Government (2015) *Rangitāne o Manawatū deed of settlement*, Wellington, New Zealand Government

Orbell, Margaret (1995) *The illustrated encyclopedia of Māori myth and legend*, Christchurch, Canterbury University Press

OURS. The Manawatū River Leaders' Accord (n.d.) *Story of Tū te Manawa*. Available online at https://www.manawaturiver.co.nz/activities/tu-te-manawa/

Palmerston North City Council (2016) *Manawatū River framework*, Palmerston North City Council. Available online at https://indd.adobe.com/view/4b1a932f-b476-4bcf-a910-c9698b82f499

Palmerston North City Council (2018) *The Manawatū River plan*, Palmerston North. Available online at https://www.pncc.govt.nz/media/3130986/manawatu-river-plan-2018.pdf

Pawson, Eric and Brooking, Tom (eds) (2011) *Seeds of empire: The environmental transformation of New Zealand*, London, I.B. Tauris

Pearce, Margaret and Louis, Renee (2008) Mapping Indigenous depth of place, *American Indian Culture & Research Journal*, Vol. 32, No. 3 pp 107–126. DOI: 10.17953/aicr.32.3.n7g22w816486567j

Phillipson, Grant (1995) *The northern South Island*, Rangahaua Whanui Series, Wellington, Waitangi Tribunal

Proctor, Jonathan and Harmsworth, Garth (2021) He Tātai Whenua: Towards developing a Māori landscape classification framework, Hill, Carolyn (ed.) *Kia whakanuia te whenua. People, place, landscape*, Auckland, Mary Egan Publishing pp 258–268

Royal, Te Ahukaramū Charles (1998) Te ao mārama: A research paradigm, *He Pukenga Kōrero*, Vol. 4, No. 1 pp 1–8

Royal, Te Ahukaramū Charles (2003) *The woven universe: Selected writings of Rev. Māori Marsden*, Ōtaki, the Estate of Rev. Māori Marsden

Sadler, Hone (2007) Mātauranga Māori (Māori epistemology), *International Journal of the Humanities* Vol. 4 pp 33–45

Simmonds, Naomi (2009) *Mana wāhine geographies: Spiritual, spatial and embodied understandings of Papatūānuku*. Unpublished Master's thesis, Hamilton, University of Waikato

Smith, Linda Tuhiwai (1999) *Decolonizing methodologies: Research and Indigenous peoples*, London, Zed Books

Syme, Tony (2020) Localizing landscapes: A call for respectful design in Indigenous counter mapping, *Information, Communication & Society*, Vol. 23, No. 8 pp 1106–1122. DOI: 10.1080/1369118X.2019.1701695

Te Atawhai o te Ao (2019) He ara uru ora: Traditional Māori understandings of trauma and wellbeing, Wanganui. Available online at https://teatawhai.maori.nz/wp-content/

uploads/2020/04/He-Ara-Uru-Ora.pdf

Te Rito, Joseph (2007) Whakapapa: A framework for understanding identity, *MAI Review* pp 1–10

Te Tau Ihu o te Waka a Māui v.1 (2008) Waitangi Tribunal report, Wai 785. Wellington, Legislation Direct. Available online at https://forms.justice.govt.nz/search/Documents/WT/wt_DOC_68199155/Te%20Tau%20Ihu%20Vol%201.pdf

Walker, Ranginui (1990) *Ka whawhai tonu mātou: Struggle without end*, Auckland, Penguin

Walter, Richard, Buckley, Hallie, Jacomb, Chris and Matisoo-Smith, Elizabeth (2017) Mass migration and the Polynesian settlement of New Zealand, *Journal of World Prehistory*, Vol. 30 pp 351–376. DOI: 10.1007/s10963-017-9110-y

Young, David (2004) *Our islands, our selves*, Dunedin, University of Otago Press

Note on the contributors

Margaret Forster (Ngāti Kahungunu, Rongomaiwāhine) is an Indigenous educator and researcher passionate about ensuring Māori worldviews and voices are part of the solution to the challenges of contemporary living. She has a particular interest in normalising human interactions with the environment that reflect our obligations to ancestors and future generations.

Peter Meihana is from Te Tauihu o Te-Waka-a-Maui, and is of Ngāti Kuia, Rangitāne, Ngāti Apa ki Te Rā Tō and Ngāi Tahu descent. He is a trustee on Te Rūnanga o Rangitāne o Wairau and sits on committees for Ngāti Apa ki Te Rā Tō. Peter publishes histories and traditions of the Kurahaupō peoples of Te Tauihu. He is a senior lecturer in History at Te Kunenga ki Purehūroa-Massey University.

Acknowledgements/Conflict of interest

The authors would like to acknowledge the incredible work that is being done by descendents of Whātonga to reclaim mana whenua over Te Tapuwae Tahi a Rangitāne-nui-a-Rangi. The Tātai Whenua project was supported by an Endeavour Fund grant from the Ministry of Business, Innovation and Employment.

PAPER

Ashlea Gillon (Ngāti Awa, Ngāpuhi, Ngāiterangi)
Samantha Keaulana-Scott (Kānaka Māoli)
Kiri West (Ngāti Marutūāhu)
Mapuana Antonio (Kānaka Māoli)

Tautitotito – Kamaʻilio: Talking Story – health storytelling between relations

Storytelling was, is and will be a vital part of the ways in which Indigenous Peoples create and maintain connection with each other, our ancestors and our relations. Storytelling and talking story create generative spaces and connections that emphasise and reiterate the importance of stories of strength, resilience, healing, survival and thriving, as well as and opposed to only stories of kaumaha, taumaha and trauma. Further, these interactions create reciprocal spaces that often ensure ethical, reciprocal communication and relationships, and (re)centre our Indigenous ways of conceptualising and enacting our sovereignty and self-determination. In this paper, we talk story with each other to share experiences of storytelling and health. As Indigenous wāhine, Kānaka Māoli and Māori, we Tautitotito and Kamaʻilio with each other and explore how we utilise storytelling within our practice as Indigenous researchers and educators and how this relates to Indigenous health. This paper explores our context and how we shape these communication land and seascapes to enhance and create ethical, reciprocal connections and seek restoration within the Westernised institutional spaces within which we occupy.

Key words: storywork, storytelling, talking story, Indigenous communication, data sovereignty, story sovereignty, Indigenous health

Introduction

Indigenous Peoples have engaged in practices of storytelling for generations, for multiple reasons. We do so because we as '… tellers, listeners, practitioners, and researchers are always conscious of the insider out, because like our trees, pūrākau are always and only relational' (Archibald et al. 2019: 165). This for us, reiterates the importance of Indigenous connection and communication landscapes. In this way, storytelling and, importantly, storylistening provide us with ways in which to relate, connect and engage with each other across lands, oceans, cultures and contexts. Within this paper, we engage in talk story about storytelling and storywork, we talk across oceans and Indigeneities to share, to understand, to listen, to connect, and ultimately, to restore.

Talk Story as a culturally grounded method(ology) allows Indigenous[1] Peoples to connect through the sharing of stories and of the ways in which we become storytellers. Connecting in these ways (re)creates the potential of possibility and spiritual connection that allow us to interrogate our ways of being, knowing and understanding in culturally specific and relevant methods. At times this may mean utilising Indigenous practices of song, prayer, art, talking, listening, practising, and much more. Storywork in this way centres on relationality (Affonso et al. 1996; Archibald et al. 2019; Au and Kawakami 1985). As Indigenous peoples, we know our storytelling has been and is restricted by colonisation. Colonisation and (un)settlers (Hokowhitu 2022) sought to re-write (the stories of) our lives, and to re-tell our realities. Colonisers wrote new stories:

> … that deliberately misremembered and obscured the injustice of what they were doing. History became a kind of rebranding in which colonisation was not seen as a violent home invasion but a grand if sometimes flawed adventure that was somehow 'better'… the new stories never found an easy place in this land. Rather, they sat uneasily upon it like the new place names and fences that were being strung across the new private properties. They were intruder stories on a land that needed no such embellishment (Jackson 2020: 145).

The impact of (un)settlers and colonisation has meant that often these re-tellings hold little of our truths, and illustrate more, colonial assumptions of our communities. We see this illustrated in the ways in which Indigenous health stories and health outcomes reflect a biased system which is not responsive to Indigenous peoples and is founded on ill health and inequity under the guise of care and wellbeing for all (Reid et al. 2017, 2019).

In this way, our stories and storytelling are sites within which resistance, reclamation and restoration (of our health) are possible and bountiful; for us, stories offer a means through which to 'ease the hurt and hara that colonisation causes' (Jackson 2020: 148). Through our relationality and connectivity, stories offer depths into our identities, our lives, our ontologies and axiologies, and how we share these with each other through notions of un-doing, as Matua Moana Jackson notes:

Ashlea Gillon

Samantha
Keaulana-Scott

Kiri West

Mapuana
Antonio

Because whakapapa traverses time between the past, present and future, the building of new relationships and the telling of new stories begins with the identification and 'un-telling' of colonisation's past and present lies. Stories for and about transformation rely on honesty about the misremembered stories and the foresight to see where different stories might lead. That is the ethic of restoration. It offers the chance, or challenge, to clutch truth and justice for 'future flowerings' (ibid: 154).

Our positionalities

Ko wai mātou? 'O wai mākou? We are four Indigenous scholars. We are Māori from Aotearoa New Zealand, and Kānaka Māoli from Ka Pae 'Āina O Hawai'i. We talk this paper into existence through our Indigenous epistemologies and through our connections. Our identities, our whakapapa and mo'okū'auhau, our 'ohana and whānau, our kaiako and kumu, all our relationships, experiences and identities inform how we make sense of the world, the ways in which we move through it and how we engage. All of these elements inform how we Tautitotito and Kama'ilio, how we do storytelling, storywork, how we talk story. Our positionalities help shape our storytelling and our storylistening. We share these here, as stories, to give the reader an introduction to us, as storytellers, so that we may engage in this way as relations, with reciprocal responsibilities to each other, to our whanaunga, and to these stories.

> Ash: He uri au nō Wairaka, he wahine, he Māori, he tamahine, tuahine, he hoa rangatira ahau. I define myself often in relation to those I value most, in relationship. I do so, not in a hierarchical Westernised way, but in an Indigenous way, within which my relationships and those I share space with inform each and every step of my practice and movement through the worlds I occupy and I exist in relation with. Within this context, I position myself as wahine Māori amongst and in relation and in story with other wāhine taketake. I engage in storywork from this place of wāhinetanga, of taketaketanga, of tauiratanga and kaiakotanga. Within a Westernised context, I exist as all these identities, and have been a student and teacher of Te Ao Māori, Kaupapa Māori, Mātauranga Māori, Indigenous health, Indigenous studies, and sociology, and public health.

> Sam: I am Kānaka 'Ōiwi, a māmā, a lover, a daughter, and a granddaughter. All hana that I engage in is in pursuit of rematriation and the optimal health and well-being of Kānaka 'Ōiwi. I am a student of Western social work, public health and policy, and actively search for ways to reclaim these disciplines through Indigenous practices and ways of being. However, I constantly battle with my own unlearning of colonialist conditioned behaviour and rely heavily on my kumu to activate the 'ōiwi in my kōkō through their mana'o, 'ike, and mo'olelo.

Kiri: Positionalities are deeply relational, and therefore shift according to the particular context we are situated within. In this space, one that I am sharing with Indigenous wāhine, I am most comfortable identifying myself through my matrilineal whakapapa as a mokopuna of Pare Hauraki. When writing from this positionality, there is an element of 'mokopunatanga' that is ever-present. That is, I write from the knowledge that I am in continuous relation to my tupuna and to my future mokopuna – my identity then, traverses time and place as I am simultaneously a mokopuna, a tamahine, a wahine, a mama and a future kuia. Academically, I have been socialised and disciplined by the fields of sociology, politics and Indigenous studies.

Mapuana: As beautifully described above, our positionality is deeply shaped by our relationships that we hold across various spaces, and thus, an exploration of our positionality requires our recognition of who are in different spaces, including the way in which intersectionality may play a role. I am wahine Kānaka 'Ōiwi, born and raised in Wahiawā on the island of O'ahu. I am a mother, daughter, granddaughter, sister and lover who is intricately connected to our generations of past and future. I am passionate about promoting mauli ola and addressing the root causes of health disparities that exist among Kānaka 'Ōiwi and other Indigenous communities, with a vision of seeing our people thrive through 'Āina mōmona and Ea. I have been trained in various spaces, including in Hawaiian ways of knowing and in Western schools of thought. I humbly receive and give 'ike as both a haumana and kumu in these spaces.

Tautitotito – Kama'ilio: Methods

Within our storywork, we see the value in our Indigenous languages which provide insight into the importance we place upon our practices, as Kānaka Māoli and Māori, we chose to utilise our languages to conceptualise our processes of storytelling and talk story within this paper.

We Tautitotito and Kama'ilio. Kama'ilio is understood as conversational Hawaiian and talking story. The word Tautitotito, illustrates the ways we 'song-in-reply'. The addition of the passive ending 'ngia' or 'a' transforms the kupu to a verb and so Tautitotitongia becomes to sing songs in response to one another, reciprocate with songs, recite alternatively (verses or parts of a song). It is a word reminiscent of the way that manu chitter chatter and talk story between one another in the ngāhere. Most commonly, Tautitotito is a kupu used to refer to traditional oratory practices of storytelling including the composition of waiata and mōteatea. The 'back and forth' elements speak to relationality and reciprocity. To use this kupu in the context of this paper is to remind us that our stories are never monologues, spoken by and of the 'self'.

This paper provides a space and opportunity to describe the way we

Ashlea Gillon

Samantha Keaulana-Scott

Kiri West

Mapuana Antonio

engage in the practice of storytelling as a way of knowing but also in the context of our work. While the full conceptualisations and actualisations of these practices and words cannot be captured in English, we attempt to elaborate on the ways in which we engage in these practices within this paper. Stories are always dialogues, their meanings are derived from relationships.

When beginning discussions about this paper, about our talking story and storytelling, Ash had asked Sam about ʻōlelo Hawaiʻi and what concepts capture our thinking in this storywork space. Sam asked her cultural advisor, friend and nephew, Pahonu Coleman, who provided insight into which words and concepts to use, and Kamaʻilio was chosen. Kamaʻilio means to converse, to talk story; within the context of our storywork we understand Kamaʻilio as talk story. Given the similarities of our Indigenous languages and relating, Ash found that the idea of Tautitotito would be a meaningful way of connecting Māori ideas and practices with those of Kānaka Māoli, further strengthening our relationships through our storying processes and practices.

We see storytelling as an opportunity for restoration, connection, sovereignty, reclamation, healing and moʻokūauhau. In this paper we engage in Kamaʻilio and Tautitotito across oceans to share space and talk story and discuss storytelling and storywork using.

What is storytelling to you, how would you describe the process of storytelling?

> Ash: Storytelling to me is whakawhanaungatanga, hononga, hauora, utu. Storytelling is a process of aroha, of manaakitanga, of all things that are Te Ao Māori, Te Ao Taketake. Storytelling to me is sharing your truth, your experiences, your realities, with those who you feel connection, relationships, restoration, movement can be made, in the hope that a story sparks another story, an idea, a thought, a moment, that it provides oranga, māramatanga, and hononga.
>
> Sam: Storytelling is a space to reconnect, reimagine and remember, specifically our identities and our relationships with each other, our kūpuna, and our ʻĀina.
>
> Kiri: Storytelling in my practice is about sense-making and having an opportunity to understand abstract concepts and theories in a way that is meaningful. When I draw from whānau stories I can traverse time and place and sit authentically across the multiple identities I hold space for (Māmā, wahine, mokopuna, scholar and more).
>
> Mapuana: Storytelling is a way of life and a way of knowing that allows for the perpetuation of ʻike over time. Those who are privileged to hear a story become knowledge seekers, but also knowledge keepers, of the wealth of ʻike that is shared through these stories. Storytelling can allow for the sharing of stories that might range from intergenerational stories that have been passed

on over time to a recreation of a lived experience, sacred to the storyteller. The reciprocal nature of storytelling and story listening can also provide a healing space that becomes intentional and can have deeper meanings about who we are, where we come from, the land we come from, our identities as a person. Now, I realise I am responding to our first question with another question, but this question also sparked a memory, where someone had asked me, 'Is there a difference between talk story and storytelling?' Interestingly, this has been a question that has come up time and time again. When I was first asked this question, I gave it some thought and reflection, especially since these concepts might seem similar in nature. Yet, at the same time, I acknowledge there is in fact a difference. What are your thoughts?

Ash: Your question seems straightforward, Mapuana, but the deeper you think about it, the more layers it has. I would say yes, there is definitely a difference between the two, and that they are intertwined and feed into each other. I guess storytelling for me is a kaupapa, it is Indigenous practice of connection, it is a chance to be an agent in our vulnerabilities and to re-author and (re)share our stories. I use storytelling a lot in my teaching, it creates a relatability that helps whakawhanaungatanga, that building, creating, and sustaining relationships and connections.

Kiri: I had never really considered the distinction before. I would say, more of my mahi sits in the storytelling space. I really love the way you frame it Ash around being an 'agent in our vulnerabilities' because so much of my storytelling is about making myself vulnerable. I should be clear and say that I tend to use personal narrative and whānau stories in my research and as a Māori data sovereignty scholar, I see storytelling as an opportunity for reclamation and taking back control of the narrative. Yes, I might be speaking about structural violence and colonial harms, but I am doing so on my terms. A really beautiful element of storytelling for me has been the opportunity to connect with my nanny through her memoirs in a way that I could never have done while she was still alive. So connection is a critical element of storytelling for me.

Sam: Love this question. Reminds me of a time when Uncle Earl Kawa'a shared the moʻolelo of Hāloanakalaukapalili (the taro plant, the eldest sibling of Kānaka ʻŌiwi). It wasn't the first time I heard this story. I was very familiar, yet with his voice, I was able to vividly imagine Hāloa's mother, Hoʻohōkūkalani, bathing in a stream, flipping her long, black, hair, revealing thousands of stars. When he described her birth to her stillborn son, Hāloa, I felt pain. So yes, I agree.

Ashlea Gillon

Samantha Keaulana-Scott

Kiri West

Mapuana Antonio

Why is storytelling important in health spaces?

Ash: From a Māori perspective, every single piece of (quantitative) data is a taonga, it is a treasure, it is part of someone, it is someone, or part of our story. The fabulous Dr Kiri West talks about data being tākoha, which I think is really important in terms of storytelling in these spaces. Kiri, can you elaborate so I don't mess it up?

Kiri: Yeah, so I think, in the Aotearoa context, the concept of koha has become really ingrained in institutional research ethics and has been in many ways co-opted into the language of 'reciprocity' and 'recognition' (as understood by colonial institutions). The consequence of this is that the critical element of relationality is stripped from the practice of koha and what we're left with is a transactionary interaction, that emulates a capitalist exchange of goods – you give me your story and I reciprocate with a $50 petrol voucher. Once this happens, the 'participant' loses all control over the storage, future transmission and expression of their story. Tākoha (re)centres relationality as critical and indicates that there are conditions which will be applied to the taonga (in this case story or data) being gifted. These conditions could be about limiting who has access – or indeed, who can make decisions about who has access – to the gift, they could also indicate a timeframe for use of the gift as well as establish the process for returning the gift. In this way the storyteller retains authority and agency, and there is an ethical responsibility on both ends to honour the taonga and act as guardians, as opposed to 'owners' or 'experts'.

Mapuana: Yes. And this also reminds me of the importance of acknowledging the idea that this story is still 'owned' and retained by the storyteller themselves. We are being honoured and privileged through the opportunity to hear about this story, which serves as a gift for us. This story contains knowledge, sometimes intergenerational, sometimes interconnected knowledge and sometimes deeper levels of meaning. And thus, the process of storytelling is truly a gift. So often in research, there is this claiming of knowledge, and this is why from an Indigenous lens, it is critically important to ensure proper protocols are in place to allow for this honouring of storytelling while also ensuring these individuals, 'ohana, and communities still retain these stories. That idea of relationality also deeply resonated with the importance of mo'olelo, especially as a mechanism of identifying certain messages or hō'ailona that are intended to be shared but also received. Even setting the tone of spaces of simply allowing for introductions and sharing who we are, where we come from or the 'Āina that we bring into our various spaces, the different kūpuna that we are channelling or bringing into various spaces, and even simply thinking about 'how are we doing?' allows for the opportunity to build and sustain our connections and relations and resonates well with many of our Indigenous brothers and sisters. Sam, I know you're familiar with aloha circles and concepts around moʻolelo. Would you mind sharing some of your manaʻo about this matter?

Sam: I am. I believe at the piko of it all is Moʻokūʻauhau. Sharing genealogies and stories of our genealogies contextualises our relationships and our being in various spaces. Through such a practice, we understand how we are woven together or NOT woven together. There is a common misconception in Hawaiʻi among 'locals' and settlers that pilina and aloha is for everyone, and that the continual prostitution of Hawaiian culture is okay. In fact, they say they celebrate Hawaiian culture by appropriating and selling our practices, even in health spaces. ʻAʻole! Moʻokūʻauhau gives us, as Indigenous Peoples, credentials in health spaces! Utilising Hawaiianness in health spaces or practices like storytelling is not for everyone. It is not for culturally grounding practice and it does not check off cultural competency. I think the issue is that Moʻokūʻauhau is an absent practice in health systems. We don't have that kind of exchange and therefore a lack of relationships with our providers. We should also be careful when attempting to plug Moʻokūʻauhau within health systems, it is very us, and not meant to be appropriated. In essence, simply plugging our practices into systems that are not ours, is not enough.

Ash: I was just reading Linda Tuhiwai Smith's recent chapter 'A story about the time we had a global pandemic and how it affected my life and work as a critical Indigenous scholar' and she uses storytelling to share her experiences throughout the pandemic and tells two stories in the beginning of the chapter, then returns to the first story to interrogate her own words, asking critical questions:

> [Who gets to name it? How is this pandemic worse than the one our peoples have experienced before?] … *The virus has successfully shut down much of the world's economies* [You mean the economies that excluded and exploit IPs?], *challenged the world's leaders* [… of nation states, settler colonial states and former empires?] … *The virus has been lethal for those who are old, black, brown and already vulnerable with chronic health conditions* [How many Indigenous communities enjoy good health anyway? Our peoples live with multiple co-morbidities, heart, lungs, diabetes and simply being Indigenous]. *It has enjoyed those social contexts where humans interact such as care homes, group activities and special events able to spread its infection with maximum efficiency* [Including Indigenous ceremonies and gatherings]. *It has overwhelmed the best public health systems in the world* [The systems that have been proven to be inequitable and racist?] (Tuhiwai-Smith 2021: 366).

I think in her storying, she highlights what we know as Indigenous health scholars, that who is telling the story, whose story is being told, and what version of the story, and how you relate, are all

Ashlea Gillon

Samantha Keaulana-Scott

Kiri West

Mapuana Antonio

critically important in seeking radical transformation within health spaces, which are so often not designed for us.

Kiri: I think this is a really provocative question. It pushes me to think about why I have shared stories in my doctoral research and in my teaching. Often the stories I share centre pain and trauma and really attempt to provide a human element to broader conversations around structural violence and persistent inequities. Sometimes, my goal is to shock the reader or listener and produce a sense of discomfort that confronts their own sensibilities and what they believe to be 'true'. I think the persistence of inequities and racism in health settings has become so embedded in the 'norm' that we almost accept that they are a natural feature of our health systems. Sharing stories then plays an important role in making all the data and all the statistics real and meaningful. This is incredibly important as we are increasingly reliant on data driven decision-making and automated technologies in health.

What stories do you tell in these spaces?

Mapuana: So often, I bring my ʻohana in my stories and in these spaces. I feel like it is critically important that we set the tone and demonstrate the way we are part of the story and the way our ʻohana are also part of this health narrative. And as an Indigenous person, I am not bringing just myself, I am bringing my whole self – physically, mentally, spiritually and emotionally – and also my ʻohana, my kumu, my haumāna, my community, our lāhui. These are the different people, experiences and stories that help to shape the way I think about health and it's critically important that I acknowledge them in the process.

Ash: Absolutely, all those relationships, those experiences, those connections help shape how I make sense of the world and the spaces that I occupy. I definitely always share my own stories and stories of my whānau because we are, ever-so politely put, high users of the health system. We all engage with it as people with chronic diseases and disabilities, and different intersecting identities that are used to provide us with inequitable treatment. When I share data, I am sharing stories of people, of myself, of my whānau, my traumas, my triumphs, I am sharing people. The numbers are people, and that's something one of my kaiako, Professor Papaarangi Reid always would say. The data are people.

Mapuana: Yes, absolutely! And in fact, your sharing of this reminds me of an activity that I incorporate in one of my NHIH courses, where we talk about Indigenising the academy and decolonising research methodologies where I have students bring a photo to class to introduce an ʻohana member that they identified as being an important part of their moʻokūʻauhau, both genealogically but also intellectually. During this activity, the students introduce the person (sometimes people) as if they are sitting in the room with us. And we envision what health looks like collectively, for us, for the person they have brought in the room with us today, and if we were to envision our future generations having a similar conversation in the generations to come. This is a beautiful way of demonstrating the importance of these stories, and students are reminded to remember these stories associated with the numbers and data that are presented in public health and in our health systems. This also aligns with the teachings from other Indigenous scholars, like Nālani Wilson-Hokowhitu (2019) who talks about moʻokūʻauhau as a methodology and the emphasis of recovering, representing, and retelling history and science through the lens of the storyteller.

Kiri: 'The numbers are people' is something I feel like I am constantly reminding people of, especially in the algorithm spaces I find myself in. There's this paragraph in my PhD thesis that comes immediately after a story, and I feel like it sits comfortably in this kōrero that we're having:

> There is nothing necessarily unique about my story above, in fact, I assume it is a story that will resonate with many people, if not in its entirety, then certainly in its fragments. There are of course stories nestled within stories here, this is a much-abbreviated version of the events that took place. I contemplated whether it was appropriate to share this story on such an open platform, and in the end, as confronting as it was, it was important for me to be able to reiterate how deeply personal the issue of data sovereignty is for all of us. Highlighting the entanglement of the personal and the political is especially critical in this case study because algorithms and predictive risk models are designed in ways that simultaneously strip us of our stories and strip our stories of us. We are laid bare before the system, disjointed from our digital selves, represented as a series of zeros and ones in exponential datasets, sitting within machines designed to learn from our mistakes (West 2022: 96).

Sam: Kiri, that made me weep. My ʻohana represents a series, if not, an entire catalogue of ones in those exponential datasets. In conversation with a clinician once, they told me they served 'too many ice heads', and as a result, lack the experience of working with other types of patients. Moʻolelo in health spaces is needed to remind folk who took an oath to care for all to look past a diagnosis, reinstall aloha in practice, and see everyone as deserving of aloha. I believe it also has the power to remind privileged individuals to reflect on their position, all their isms, and confront the ways in which they contribute to ongoing violence and historical trauma.

Ashlea Gillon

Samantha Keaulana-Scott

Kiri West

Mapuana Antonio

What are the ethical responsibilities of a storyteller and of the storylistener?

Kiri: sitting back in reflection, from an Indigenous perspective, a significant focus in the theorising around storywork, talking story and pūrakau has been about our ethical responsibilities as storytellers and as listeners. Jo-ann Archibald in her seminal work really emphasised that notion of ethical storytelling, and others like Jenny Lee-Morgan have built from there. I have become increasingly interested in thinking about the ethical responsibilities of the audience, and I think my first introduction to this idea was in reading my great grandmother's memoirs where she asks this of the readers:

> Please read these bits and pieces with kindly patience. Repetitions here and there, quite unavoidable in the very style of your ninety-year-old matriarch, whose eyesight is limited to half an eye and fingers growing less willing to hold a pen (Angeline Ahirata Ryan, personal communication).

Taking a lead from nan, I asked that readers approach my mahi with an open mind and generosity of spirit and a recognition that even if they can't understand my experiences, then at the very least, my hope is that they can be seen as real, valid and legitimate. With these ideas bubbling away in my subconscious, I was excited to come across these same ideas in the *Mana Wahine reader* (2019) that if we, as Indigenous women, have been rendered silent, it isn't because we are voiceless, or mute, it's because we are not being listened to and this is far more dangerous. 'Speaking and listening cannot be split into productive and receptive modes, abdicating the listener of any responsibility in the communicative act' (Waitere and Johnston 2009: 14). There has to be a responsibility put on the audience in terms of listening, giving space, not being defensive or coming in with preconceived ideas. We need to think creatively about how we might generate that ethical responsibility beyond a research team.

Ash: I love that, that's exactly what it is. A good friend of mine, MahMah, always says 'never let your defensiveness override your willingness to learn'. The ethic of storytelling, storylistening and story sovereignty also remind me of our beloved Matua Moana Jackson, and how he talks about sovereignty and being sovereign, and how I've used that in my work around mana and sovereignty, is that, he talks about how we didn't cede sovereignty, our sovereignty is continuously disregarded, not acknowledged, omitted and ignored, rather than being 'lost' or ceded. So often our experiences, our sovereignties, our mana, our tikanga, our pūrākau, our everything, really, are disregarded, not heard or validated, and so often within health spaces. I know within Westernised settings this idea of listening is often talked about in terms of active listening, or listening to listen, rather than listening to respond (in positive or negative ways). I feel like I see your Nan's statement of ethical care as a beautiful thing, because I would like to think that the ways I think and engage in storytelling, storywork and storylistening, are with an ethic of care and whakamōmona ngā whanaungatanga, seek to nurture and nourish relationships. So, of course, that makes sense to me. I can also imagine that people who don't relate in these ways might not understand that at the centre of storying are relationships, are connections, are aroha, manaaki and tautoko. I come back to Jenny Lee-Morgan (2019: 165) who talks about this as well; she says that '… tellers, listeners, practitioners, and researchers are always conscious of the insider out, because like our trees, pūrākau are always and only relational'. It makes me think about relationships, story sovereignty, ngā mana pūrākau, mana Tautitotito, mana Kama'ilio, and the ways in which our Indigenous tikanga, epistemologies and axiologies guide us in these spaces to engage in reciprocal responsibilities and relationships within storytelling/listening. It makes me think of kuleana; does that make sense in this space Mapuana and Sam?

Mapuana: Of course. When we engage in mo'olelo, we are at the highest standard of kuleana. For instance, if we have the privilege of hearing the mo'olelo of someone, or of 'Āina, or of a deeper message, we now have kuleana, not just to this mo'olelo but also to this person, their 'ohana, and their community to honour their 'ike. We are now in pilina with each other when we create this intentional space to allow for this reciprocity – with the deep understanding that mo'olelo is an active process of sharing and listening. This allows us to listen and tell stories that we are intended to receive and to guide us in our pathway. This also allows us to think about our whole selves, but also how the story might relate to others, to the way we connect intergenerationally, the way we connect with 'Āina, the way we connect spiritually.

Sam: YES, I kako'o Mapuana, and understand storytelling as a form of bestowing kuleana upon others. We don't know what we don't know, but when we do know, what will we do about it? The receiver is privileged with relationality, understanding, and 'ike, but also with the burden to take action. I don't mean burden in a negative way, but Kānaka understand that kuleana comes with a lot of weight. For example, the kuleana to aloha 'āina involves intentional action, every day to maintain Hawai'i for our kūpuna who have passed, us in this earthly realm and for the multitudes of generations to come.

In the ethic of restoration, of reclamation, of re-storying, we pose a question to end our Tautitotito and Kama'ilio, and offer our answers at this moment in time, as we know undoubtedly, that like our stories, they will (re)grow, (re)shape, (re)shift, and will be (re)told. We do so in the hope that this question sparks curiosity, sparks ideas, sparks connection and sparks a story.

Ashlea Gillon

Samantha Keaulana-Scott

Kiri West

Mapuana Antonio

What is one word or one sentence that sums up how you feel about storytelling, storylistening, storywork for Indigenous health?

Ash: Hei oranga. Storytelling and storylistening are medicine, are restorative.

Sam: Moʻokūauhau.

Kiri: In the context of my mahi, storytelling is about sovereignty and reclamation.

Mapuana: For me, the one word I would use to summarise storytelling and story listening is healing.

Discussion

Tautitotito and Kamaʻilio offer us Indigenous ways of engaging in storywork, storytelling and talking story. They offer us methods within which to theoretically, methodologically, pedagogically and ethically centre our praxis of creating, telling, sharing and listening to stories with the necessary cultural connectedness, understanding and nuance to make sense and meaning of them (Archibald et al. 2019; Toliver 2022).

In her recent works around Black storytelling, Stephanie Toliver delves into the importance of storylistening and asks 'what elements are needed for you to care about the conflict in the story?' (2022: xxiv-xxv). Toliver relates these notions of storylistening and the multiple components and roles within Indigenous storytelling and storywork. When understanding the importance of storywork for Indigenous and minoritised peoples, Toliver explores the ways Joann Archibald Q'um Q'um Xiiem and Linda Tuhiwai Smith discuss story(ing), Toliver notes that Archibald Q'um Xiiem says: 'My dear ones, our work is about to begin' (2019: 4). This statement uses the pronoun 'our' to note that the storyteller isn't the only one doing work: instead, the collective is engaging in the work of story – the story, the storyteller and the story listener. As Ngāti Awa and Ngāti Porou scholar Linda Tuhiwai Smith said: 'The story and storyteller both serve to connect the past with the future, one generation with the other, the land with the people and the people with the story' (2012: 146).

Through the importance of ethical relationality, we see that storywork, storytelling, storylistening all offer chances to utilise and share our Indigenous knowledges and the opportunities to exist and practise our multiple identities and roles. Through this sharing, the importance of data sovereignty, story sovereignty and story catching are important. While we do not have all the answers, we offer questions to consider when engaging in storywork:

- How do we (re)create, (re)share, (re)collect, guard, and protect these stories in ways that help the communities we are a part of and work for?
- How do we uphold the mana of storytellers and storylisteners?
- How can we draw upon the ethic of (tā)koha to ensure the mana of story is (re)(main)tained?
- How do we (re)centre the ethics of storywork?
- How do we Tautitotito and Kama'ilio for health?

(Re)thinking the ethics of storywork and considering these critically reflective questions allows us to consider the ways in which data and ethics can shape our health. In every facet of health, storywork and storytelling are vital to not only the reclamation of health, but to ensuring data and story sovereignty and consent (West 2020, 2022). When considering the reciprocal relationships and responsibilities between storytellers and storylisteners we can conceptualise the ways in which Indigenous ethics are crucial within health spaces. Our stories, our data, are sacred, they are powerful, and they give us not only the opportunity to speak, be heard and listen, but they create ways for us to connect. In this way, we see storytelling and storywork as a mechanism for uncovering and re-telling truths within health spaces, related to our wellbeing. Matua Moana Jackson says that 'the stories named our right to stand in this place and provided an intellectual tradition that gave us insight into the obligations that went with the right to stand' (Jackson 2020: 137). We know that storytelling is resistance and it is our right. Storytelling is our responsibility, our kuleana, especially in the context of health and wellbeing research. Up until very recently, health narratives have marginalised and minoritised Indigenous ways of knowing and being, and relegated our truths to fantasy and fiction (Jackson 2020). We have not been the narrators of dominant discourse about us (Smith 2012), we have been denied access to be the authority. And, yet Indigenous bodies and minds occupy so much real estate in Western health contexts.

Indigenous Peoples have had poor health and education, high levels of unemployment, homelessness and incarceration forced upon us, as well as increased risk of morbidity and younger mortality rates (Reid et al. 2017, 2019). It is a dire story, that so often purposefully omits the perpetrator of these inequities, colonisation and (un)settlers (Jackson 2020; Reid et al. 2019). We know that being restricted from creating and (re)telling our stories impacts how these stories are (re)produced and whose truths they claim to speak of. Storywork, stories give us the opportunity to (re)centre our health, (re)centre our wellness, and (re)centre restoration in the hope that our stories can be reclamation, restoration and 'a guide to resolution' (Jackson 2020: 148).

Ashlea Gillon
Samantha Keaulana-Scott
Kiri West
Mapuana Antonio

Glossary

ʻŌlelo Hawaiʻi

aloha	love, compassion, empathy, caring, kindness
ʻāīna	land, earth, land that provides and feeds
ʻaʻole	no
hana	work, practice, process, task
haumāna	student, learner
ʻike	to see, to know, to feel, to greet, to experience, to understand, understanding
kākoʻo	to uphold, support
Kamaʻilio	to talk story, to converse, conversational, the connecting in conversation
Kānaka Maoli/Kānaka ʻŌiwi	Indigenous, original peoples of Ka Pae ʻĀina o Hawaiʻi
kaumaha	grief, heaviness
koko	blood
kuleana	(cultural) responsibility, privilege, right, reason
kumu	source, teacher, knowledge holder
kūpuna	ancestors, starting point, growing point, source
lāhui	nation, peoples, to gather, to assemble
mana	ancestral divine power, spiritual power, authority
manaʻo	thought, idea, belief, meaning
moʻokūʻauhau	genealogy
moʻolelo	story
ʻohana	family, relative, kin
ʻōiwi	Indigenous, native, bones
pilina	relationship, connection

Te Reo Māori

hoa rangatiratanga	partner
kaiako	(tanga) teacher (teaching, practice of teachership)
koha	gift, present, offering, contribution
kuia	grandmother, elder woman
mahi	work, to perform, accomplish
Māmā	mother

mana	ancestral divine power, spiritual power, authority
manu	bird
Māori	Indigenous peoples of Aotearoa New Zealand, normal, ordinary
mokopuna(tanga)	descendent, grandchild(ren), the place or time of descendents/grandchild(ren)
mōteatea	lament, traditional chant, to grieve
pūrākau	story
taketake	(tanga) Native, Indigenous, to be established, original, ancient, Indigeneity
tākoha	gift, present or offering, especially one maintaining relationships
tamahine	daughter taonga treasure, valuable
tauira(tanga)	student, learner, the place or time of studentship/learning
taumaha	heaviness, ailment, burden, weighed down with illness
tautitotito	to talk story, to converse backwards and forward, birds chatting
tikanga	protocol, practice, procedure, custom, process
tuahine	sister
uri	descendent, relative, kin, progeny
wahine/wāhine	feminine identifying people, often woman/women
waiata	song, chant, to sing
Wairaka	An Indigenous Wahine ancestor who saved her people
wairua(tanga)	spirit, soul, spirituality
whakamōmona	to nourish, to fertilise, to nurture
whakapapa	layers of ancestry, genealogy, ancestry
whānau	extended family, to be born, birth,
whanaungatanga	relationships, kinship, connections.

Note

[1] The re/de-capitalisations within this paper are purposeful praxis in re-centring Indigenous knowledges and challenging colonial, westernised, knowledge and grammar conventions

Ashlea Gillon

Samantha Keaulana-Scott

Kiri West

Mapuana Antonio

References

Affonso, Dyanne D., Mayberry, Linda, Inaba, Audrey, Matsuno, Rhonda and Robinson, Elaine (1996) Hawaiian-style 'talkstory': Psychosocial assessment and intervention during and after pregnancy, *Journal of Obstetrics Gynecology Neonatal Nursing*, Vol. 25, No. 9 pp 737–742. DOI: 10.1111/j.1552-6909.1996.tb01489.x

Affonso, Dyanne D., Shibuya, June Y. and Frueh, B. Christopher (2007) Talk-story: Perspective of children, parents, and community leaders on community violence in rural Hawaii, *Public Health Nursing*, Vol. 24, No. 5 pp 400–408. DOI: 10.1111/j.1525-1446.2007.00650.x

Archibald, Q'um Q'um Xiiem Joanne, Lee-Morgan, Jenny Bol Jun and De Santolo, Jason (2019) *Decolonizing research: Indigenous storywork as methodology*, London, Zed Books

Au, Kathryn Hu-pei and Kawakami, Alice J. (1985) Research currents: Talk story and learning to read, *Language Arts*, Vol. 62, No. 4. Available online at https://www.readinghalloffame.org/sites/default/files/au.kawakami.talk_.langarts.1985.pdf

Hokowhitu, Brendan, Moreton-Robinson, Aileen, Tuhiwai-Smith, Linda, Andersen, Chris and Larkin, Steve (2022) *Routledge handbook of critical Indigenous studies,* Abingdon, Oxon, Routledge

Jackson, Moana (2020) Where to next? Decolonisation and the stories in the land, Elkington, Bianca, Jackson, Moana, Kiddle, Rebecca, Mercier, Ocean Ripeka, Ross, Mike, Smeaton, Jennie and Thomas, Amanda (eds) *Imagining decolonization*,Wellington, New Zealand, Bridget Williams Books

Reid, Papaarangi, Paine, Sarah-Jane, Curtis, Elana, Jones, Rhys, Anderson, Anneka, Willing, Esther and Harwood, Matire (2017) Achieving health equity in Aotearoa: Strengthening responsiveness to Maori in health research, *New Zealand Medical Association,* Vol. 130, No. 1465 pp 96–103

Reid, Papaarangi, Cormack, Donna and Paine, Sarah-Jane (2019) Colonial histories, racism and health: The experience of Maori and Indigenous peoples, *Public Health,* Vol. 172, No. 2019 pp 119-124. DOI: 10.1016/j.puhe.2019.03.027

Toliver, Stephanie R. (2022) *Recovering Black storytelling in qualitative research (futures of data analysis in qualitative research)*, Abingdon, Oxon, Routledge

Tuhiwai-Smith, Linda (2022) A story about the time we had a global pandemic and how it affected my life and work as a critical Indigenous scholar, Hokowhitu, Brendan, Moreton-Robinson, Aileen, Tuhiwai-Smith, Linda, Andersen, Chris and Larkin, Steve (eds) *Routledge handbook of critical Indigenous studies,* Abingdon, Oxon, Routledge

Waitere, Hine and Johnston, Patricia (2009) Echoed silences: In absentia: Mana wahine in institutional contexts, *Women's Studies Journal*, Vol. 23, No. 2 pp 14–31

West, Kiri (2020) There's 'consent' and then there's consent: Mobilising Māori and Indigenous research ethics to problematise the western biomedical model, *Journal of Sociology,* Vol. 52, No. 2 pp 184–196. DOI: 10.1177/1440783319893523

West, Kiri (2022) *From a given to the taken: Theorising Māori data sovereignty in Aotearoa*, PhD Thesis, Auckland, University of Auckland

Wilson-Hokowhitu, Nālani (2019) *The past before us: Moʻokūʻauhau as methodology,* Germany, University of Hawaii Press

Yamamoto, Kathryn K. and Black, Rhonda S. (2013) Standing behind and listening to Native Hawaiian students in the transition process, *Career Development and Transition for Exceptional Individuals,* Vol. 38, No. 1. DOI: 10.1177/21651434134984123

Note on the contributors

Ashlea Gillon: He uri au nō Ngāti Awa, Ngāpuhi, me Ngāiterangi. Ko Ashlea Gillon ahau. Ashlea is a Kaupapa Māori transdisciplinary research fellow at the University of Auckland, doing a PhD in Indigenous Studies and Psychology exploring body sovereignty for fat Indigenous wāhine, and a Fulbright Scholar in Native Hawaiian and Indigenous Health at the University of Hawaiʻi at Mānoa. Ashlea's areas of interest are Indigenous health, fat studies, identity, racism, equity, Indigenous theories and methodologies.

Dr Samantha Keaulana-Scott: Aloha. O Samantha (Sam) Keaulana-Scott koʻu inoa. She is a Robert Wood Johnson Health Policy Research Scholar and has experience in community-based research and culturally grounded health programmes through various Native Hawaiian organisations and departments. She received her Master's in Social Work from the University of Hawaiʻi at Mānoa and recently completed a PhD candidate in public health. Her research interests include investigating historical and intergenerational trauma as systemic barriers of optimal health among Native Hawaiian women.

Dr Kiri West: He uri au nō Ngāti Marutūāhu. Ko Kiri West ahau. She is a critical kaupapa Māori researcher and lecturer at the University of Auckland. Previously coordinator for the multidisciplinary Indigenous and Pacific *MAI Journal*, with a background in Sociology, her work centres on Indigenous data sovereignty, data ethics, consent, sovereignty, sociology, Indigenous studies, Indigenous communications and Indigenous theories and methodologies.

Dr Mapuana Antonio: Aloha mai kākou. O Mapuana Antonio koʻu inoa. A Kanaka Maoli dedicated to advancing the health and well-being of Native Hawaiians and Indigenous peoples, Mapuana is an Assistant Professor and the specialisation head of the Native Hawaiian and Indigenous Health programme in the Office of Public Health Studies, Thompson School of Social Work and Public Health at the University of Hawaiʻi at Mānoa. Mapuana's research takes a community-based, ʻĀina-based (land-based) and holistic approach to health and resilience by addressing socio-cultural determinants of health.

Dr Charleen Charisna Fisher
Dr Nina Nikola Doering

Shijyaa haa research: Reflections on positionality, relationality and commonality in Arctic research

This paper engages an Indigenous and a non-Indigenous researcher in discussion about collaboration and co-creation between researchers and Indigenous communities that include and prioritise Indigenous knowledge. It places a focus on the preconditions for respectful and goal-oriented research relationships. The paper is structured around 'small moments' in research, as a means of analysing the need for commonality and relationality. Indigenous understandings of relationality include connection to place as a living practice with a responsibility to kin. Relationality and commonality focus on friendship, shared visioning and communication across long distances. Through discourse, Dr Charleen Fisher (Gwich'in, Tl'eeyegge Hʉt'aane, Dena'ina) and Dr Nina Doering (German) focus on positionality, relationality, communication and co-creation in a variety of communication landscapes. Long-term critical discussions during the Covid-19 pandemic about ethical research with Indigenous philosophy, epistemology and ontology normalised virtual meetings as a contemporary practice. The paper addresses research in the social and natural sciences and humanities.

Key words: relationality, positionality, commonality, co-creation, Indigenous research, Arctic research, Shijyaa haa research

Introduction

Shijyaa haa is a Gwich'in term that means 'with my friend'. Literally translated, the possessive pronoun *shi* means 'my', the stem for 'friend' is *-jyaa*, and *haa* is 'with'. *Shijyaa haa* research is how we (Dr Charleen Fisher and Dr Nina Doering) came to reference the communication style and collaborative work shared in this conversational research paper on positionality, relationality, communication and co-creation in a variety of communication landscapes.

Recent years have seen growing debate on ethical research and on possible ways to improve research relationships between Indigenous and non-Indigenous partners in the Arctic (e.g. Arctic Council Secretariat 2020: 45-48). To counter harmful research practices and ensure that the right of Indigenous peoples to have control over projects affecting their lands and waters (e.g. United Nations 2007) is acknowledged and respected, Indigenous rights organisations, researchers and youth organisations have developed guidelines (e.g. Gwich'in Tribal Council 2011; Inuit Circumpolar Council 2022; Pedersen et al. 2020; Sámediggi 2021) and frameworks (e.g. Buschman 2022a; Yua et al. 2022) and highlighted the need to centre Indigenous knowledge in research and decision-making (e.g. Buschman 2022b). Terms such as 'co-creation' and 'co-production' in research and conservation have become ubiquitous, both describing the need for equitable partnerships and the bringing together of different ways of knowing throughout all stages of research and conservation processes (e.g. Armitage et al. 2011; Buschman 2022a; Cooke et al. 2020; Degai et al. 2022; Sarkki 2020; Yua et al. 2022). Although progress has been made, research continues to exclude and dismiss Indigenous peoples across the Arctic (e.g. Inuit Tapiriit Kanatami 2018: 5) and academic and funding systems often hinder change (Buschman 2022a; Doering et al. 2022). It is our intention with this paper to add a personal perspective on the challenges we have encountered and the possibilities that have opened for us as we – a Gwich'in and a German researcher – are building our own relationship. We hope that such insights can help other researchers reflect on their own collaborative paths.

We are inspired in this paper by Dr Albert Marshall's concept of 'Two-Eyed Seeing' (Etuaptmumk in Mi'kmaw) and similar Indigenous frameworks, as described by Reid et al. (2021), both for their potential to bring together Indigenous and non-Indigenous ways of knowing, and for our joint reflections on past and present experiences with research. Two-Eyed Seeing encourages 'learning to see from one eye with the strengths of Indigenous knowledges and ways of knowing, and from the other eye with the strengths of mainstream knowledges and ways of knowing, and to use both these eyes together, for the benefit of all' (ibid: 243). We engage with research and research practices and the academic system from the perspectives of an Indigenous and a non-Indigenous researcher with the aim of exploring how our experiences relate and understanding how to improve relationships in research. We structure the sections of this paper around 'notable moments' in research as a means of analysing the need for relationality and commonality. We hope that our reflections will be meaningful to others by being personal to us.

About this paper

We first met at the 10th Summer Seminar of the 'International PhD School for the Studies of Arctic Societies' (IPSSAS) in Fairbanks in 2015 and connected on different occasions afterwards before we began to

Charleen Charisna Fisher

Nina Nikola Doering

schedule weekly Zoom calls in the early summer of 2021 – 'visiting' each other virtually in our living rooms and office spaces for informal conversations. Our joint reflection process took place during the Covid-19 pandemic online and was sometimes interrupted by unstable internet connections and health challenges. All of this raised questions for us about what it takes to build relationships and co-work across large distances. Relationality and positionality through research are not well expressed in the academic system and we converse in this paper about how friendship and strategy can overcome structure. Relationality is not necessarily tied to literacy and our early conversations focused on listening and establishing shared understanding. In Gwich'in culture, 'visiting' constitutes a common method for communication and knowledge transfer. Only later did we turn these conversations into written notes contained in shared documents when our joint goals were turned to action in the form of presentations and co-authorship.

Positionality

Charleen: *Drin Gwinzii Ch'anjaa naii, Khehkwaii naii, ts'a' shalak naii, nakhweenjit dagoonchy'aa? Shoozhri' Charleen Fisher oozhii. Beaver, Alaska gwats'an ihłii. Tseenduu Gwich'in, Dena'ina, Tl'eeyegge Hʉt'aane ihłii.* Good Afternoon Elders, chiefs and all my relations, how are you all? My name is Charleen Fisher. I am from Beaver, Alaska. I am a Gwich'in, Dena'ina and Tl'eeyegge Hʉt'aane.

Nina: Thank you, Charleen! My name is Nina Doering. I grew up near Munich in the south of Germany, before moving to the UK during my studies. I now live and work in Potsdam, Germany.

Charleen: Mahsi' or thank you for sharing your introduction with me. The Gwich'in formal introduction is at least twice as long as the one I just shared and really situates a person to the land, their clans and family as part of the larger Gwich'in community. What is your connection to land, to the earth? Connection to place shapes who we are and how we think. I am very conscious of how I was taught and the foundational experiences that shaped who I am and how that impacts my children's experiences. As an educator, I found a path where I could work in my home and allow my children to live in our homeland and participate in ancestral hunting, fishing and gathering practices. Cultural connections to place have been integral to my work and personal motivation to pursue a terminal degree and research. As Margaret Kovach states: 'Indigenous methodologies require a purpose statement about self in relation to the world' (2021: 150).

Nina: I did not grow up with a practice of formal introductions in the sense that you just described. While my connections with people and places have made me who I am, in most official settings in Germany that I am familiar with, a focus tends to be placed on people's occupations and professional achievements. Among white,[1] university-educated, middle-class Germans such as myself, it has been my experience that asking someone where they are from indicates interest in a person, but does not generally establish a deeper understanding about belonging and relationships.[2] Thinking about this, I am reminded of researchers, authors and activists from around the world who have noted that the possibility to go about life without constantly being prompted to reflect upon one's own identity and relation to the world is both a cause and symptom of racism and continued colonial exploitation. Reni Eddo-Lodge writes of white privilege as 'the fact that if you're white, your race will almost certainly positively impact your life's trajectory in some way. *And you probably won't even notice it*' (2017: 87, emphasis added). Similarly, Shawn Wilson notes that 'as part of [dominant system academics'] white privilege, there is no requirement for white academics 'to be able to see other ways of being and doing, or even to recognize that they exist' (2008: 44). I grew up in a system that views whiteness as the norm and was educated in academic institutions, in which voices of BIPoC [Black, Indigenous and People of Colour] scholars had often been under-represented or rendered invisible.[3] As I have reflected on these dynamics and my own positionality with you, I keep coming back to Zoe Todd's (2016) article on the 'ontological turn', in which she illustrates how Indigenous thinkers continue to be excluded and Indigenous thought denied credit in the European academy. In my own studies and work, I was motivated to understand the global inequalities that have afforded me my own privileges and to learn how I could contribute to addressing them. This was not the result of abstract reflections on systemic and structural violence and exclusion: I am German, the generation of my grandparents is responsible for the atrocities of the Second World War and I had long realised that the clothes I was wearing and things I was using were produced under violent conditions. I had a deep feeling that my privileges demand that I take responsibility for them, but I did not question my own knowledge system and its role – and thus my own role – in reproducing these inequalities in my work and research.

Charleen: What do you research? I research education, Gwich'in pedagogy or as Stan Wilson has coined, Indigegogy (Wilson and Schellhammer 2021: 50), Indigenous studies and co-creation. With a K-12 teaching certificate, principal endorsement and a Master's degree in Education I took particular interest in the common ancestral stories and curriculum. I took my doctoral research as an opportunity to reflect on these topics. It was a joy to listen to the now passed Elders, to hear the stories that they told. I treasure the interviews and still have concerns about the way that I honoured the precious stories that were communicated to me. I think of the times sitting on a porch or at the table listening to stories on ancestral homelands as sacred times. As a result of my doctoral research experience, I feel that academic writing processes are not the proper way to honour our ancestral knowledge and, in many circumstances, it should be honoured in our traditional ways only without the expectations of academia.

Nina: For my PhD, which focused on public participation in extractive resource management, I spent nine months in Aasiaat and several other

Charleen Charisna Fisher

Nina Nikola Doering

towns along the west coast of Kalaaliit Nunaat. I had spent some time in Aasiaat before while working on my Master's thesis on hopes, concerns and expectations triggered by oil exploration activities. During my PhD I began to question my own approach to research and since I moved back to Germany three years ago, I have worked together with Indigenous and non-Indigenous partners to gain a better understanding of the changes necessary within my work and my institution to enable co-creation in ethical and equitable research relationships. I am motivated to learn how to address my own biases, to understand and move away from the colonial and exploitative structures and practices that I am a part of and that I have helped carry forward. Over the past year, discussing our respective positionalities has formed the foundation for our conversations. As we have told each other stories about experiences in life and research, jointly analysed and re-interpreted them, I have gained helpful new insights into my own positionality that would not have been possible outside of our shared reflection.

Charleen: Research is part of a person's life's journey. My research journey is centred in identity, culture, language, family and community and transmission to future generations. It is only through establishing close connections with allied researchers who share common interests that I feel collaborative research between Indigenous and non-Indigenous partners takes place. I appreciate your work to break down colonial extractive practices.

Nina: I know that I am at the very beginning of this learning journey. I have learned tremendously from you, Charleen, about taking the first steps toward becoming an ally.

Charleen: *Aaha', shii chan*. Yes, me also. There is a need for critical allyship, linguists working on languages etc, to bridge these systems. To me, Indigenous research is not about devaluing someone else, decolonising is a positive construct and decolonising work is additive to secular cultural understandings. Weaving experiences from historical, institutional oppressive frameworks with advocacy work between generations creates positive social movements that decolonise systems, minds and hearts. Work-based on personal relationships and shared experiences that express vulnerability and relieve stresses that we feel help young researchers to frame research positively.

Relationality

> [T]he shared aspect of an Indigenous ontology and epistemology is relationality (relationships do not merely shape reality, they *are* reality). The shared aspect of an Indigenous axiology and methodology is accountability to relationships (Wilson 2008: 7).

When we began to talk about how we had first met and started to build a relationship, we remembered many 'small moments' – of spending time together on- and offline, chatting informally, sharing about ourselves and our thoughts. However, as we reflected more upon them, we realised that these moments had not been 'small' or mundane after all, they had required openness, energy, intention and a willingness to be vulnerable; and each of them had been consequential. We began to call them 'notable'. In particular, we feel that the work on this paper has been the result of each of us continuing to reach out. As we turned to the Two-Eyed Seeing framework to reflect, we noticed that 'seeing together' in a literal sense had been crucial: Charleen taking Nina to see places around Fairbanks that held meaning for her, seeing each other through our computer screens, sharing glimpses of our lives via camera, Nina inviting Charleen to Germany to see where she lives and works and both of us together looking at and editing pieces of text online. Many of the themes we discussed did not make it into this paper but formed an important part of our process. For example, we repeatedly discussed the role of humour as a form of resistance and a means of connecting and shared humour helped us deepen our own relationship and deal with difficult topics.

Figure 1. (a) Charleen and Nina in Fairbanks in front of the church of Charleen's father in 2015, (b) Charleen and Nina in Potsdam in 2022 and (c) on Zoom in 2022

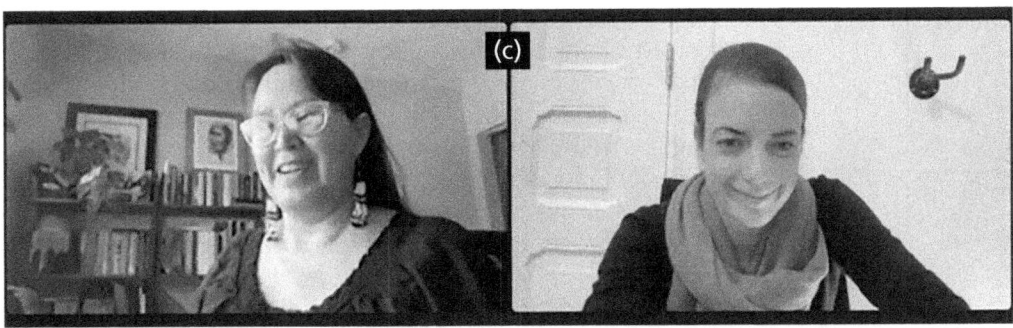

Charleen
Charisna Fisher

Nina Nikola
Doering

Charleen: Small moments of care, concern and friendship led to our established relationality. We initially toured Fairbanks and shared meals 10 years ago at IPSSAS when we were both in PhD programmes. I was thankful that you reached out and kept in touch virtually and on social media. Eventually, we worked together, and this led to a visit and collaboration in Germany. Relationships are critical to the co-creation of knowledge and collaborative research. It is difficult to work to understand our own bias and how our cultural knowledge systems are impacted by research in a way that is comprehensible and contextual. Expressing Indigeneity through the medium of western languages and society should be done with careful consideration of power, bias and reflection to make sure that important Indigenous protocols aren't overlooked or diminished. Our circular planning and writing discussions also helped us be conscious of our own biases and the critical nature of our work.

Nina: I reached out to you in a moment of uncertainty. I had felt increasingly unsettled by my own practices during my PhD and realised that I had come to a point at which I needed to re-learn how to work in academia. I was planning a workshop on 'Ethics and methods in Arctic transformative research' (www.arctic-ethics.org) to address some of the fundamental questions I had but did not want to put my need to learn as a burden onto others or dominate the agenda. I was also conscious of the problematic focus on 'decolonisation', often employed to serve the image of western people and institutions (see also Tuck and Yang 2012). We had many conversations while I worked with colleagues to develop a programme that I hoped would be meaningful and beneficial to all workshop contributors and we continued to speak online every week after the workshop had taken place. We met and talked with intention – to learn together and seek out possibilities to effect change from our respective positionalities – but without any plans for specific 'measurable' outputs. The relationship we have built has formed a foundation for other projects. However, this was not our goal and I now feel it would have been prohibitive. Indigenous scholars have written about the importance of time and reciprocity in relationship-building (e.g. Tynan 2021; Wilson 2008), reminding us that relationality needs to be felt and practised to be realised (Tynan 2021). I am grateful to you for not only having patiently explained, but practised with me.

Charleen: I was happy to hear from you and had finished my doctoral programme and had concerns about research also. That first workshop was interesting for me and a bit intimidating since offering the workshop session was tied to Indigenous research ethics, but I chose to share about myself and the community priorities that were important to me as an Indigenous person. It is difficult to establish relationality as your authentic self with strangers without an ally. Relationality is expressed in every part of the Gwich'in language whether creating context from the conversation, directional terms or the subjective nature of stem languages. Indigenous protocols are often overlooked and misinterpreted by non-Indigenous people and by

Indigenous people who haven't been raised with these protocols. For example, the knowledge of Elders should be accepted as given. Elders' knowledge may be understood and contextualised at a later date as the researcher learns more and their lived experiences grow. Protocols are an expression of the important connections between the systems, a way to express connection and respect between lands, water, air and animals. Protocols are also ceremony and communication. It is a spiritual connection that ties us together and to the earth, water, air and all other living creatures:

> Knowledge comes from multiple sources, such as humans, animals, birds, fish, insects, the earth, land, sky, and spirit. Indigenous epistemologies are not human centric, meaning that all species, not solely the human species, are a source of knowledge. Neither is knowledge limited solely to cognitive reasoning, though holism encompasses this source of knowing (Kovach 2021: 69).

While working on this paper, ensuring extra care to listen to each other was important to establish relationality from the beginning to address difficult subjects with sensitivity. Establishing relationality in a colonial era is laden with emotion but honest conversations and intention has been our practice. Connecting on a level of humanity brings us together in our co-creative research to understand the knowledge and ready ourselves to share with future generations. Spiritual connection, clan connection and community connection are all parts of my values-based lived experience with relationships. I feel blessed to live with a seasonal understanding of the Arctic.

Nina: I remember that early on in our conversations, you told me you were extending a hand to build a relationship that could last. It was clear that this offer contained a reciprocal responsibility to care for our relationship, to take seriously our collaborative work and to face up to the sometimes difficult and uncomfortable discussions we engaged in. I have also felt this responsibility in the relationships I built – and continue to value – during the work for my thesis. However, our discussions and our joint projects have provided me with a better understanding of how this responsibility extends to research practices, which form part of our relationships. Basing my research solely on Western concepts had rendered my efforts for ethical conduct incomplete and I understand the focus of my current work to constitute part of fulfilling my responsibilities as a researcher working in a colonial context.

Charleen: As an Alaska Native in America, with no governmental reconciliation and reclamation for past offences, I limit academic relationships to those who share common goals. Relationality and commonality create shared goals and there are many opportunities for friendship and mutual care. As an Indigenous researcher, I do end up being quite guarded and have a close-knit community of researchers that I work with on similar goals. For an outsider, it would be very difficult to break into this close-knit community without friendship and shared goals. I appreciate you reaching out and expressing your

Charleen Charisna Fisher

Nina Nikola Doering

opinions honestly. Establishing shared goals requires open discussions about difficult topics.

Nina: As I am learning, I have found the work of Eve Tuck and K. Wayne Yang helpful, who remind us that '[s]olidarity is an uneasy, reserved, and unsettled matter that neither reconciles present grievances nor forecloses future conflict' (2012: 3). I understand their work on '"settler moves to innocence", that problematically attempt to reconcile settler guilt and complicity, and rescue settler futurity' (ibid: 1) to highlight that engagement with our (i.e. Western researchers') uncomfortable emotions must be decentred and addressing them is work that we need to do amongst ourselves and within our institutions. Not with an aim of resolving them (this is neither possible nor relevant), but to understand how they may keep us from honestly addressing the root causes of exploitation. I grew up in Germany with deeply personal conversations among friends and schoolmates discussing the Holocaust and how much guilt had been passed down to us. From my perspective, it is a question that is mostly not only unproductive; as Astrid Messerschmidt (2008) illustrates, the showcasing and simultaneous denial of guilt have enabled German society to divert attention from continued anti-semitism *and* have contributed to a broad refusal to address racism in Germany, which does not fit a national self-image of having faced up to the past. Statistics on anti-semitic and right-wing offences in Germany (e.g. Federal Ministry of the Interior and Community 2021) and experiences of BIPoC students at German universities (e.g. Kuria 2015) make clear that German antisemitism and racism are neither remnants of the past nor attributable to isolated incidents; both are deeply embedded in German society and institutions. Where remembrance of and engagement with the Holocaust may be described as fragile (see also Messerschmidt 2008), conversations about our colonial history and the ways in which we continue to benefit from institutions built upon extraction from Indigenous peoples and lands have barely begun. Trying to understand how I have carried forward exploitative practices in my own research and learning how to do better is what motivates me on a personal level and an attempt to engage with my own guilt. As you mention, pushing back requires constant reflection on my own biases as well as the exploitative logics of the academic system within which I work. This extends to our joint efforts for co-creation, where we have felt ourselves how the deadline- and output-driven culture of academia leads to pressures that immediately render this work meaningless. I have learned that it is sometimes better to step back to avoid contributing to these practices and pressures.

Charleen: I am conscious of the heavy weight of colonisation in many parts of my personal life and work. It is important to privilege, prioritise and honour the work of decolonisation and find a path forward through establishing shared priorities. Our path forward includes respecting each other, working toward a shared understanding and being allies. It doesn't mean we have to agree on every topic, but acknowledge each other's truths and ensure agency in our own experiences. Indigenous and non-Indigenous researchers have the opportunity to co-create knowledge by knowing their own story and finding their place in an inter-connected world governed by sacred ceremonies and respect for all.

Western knowledge structures must remedy historical wrongs, critically and strategically fight oppression, and help Indigenous people to continue living in a sacred relational way. Indigenous ontology is a life lived with respect and protocols within an epistemological context and following axiological principles. The role of ceremony in decolonisation requires relationality, shared positionality and shared co-creation goals (see also Wilson 2008).

Co-creating commonality: Aligning goals around internalised colonisation and resurgence

When we started our conversations on Zoom a year ago, we let them flow freely, going where our thoughts and reflections took us. Over time, we kept circling back to the very different historical, relational, epistemological and institutional contexts we each find ourselves in, and consequently the different goals we strive to work towards, both personally and professionally. Yet on a deeper level, the problems we are trying to address – i.e. the consequences of continued colonial, economic and academic exploitation – are deeply interlinked. Returning to the Two-Eyed Seeing framework (Reid et al. 2021), we are seeing them from two perspectives/positions, which holds potential for mutually beneficial progress.

Nina: When I first reached out to you, my goal was to learn what changes were necessary within myself and my institution to improve my/our research practices – and to understand the aims of your work to find out if we could connect in a mutually beneficial way.

Charleen: I appreciate you reaching out and sharing these concerns. Indigenous knowledge documentation, revitalisation and education are work framed with urgency. Indigenous knowledge holders and youth both have a crisis in transmitting and receiving knowledge. Youth suffer from loss of cultural identity and traditional knowledge systems have encountered disruption, so opportunities for youth to learn from Elders are often programme dependent. To simply be Indigenous and to live our cultures is our resistance to colonisation. Our Indigenous agency is represented by every Indigenous voice spoken to honour our ancestral ways in our languages. One of the most difficult things for me in my dissertation writing experience was that the main elder whom I was working with passed away. Apart from the grief, this led me to have a deeper understanding of the urgency of working with our Indigenous Elders who are holding Indigenous knowledge and language. Since this time, all of the Elders whom I was working with have passed on. I feel as if I barely scratched the surface of their knowledge with the interview questions approved by my university's institutional review board. As an Indigenous person and researcher, I feel that some

Charleen Charisna Fisher

Nina Nikola Doering

Indigenous knowledge can and should be shared within the culture and community outside of research and Western systems because system processes don't appreciate the urgency of documenting first language speakers.

Nina: In my experience, this urgency that you describe has not been recognised widely in Germany, one of the centres of colonialism. Kien Nghi Ha (2018) traces German (dis)engagement with its colonial role, which has long been largely absent from political and dominant public discourse and emerged relatively late as a subject of inquiry in academic debate in Germany, crucially advanced by black German and African scholars and scholars of colour, whose voices continue to be under-represented in the German academy.[4] This has been tied with a broadly communicated public misconception that the effects of Germany's colonial rule have been relatively insignificant.[5] In recent decades, critical engagement has become more visible, as seen for instance in the work of local activist groups (e.g. Decolonize Berlin, www.decolonize-berlin.de), museums (e.g. GRASSI Museum für Völkerkunde zu Leipzig, n.d.) and calls for decolonial approaches to academic disciplines in Germany are growing (e.g. Ndlovu-Gatshen et al. 2022 on African Studies; Layne 2019 on German Studies; Arghavan et al. 2019 on American Studies/ the Humanities). Yet despite increasing public and academic debate, sincere political efforts and a general culture of remembrance remain lacking. The topic took up minimal space in my school curriculum and little seems to have changed since in many German schools. When I moved to the UK for my Master's degree in Development Studies, my experience did not change fundamentally. While the programme introduced me to diverse literatures and perspectives and facilitated critical thinking, I can remember only few instances where we were introduced to Indigenous or other non-Western research methods and ethical clearance for my fieldwork was provided by the university ethics committee without critical reflection on the appropriateness of such procedures in the context of research taking place on Indigenous lands. Meanwhile, in Germany, many universities and research institutes continue to operate without ethics committees. At the same time, there is growing recognition among Arctic researchers in Germany that change is necessary. Debate across the Arctic on ethical research (e.g. Arctic Council Secretariat 2020), and requirements for research permits and funding applications have spurred some discussions in Germany, albeit with the often-voiced addendum that this will require a learning process.

Charleen: Our communicative research process has forced me to think about how collaborative research partnerships can benefit Indigenous people. My research has been largely documenting Indigenous cultural practices for future generations. Indigenous communities communicate learned experiences through shared experiences tied to ancestral land, cultural knowledge and language. Researchers seeking to work with Indigenous people must understand the priorities of the Indigenous community. They should ask themselves if their research contributes to language revitalisation, culture revitalisation, resurgence, reclamation or advocacy, etc? Putting the burden and responsibility of policing opportunistic research about Indigenous knowledge on traditional governing structures (for example, Alaskan tribes) should not be a question of their capacity. Our ancestors have lived here for thousands of years in a sustainable way and research can help non-Indigenous and Indigenous researchers to learn how to live in a relational way with each other, land, waters, air and animals. Researchers and scientists must view Indigenous communities as partners and not as an opportunity for information extraction.

Nina: This will require a structural transformation of the Western academic system, including funding, hiring procedures, set-up of projects, research methodologies, outcome evaluations and school and university curricula. As we have seen in our joint work on funding, it is not sufficient to provide financial resources for co-creative research. Funding programmes themselves need to be co-developed, eligibility criteria need to change, timelines need to be extended and be made flexible and long-term care for research relationships needs to be acknowledged as part of the research cycle (Doering et al. 2022). And as you have noted, there are deeper conversations to be had on how far Western systems can change to accommodate Indigenous epistemologies and ontologies. There is also a risk that 'co-production' and collaboration become mere boxes to tick for Western researchers as the concepts are emptied of any meaning (see also Buschman 2022a: 5; Yua et al. 2022). As Linda Tuhiwai Smith (2012) has so eloquently illustrated, our academic system is built on a foundation of colonial exclusion. Pedersen et al. (2020) highlight that, beyond respecting the rights of Indigenous peoples, Western researchers can improve the quality of their research if they learn to understand and treat Indigenous knowledge as more than 'data' to be collected for (or ignored in) scientific projects by establishing respectful and equitable research relationships.

Charleen: I am struggling to find a balance between how much time and effort I spend on decolonising or Indigenising Western systems when I can't speak my own language fluently in my own culture. When questioning my mother once about my future career path, she told me in jest: 'All you have to do is stay Native (Dinjii zhuh, Dena'ina, Denaa) until you die.' She followed up with some statements about how I should be happy and proud of my identity and feel like I am contributing in a positive way but this is it. Transformational impacts to academic institutions are a secondary impact for Indigenous research. Contributing to academia is secondary to transformational change that supports and advocates for Indigenous reclamation and resurgence. Why do I have to change the Western world when I can actively contribute to 10,000 years of knowledge transmission within my own community? Are colonists or settlers having discussions and committing lifetimes of work to ensure that their knowledge is included in Gwich'in decision-making or governance or do they make the

Charleen Charisna Fisher

Nina Nikola Doering

assumption that their knowledge replaces it? Transformative research must not recolonise Indigeneity. Recolonisation by our own people reinforces colonial structures, systems and power instead of our own, by using English content and system codification to make parallels to Indigenous knowledge.

Nina: The responsibility to push for change in Western academic institutions must lie with us Western researchers. This is slow and often invisible but important work. Together with partners from the Saami Council, I worked for several months on a project proposal last year trying to achieve greater equality in the distribution of overhead costs factored into the project budget between Indigenous and non-Indigenous partner institutions. For me, this was a powerful experience and it highlighted that the foundation for co-creation is laid long before the start of a research project. Yet working on these details of the proposal together also helped us establish stronger relationships for the project work we are now engaged in.

I believe that we also have to recognise that the urgency you describe above does not only apply to Indigenous peoples. Our extractive-based Western lifestyle of over-consumption has led the world to the brink of catastrophe (although Indigenous and other marginalised communities once again will be and are already harmed disproportionately). Across the world, Indigenous lands are degrading less quickly and exhibit higher biodiversity. We cannot afford to ignore and disregard Indigenous expertise (see also Buschman 2022a).

Charleen: Western academic scholarship doesn't understand its role in healing wounds from colonisation or relating ceremonial rights of passage to a student's experience in post-secondary education. Surface discussions in westernised academia have begun to understand the cultural obligations of protocol and honouring Elders, place and knowledge systems. The academy's role is to foster research and that is what is so exciting about Indigenous studies, Indigenous researchers and co-creation. We have this wonderful opportunity to work on shared goals to learn, share, heal, revitalise, reclaim and transform systems to include those that have traditionally been oppressed.

Non-Indigenous and Indigenous researchers must endeavour to learn Indigenous language to comprehend Indigenous knowledge. Systemic transformation to the academy can eventually require Indigenous vetting of research cultural and language metrics to help situate and contextualise the knowledge. Indigenous and non-Indigenous researchers must seek help to establish cultural and linguistic relevance in research. If researchers want to participate in Indigenous research, they have to step outside their own cultural understandings to learn about Indigenous priorities (Brayboy et al. 2012). Reframing academic discussions that align research priorities to community issues and language and cultural knowledge revitalisation goals should be held prior to project proposals and be embedded throughout the entire research process (Kovach 2021).

Participatory-based research can create valuable knowledge that accompanies the research content. Indigenous perspectives have different ways of knowing (Smith 2012; Wilson 2008), different ways of teaching and different ways of transmitting knowledge from one generation to the next with the intent of understanding five or seven generations down the line. Understanding your place and understanding your role contribute to understanding Indigeneity. Collaboration without true co-creation leads to extraction that unevenly benefits Western knowledge systems. Contributing to Indigenous bodies of knowledge without contributing to Indigenous goals is a one-sided colonial-constructed understanding that omits the community perspective.

Nina: Thank you for sharing your insights into the 'how to' of collaboration and co-creation! This brings me back to another point that you raised above and that you and fellow Indigenous scholars have brought up repeatedly in our discussions: how can we non-Indigenous researchers learn to do things differently without reproducing what Nora Berenstain (2016) has termed 'epistemic exploitation' by expecting our Indigenous friends and colleagues to teach us how to transform our western institutions and challenge the epistemic oppressions that are built into their fabric (on 'building self-capacity' see also Buschman 2022a: 5)? I find your focus on contributing to Indigenous goals helpful as an analytical tool to assessing the projects we choose to pursue. I have been conscious over the past year that you shared many hours with me on Zoom despite the limited time you have available. I am grateful for all I have learned from you and I have tried to reciprocate by using the resources available to me to support efforts for change in research.

Charleen: I research with strategic purpose and intention and it is usually deeply personal. This purpose is multi-faceted, loaded with the representation of accurate understandings of Gwich'in knowledge, Gwich'in language and Indigenous pedagogy. This purpose is built on the years of teaching in the K-12 classroom on my ancestral lands and years of decentring Western content in a way that is reframed in the context of my own Indigenous perspective. For years and years, I became conscious that the information I was employed to teach was biased, historically inaccurate, and lacked a connection to the very place where we had the honour to steward for future generations. Having my students, my children, nieces and nephews be required to learn information laden with obvious bias led me to reframe, decolonise and resituate knowledge and truths to make sense to me and to my blood memory. I wasn't aware of what Critical Indigenous Research Methodologies (CIRM) (Brayboy et al. 2012) were when I began the Indigenous Studies PhD programme, I just knew that we had our own ways of knowing, being, teaching and understanding that had to be represented in academia to impact systemic change in Western education.

Nina: As I reflect on this past year, I feel that in aligning our goals and

Charleen Charisna Fisher

Nina Nikola Doering

in placing a focus on 'notable' moments in our interactions – by first discussing them, acknowledging and valuing them as enabling and then seeking them out and creating them with intention – we achieved more than our initial plan to 'reflect and write together'. We found ways of working and thinking together, built connections not only between ourselves but with a growing network of colleagues seeking to effect change, and experienced joy and friendship that will form a basis for future connection. However, in line with the trade-offs you describe, I think that it is your assessment that counts regarding whether the time you invested has contributed towards your communities' goals.

Charleen: Indigenous people have been careful about how and what to share with outside researchers. Scholarship has become a path for Indigenous knowledge to be included in Western educational systems with the goal of transformation. Centring Indigenous knowledge is good for all people. In my dissertation, I was also careful to present Indigenous knowledge so that it is represented as it is within the culture. Academic research cannot replace innate cultural knowledge or blood memory instilled from birth by family, clan and community systems. The work of Indigenous researchers in western academic systems of power support inclusive knowledge co-creation, language, cultural revitalisation and advocacy but these systems are based on western thought and priorities. Indigenous researchers spend a lot of time navigating western systems to purposely advocate for their own community priorities. Indigenous knowledge is sacred and exists independently of and has value outside of Western academic systems. Indigenous research priorities established through commonality can include transformation in the academy but also includes Indigenous community priorities. I am motivated to learn my language and to participate in the generational transmission of epistemological, ontological and axiological practices. My motivation to participate in research is strategic with communicative goals and I am so happy to welcome allies who share these goals. In some circumstances, I do believe that Indigenous knowledge should be honoured in the community only but most areas are places where allies help restore traditions. Thank you for your time and friendship over all these years. I have grown considerably in this process.

Conclusion

Shijyaa haa research establishes cooperative relationality that is initiated in small moments and can grow from communication over time and across distance. Meaningful co-creative research requires work to establish relational tenets and time together virtually and/or in-person to understand positionality and strategic and thoughtful commonality. Sensitivity and careful listening are key to establishing relationality and aligning goals especially when communicating across cultures. Co-creative research is a journey and going through it together and learning about each other's processes taught us unintentional lessons along the way as we established relationality. The distance between Alaska and Germany did not prohibit us from making connections – friendship, trust and collegiality can be established virtually, but must be enhanced with in-person visits. Learning about and experiencing each other within our communities – understanding each other in place and in context – strengthened our relationship in ways that video calls cannot accomplish. We encourage co-creative researchers across disciplines to be careful about being dismissive of someone else's perspective and to participate in active listening to cultivate co-creative research. Our hope is that our work together will impact other Indigenous and non-Indigenous researchers who engage in collaborative research with Indigenous communities to be reflective and think deeply and intentionally about how 'small' moments can initiate, and eventually constitute, relationships. Work on relationality includes knowing firmly your positionality to create a deeper understanding of shared goals that can clarify and grow future collaboration. Relationality may form the foundation for future research projects – but this is not necessary; relationships are valuable in and of themselves. In our conversations, we addressed uncomfortable topics, but committing to showing up online every week to communicate openly helped us establish a longer-term relationship. As Charleen's grandma, the late Charlotte Adams and most Gwich'in grandmothers would say:, 'Listen!'

Glossary

Dinjii zhuh, Dena'ina, Denaa	mean 'people of place' in slightly different ways; for more information on the language families, see Krauss, Holton, Kerr and West (2011)
Shijyaa haa	'with my friend' (Gwich'in)
Tl'eeyegge Hʉt'aane	'people of the very place pointing down to the land' (Jetté and Jones 2000, p. l).

Notes

[1] I (Nina) lowercase 'white' here to avoid aligning with right-wing use of the term, and understand it as a socially constructed category

[2] It is important to note that for BIPoC Germans, being asked 'where one is from' is often an experience of racism and othering (see, for example, Obute 201: 88)

[3] See Eggers et al. (2018) for perspectives on the German context and Florvil (2020) for insights into resistance, the black German movement and black German women's intellectual activism

[4] Emily Ngubia Kuria (2015) writes about student experiences of racism and strategies of resistance

[5] Ha (2018) notes that the German Federal Agency for Civic Education ('Bundeszentrale für Politische Bildung') provided support to a book that diminishes the extent of German colonialism

Charleen
Charisna Fisher

Nina Nikola
Doering

References

Arctic Council Secretariat (2020) Arctic Resilience Forum 2020. Available online at https://oaarchive.arctic-council.org/bitstream/handle/11374/2614/arctic-resilience-forum-2020_web.pdf?sequence=1&isAllowed=y

Arghavan, Mahmoud, Hirschfelder, Nicole and Motyl, Katharina (2019) Who can speak and who is heard/hurt? Facing problems of race, racism and ethnic diversity in the humanities in Germany: A survey of the issues at stake, Arghavan, Mahmoud, Hirschfelder, Nicole, Kopp, Luvena and Motyl, Katharina (eds) *Who can speak and who is heard/hurt? Facing problems of race, racism and ethnic diversity in the humanities in Germany*, Bielefeld, transcript Verlag pp 9–44

Armitage, Derek, Berkes, Fikret, Dale, Aron, Kocho-Schellenberg, Erik and Patton, Eva (2011) Co-management and the co-production of knowledge: Learning to adapt in Canada's Arctic, *Global Environmental Change*, Vol. 21, No. 3. DOI: 10.1016/j.gloenvcha.2011.04.006

Berenstain, Nora (2016) Epistemic exploitation, *Ergo: An Open Access Journal of Philosophy*, Vol. 3, No. 26. Available online at http://dx.doi.org/10.3998/ergo.12405314.0003.022

Brayboy, Bryan, McKinley, Jones, Gough, Heather R., Leonard, Beth, Roehl, Roy F. II and Solyom, Jessica A. (2012) Reclaiming scholarship: Critical Indigenous research methodologies, Laplan, Stephen D., Quartarolo, Marylynn, T. and Riemer, Frances J. (eds) *Qualitative research: An introduction to methods and designs*, San Francisco, John Wiley & Sons pp 423–450

Buschman, Victoria Qutuuq (2022a) Framing co-productive conservation in partnership with Arctic Indigenous Peoples, *Conservation Biology*, Vol. 36. DOI: 10.1111/cobi.13972

Buschman, Victoria Qutuuq (2022b) Arctic conservation in the hands of Indigenous peoples. Available online at https://www.wilsonquarterly.com/quarterly/the-new-north/arctic conservation-in the-hands-of-indigenous-peoples

Cooke, Steven J., Nguyen, Vivian M., Chapman, Jaqueline M., Reid, Andrea J., Landsman, Sean J., Young, Nathan, Hinch, Scott G., Schott, Stephen, Mandrak, Nicholas E. and Semeniuk, Christina A. D. (2020) Knowledge co-production: A pathway to effective fisheries management, conservation, and governance, *Fisheries*, Vol. 46 p 46. DOI: 10.1002/fsh.10512

Degai, Tatiana, Petrov, Andrey N., Badhe, Renuka, Dahl, Parnuna Egede, Döring, Nina, Dudeck, Stephan, Herrmann, Thora, Golovnev, Andrei, Mack, Liza, Omma, Elle Merete, Retter, Gunn-Britt, Saxinger, Gertrude, Scheepstra, Annette J. M., Shadrin, Chief Vyachelav, Shorty, Norma and Strawhacker, Colleen (2022) Shaping Arctic's tomorrow through Indigenous knowledge engagement and knowledge co-production, *Sustainability*, Vol. 14, No. 3. Available online at https://doi.org/10.3390/su14031331

Doering, Nina, Dudeck, Stephan, Elverum, Shelly, Fisher, Charleen, Henriksen, Jan Erik, Herrmann, Thora Martina, Kramvig, Britt, Laptander, Roza, Milton, Justin, Omma, Elle Merete, Saxinger, Gertrude, Scheepstra, Annette J. M. and Wilson, Katherine (2022) Improving the relationships between Indigenous rights holders and researchers in the Arctic: An invitation for change in funding and collaboration, *Environmental Research Letters*, Vol. 17, No 6. Available online at https://doi.org/10.1088/1748-9326/ac72b5

Eggers, Maureen Maisha, Kilomba, Grada, Piesche, Peggy and Arndt, Susan (eds) (2018) *Mythen, Masken und Subjekte: Kritische Weißseinsforschung in Deutschland* [*Myths, masks and subjects: Critical whiteness studies in Germany*], Münster, UNRAST Verlag, third edition, e-book

Federal Ministry of the Interior and Community (2021) Politisch motivierte Kriminalität im Jahr 2021: Bundesweite Fallzahlen [Politically motivated crime in 2021: Nationwide case figures]. Available online at https://www.bmi.bund.de/SharedDocs/downloads/DE/veroeffentlichungen/nachrichten/2022/pmk2021-factsheets.pdf;jsessionid=3BCBC6E7863144FF55CFEBF667903391.2_cid287?__blob=publicationFile&v=2

Florvil, Tiffany Nicole (2020) *Mobilizing Black Germany: Afro-German women and the making of a transnational movement*, Urbana, University of Illinois Press

GRASSI Museum für Völkerkunde zu Leipzig (n.d.) Steps toward decolonisation. Available online at https://docs.google.com/document/d/1EULngskirMF6z1N_-WS_sDmQLOXZnuluNm3n8T3i3QY/edit#

Gwich'in Tribal Council (2011) Conducting traditional knowledge research in the Gwich'in settlement area: A guide for researchers. Available online at https://nwtresearch.com/sites/default/files/gwich-in-social-and-cultural institute_0.pdf

Ha, Kien Nghi (2018) Macht(t)raum(a) Berlin: Deutschland als Kolonialgesellschaft, Eggers, Maureen Maisha, Kilomba, Grada, Piesche, Peggy and Arndt, Susan (eds) *Mythen, Masken und Subjekte: Kritische Weißseinsforschung in Deutschland* [*Myths, masks and subjects: Critical whiteness studies in Germany*], Münster, UNRAST Verlag, third edition, e-book

Inuit Circumpolar Council (2022) Circumpolar Inuit protocols for equitable and ethical engagement. Available online at https://hh30e7.p3cdn1.secureserver.net/wp-content/uploads/EEE-Protocols-LR-WEB.pdf

Inuit Tapiriit Kanatami (2018) National Inuit strategy on research. Available online at https://www.itk.ca/wp-content/uploads/2020/10/ITK-National-Inuit-Strategy-on-Research.pdf

Jetté, Jules and Jones, Eliza (2000) *Koyukon Athabaskan dictionary*, Fairbanks, Alaska Native Language Center, University of Alaska Fairbanks

Kovach, Margaret (2021) *Indigenous methodologies: Characteristics, conversations, and contexts*, Toronto, University of Toronto Press

Krauss, Michael, Holton, Gary, Kerr, Jim and West, Colin T. (2011) Indigenous peoples and languages of Alaska, Fairbanks and Anchorage, Alaska Native Language Center and UAA Institute of Social and Economic Research. Available online at https://www.uaf.edu/anla/collections/map/

Kuria, Emily Ngubia (2015) *Eingeschrieben: Zeichen setzen gegen Rassismus an deutschen Hochschulen* [*Enrolled: Taking a stand against racism at German universities*], Berlin: w_orten & meer

Layne, Pricscilla (2019) On racism without race: The need to diversify Germanistik and the German academy, Arghavan, Mahmoud, Hirschfelder, Nicole, Kopp, Luvena and Motyl, Katharina (eds) *Who can speak and who is heard/hurt? Facing problems of race, racism, and ethnic diversity in the humanities in Germany*, Bielefeld, transcript Verlag pp 217–238

Lewis, Jordan P. (2021) *Generativity and aging well for Alaska Natives*, Selin, Helaine (ed.) *Aging across cultures: Growing old in the non-Western world*, Cham, Springer. Available online at https://doi.org/10.1007/978-3-030-76501-9_21

Messerschmidt, Astrid (2008) Postkoloniale Erinnerungsprozesse in einer postnationalsozialistischen Gesellschaft: Vom Umgang mit Rassismus und Antisemitismus [Postcolonial memory processes in a post-national socialist society: On dealing with racism and antisemitism], *PERIPHERIE*, Vol. 28, Nos 109 and 110 pp 42–60

Ndlovu-Gatsheni, Sabelo, Seesemann, Rüdiger and Vogt-William, Christine (2022) African studies in distress: German scholarship on Africa and the neglected challenge of decoloniality, *Africa Spectrum*, Vol. 57, No. 1. DOI: 10.1177/00020397221080179

Obute, Anthony (2019) *Beyond a trifling presence: Afro-Germans and identity boundaries in Germany*, Arghavan, Mahmoud, Hirschfelder, Nicole, Kopp, Luvena and Motyl, Katharina (eds) *Who can speak and who is heard/hurt? Facing problems of race, racism, and ethnic diversity in the humanities in Germany*, Bielefeld, transcript Verlag pp 83–100

Pedersen, C., Otokiak, M., Koonoo, I., Milton, J., Maktar, E., Anaviapik, A., Milton, M., Porter, G., Scott, A., Newman, C., Porter, C., Aaluk, T., Tiriraniaq, B., Pedersen, A., Riffi, M., Solomon, E. and Elverum, S. (2020) SciQ: An invitation and recommendations to combine science and Inuit Qaujimajatuqangit for meaningful engagement of Inuit communities in research, *Arctic Science*, Vol. 6, No. 3. Available online at https://doi.org/10.1139/as-2020-0015

Charleen Charisna Fisher

Nina Nikola Doering

Reid, Andrea J. Eckert, Lauren E. Lane, John-Francis, Young, Nathan, Hinch, Scott G. Darimont, Chris T. Cooke, Steven J., Ban, Natalie C. and Marshall, Albert (2021) 'Two-eyed seeing': An Indigenous framework to transform fisheries research and management, *Fish and Fisheries*, Vol. 22, No. 2 pp 243–261

Sámediggi (2021) Etiske retningslinjer for samisk helseforskning [Ethical guidelines for Sámi health research]. Available online at https://sametinget.no/_f/p1/iab4f8a7f-1c05-4f9f-a5e2-1d4f6196671d/etiske-retningslinjer-for-samisk-helseforskning-ny.pdf

Sarkki, Simo, Rasmus, Sirpa, Landauer, Mia, Lépy, Élise and Heikkinen, Hannu I. (2020) Matching societal knowledge demand, research funding and scientific knowledge supply: Trends and co-creation dynamics around reindeer management in Finland, *Polar Geography*, Vol. 44, No 2. Available online at https://doi.org/10.1080/1088937x.2020.1755905

Smith, Linda Tuhiwei (2012) *Decolonizing methodologies: Research and Indigenous peoples*, London, Zed Books, second edition

Todd, Zoe (2016) An Indigenous feminist's take on the ontological turn: 'Ontology' is just another word for colonialism, *Journal of Historical Sociology*, Vol. 29, No. 1. Available online at https://doi.org/10.1111/johs.12124

Tuck, Eve and Yang, K. Wayne (2012) Decolonization is not a metaphor, *Decolonization: Indigeneity, Education & Society*, Vol. 1, No. 1 pp 1–40

Tynan, Lauren (2021) What is relationality? Indigenous knowledges, practices and responsibilities with kin, *Cultural Geographies*, Vol. 28, No. 4 pp 597–610

United Nations (2007) United Nations declaration on the rights of Indigenous peoples (A/RES/61/295). Available online at https://www.un.org/development/desa/indigenouspeoples/wp-content/uploads/sites/19/2018/11/UNDRIP_E_web.pdf

Wilson, Shawn (2008) *Research is ceremony: Indigenous research methods*, Halifax, Fernwood Publishing

Wilson, Stan and Schellhammer, Barbara (2021) *Indigegogy: Invitation to learning in a relational way*, Darmstadt, wbg Academic

Yua, Ellam, Raymond-Yakoubian, Julie, Raychelle, Aluaq Daniel and Behe, Carolina (2022) A framework for co-production of knowledge in the context of Arctic research, *Ecology and Society*, Vol. 27, No. 1. Available online at https://doi.org/10.5751/ES-12960-270134

Note on the contributors

Dr Charleen Fisher is Dinjii zhuh (Gwich'in), Tl'eeyegge Hʉt'aane and Dena'ina and a tribal member from Beaver, Alaska. She currently teaches at the University of Alaska Fairbanks as an Assistant Professor. She has many years of experience as a K-12 certified teacher, principal and in administration in Alaskan school districts. She has also been the executive director with the Council of Athabascan Tribal Governments, and has served as the chief of Beaver Village Council and in other positions of leadership. She has a BA in Political Science, MEd in Language and Literacy, a Graduate Certificate in Educational Leadership from the University of Alaska Anchorage and a PhD in Indigenous Studies from the University of Alaska Fairbanks.

Dr Nina Doering works as research group leader at the Research Institute for Sustainability, Helmholtz Centre Potsdam (RIFS) in Potsdam, Germany. Her research has focused on public participation, extractive resource management, anticipation and change in the Arctic. She has become particularly interested in research ethics, co-creative research, research relationships and Indigenous rights. Following her studies in International Economics and Development Studies at the University of Bayreuth and the University of Oxford, she completed a DPhil (PhD) at the University of Oxford's School of Geography and the Environment.

Conflict of interest and acknowledgements

We are grateful for the very helpful comments of two reviewers. We have no conflicts of interests to declare.

PAPER

Tanya Allport
Tom Johnson
Meretini Bennett-Huxtable

Traversing Indigenous communication landscapes: Translation, uptake and impact of Māori research

As Indigenous researchers we are supported and guided by an integral understanding to conduct research in accordance with our own Indigenous ethics (tikanga). By taking greater control of research methodologies and processes, we are reclaiming our ancient knowledges and ways of passing on or disseminating those knowledges. One of the less widely understood components of Māori research is around Indigenous-based, effective modes for communicating research findings to effect aspirational change for Māori. This paper explores the components of a new framework rooted in the strengths, wisdom and world views of Indigenous peoples. The TUI (Translation, Uptake and Impact) framework is designed to communicate new Māori research knowledge. This paper looks at using the TUI framework as a way to build awareness methods to engage whānau, hapū, Iwi and Māori communities, and a way to use communication to rebalance inequities. Inclusive, Māori led and Māori focused research translation thereby has the potential to contribute to more sustainable and transformative change.

Key words: Māori; Research dissemination; Indigenous ethics; Indigenous knowledge

Introduction

Persistent inequities in health outcomes are experienced globally by Indigenous populations, particularly in settler-colonial nations (Wilson et al. 2021). Indigenous peoples are cut off from the protective elements ingrained in their traditional values, beliefs and practices (Mulholland and Tawhai 2010) and experience ineffective interactions

Tanya Allport

Tom Johnson

Meretini Bennett-Huxtable

with healthcare services (Aspinall et al. 2020). Māori, the Indigenous peoples of Aotearoa New Zealand, are a group who have been studied for decades, yet continue to experience significant health disparities when compared to their Pākehā (non-Māori) counterparts (Robson and Harris 2007; Ministry of Health 2015; Houkamau 2016). While the majority Pākehā enjoy relatively good health in New Zealand (Barnes et al. 2014), deep-seated health and wellbeing inequities are a feature of New Zealand's long-term population health trajectory for Māori (Robson and Harris 2007; Ministry of Health 2015). Colonisation continues to have adverse and detrimental effects on the health, wellbeing and very existence of Māori (Durie 2012; Robson and Harris 2007) and on the Māori populations' aspirations, vitality and potential (Moewaka Barnes and McCreanor 2019). These historical disparities result from colonial policies and practices that deprive Māori of their rights, property, infrastructures, institutions and sovereignty (Smith 1999; Spoonley and Pearson 2004; Walker 1990). Language degradation, racist policies, discrimination and social exclusion are congruent with the disparate Māori healthcare outcomes (Robson and Harris 2007). Subsequently, the very concept of 'research' has a troubled past amongst Indigenous peoples, with Māori featuring as subjects of studies as the novel 'other', with the result of being harmed, exploited and traumatised (Boulton 2020).

Whakauae research

Whakauae Research is based in Whanganui, a town on the west coast of Aotearoa New Zealand's North Island. Whakauae Research holds a unique position as the only research centre in Aotearoa directly owned and accountable to an Iwi (tribal) entity. Overseen by Ngāti Hauiti an Iwi (tribe) in the Rangitīkei region, Whakauae Research is committed to transforming Māori lives by translating health research evidence into practice and driving Kaupapa Māori research (Māori centred research) as innovative, collaborative and cutting edge. Reclaiming the intellectual traditions, reviving ancient teachings and re-applying the knowledge of ancestors are part of a movement Whakauae Research is enacting toward developing research which is meaningful and useful to Māori communities (Boulton 2020). Whakauae Research is guided by tikanga (values and ethics) handed down from their Elders. Inherently, Whakauae Research has practised and adapted its ancestral communication landscape throughout its years of health research to reach the ears of its funders, the hands of its Iwi owners and most importantly, the hearts of the people they serve: hapori Māori (Māori communities). The practice of Kaupapa Māori research in this sense acknowledges that the deeply entrenched health and wellbeing inequities for Māori are tied to a range of systems that do not work for Māori. Changing these systems requires from the ground up re-framing of narratives towards the inclusion of whānau (family), hapū (sub-tribe), Iwi and hapori Māori.

Ethics and tikanga

Tikanga are a set of locally informed and specific values and practices which guide relationships between all living things. This means that tikanga represent the ethics we use in being, living and in undertaking research. Tikanga is adapted and enacted appropriately in contextually specific responses. Individual hapū and Iwi have their own localised understandings and examples of tikanga based on their specific experiences, contexts and environments (Cheung 2008) which are customary practices, or 'layers of the culture' woven from common cultural concepts, and primarily a set of values handed down from ancestors (Carter et al. 2018). These tikanga and ethics can 'speak to us through chants, songs, stories and many other forms of belief' (Smith 2020: 127). They are at the heart of Māori life and society (Mead 2003) and applied in everyday settings (Barlow and Wineti 1991). Tikanga inform and build frameworks for how groups interact, relationships are formed and address ethical issues, behaviours and practices in engaging with Māori and things that matter to them (Carter et al. 2018). For Māori, ethics is about 'tikanga' – for tikanga reflects our values, our beliefs and the way in which we view the world (Hudson et al. 2010). As a result, when conducting research with Māori, ethical considerations are based on Māori values, thus ethical behaviour then mirrors those values.

Whakauae Research follows conventional Western research ethics standards but not at the expense of their tikanga (Boulton 2020). The fundamental principles of tangata whenua (Indigenous peoples of the land) are incorporated from Whakauae Research's parent organisation, Te Rūnanga o Ngāti Hauiti. These tikanga guide researchers at Whakauae Research on the selection of a study design, the development of research questions and how the communication and dissemination of results is returned to Māori. The five tikanga that govern the mahi (work) at Whakauae Research are highlighted by Boulton (2020): a holistic view of what constitutes good health for all is embraced by the principle of *Hauora Tangata,* which recognises the dimensions of the physical body, spirituality, knowledge and understanding and the well-being of the entire whānau as the key principles of well-being. Secondly, *Rangatiratanga* affirms the freedom to choose our own Māori aspirations and the means to pursue them. In practice this means that research always is responsive to the needs of Māori. Thirdly, *Manaaki Tangata* upholds high standards of care and respect for the individuals and organisations with whom Whakauae Research interacts. Fourth, *Mātauranga* recognises the utilisation of both Māori and Western academic knowledge to support Māori ambitions. And finally, *Ngākau Tapatahi me te Aurere* is a tikanga at Whakauae Research where the team aims to create transformative change for Māori through their expertise, ethics, effort, sincere passion and commitment to excellence. From the start to the finish of every study endeavour, these tikanga that guide Whakauae Research are articulated and put into practice (Boulton 2020).

Tanya Allport
Tom Johnson
Meretini Bennett-Huxtable

Communication landscapes of our tūpuna (ancestors)

Māori communication landscapes – which we are defining here as the what, why and how of knowledge sharing for the benefit of the whānau, hapū, and Iwi – reflect the specifics of tribal land, histories and stories expressed throughout te ao Māori (the Māori world). These communication landscapes situate the importance of whakapapa (genealogy), a cornerstone of Māori wellbeing (Boulton et al. 2021) and allow the exchange of knowledge, weaving together various strands of work to collectively achieve tribal aspirations. The ancestral communication landscapes of Māori are not simply about describing the past but equally define the present; they are alive today (Kawharu 2009). The examples of Māori communication landscapes provided below are not exhaustive, but rather, they reflect aspects that Whakauae Research builds on in their development of a new communication landscape for Māori research.

Mātauranga Māori

Mātauranga Māori refers to the traditional knowledge of Māori and the embodiment of that knowledge through language, values, ethics and cultural customs (Hikuroa 2017; Mead 2003; Paul-Burke et al. 2018; Royal 2009). Because Mātauranga Māori is refined and evolved in Aotearoa for centuries, it is considered both traditional and dynamic (King et al. 2007) and applicable today. The idea of an ancestral communication landscape for Māori represents the way in which mātauranga Māori, knowledge new and old, can be a 'living thing' that is passed on for the purposes of strength and wellbeing of whānau, hapū, Iwi and hapori Māori. In this way, mātauranga Māori is communicated to impart the place of someone or something within whānau, hapū and Iwi. A Māori world view thus frames how traditional knowledge was communicated and disseminated – not only through humans – where information and conversations traversed space and time, the seen and unseen, living and non-living.

Marae and pōwhiri

One of the central physical landscapes for ancestral communication was the marae, where social interaction, discussion and collective decision-making occurred. There was tikanga on how discussion was governed on the marae such as whakawhitiwhiti kōrero (talking criss-cross) or te haere o te rākau (passing the stick) which ensures all voices are heard (Metge 2001, Metge 2014). An example of the continued practice of ancestral communication is also in pōwhiri. Pōwhiri is a traditional welcoming process which includes karanga (call) and whaikōrero (formal speech). The whaikōrero includes a tauparapara (ritual chant) where the orator begins a conversation with atua (gods), stars, the sun and the earth to honour the visitor, or new staff member and to ask for care. At Rātā Marae, a marae of Ngāti Hauiti, the ruru (native owl) is the kaitiaki (spiritual guardian) and the kaikaranga (the woman whose voice is heard first on the Marae to call on the guests) is called the kairuru.

The karanga performed by a wāhine (woman) opens the spiritual realm safely for the pōwhiri. The whaikōrero continues with paying a tribute to ngā mate (the dead) and acknowledges the tūpuna (ancestors) and descendants of those present. Finally, acknowledgement to the marae, the earth mother Papatūānuku and all living things is made. From this ceremony the pōwhiri allows communication to resonate between humans, gods, earth and the dead.

Wānanga

In te ao Māori wānanga is a centuries old concept that provides a context in which knowledge is shared and translated. Wānanga cannot be fully expressed with a direct translation to English, without the understanding of Māori epistemology. Wānanga as a concept provides a space for coming together to communicate knowledge, yet it can be both a verb and noun. Smith (Smith et al. 2019) cites Pohatu and Warmenhoven that 'through wānanga we are able to reflect and be reminded of our place in the universe' (Pohatu and Warmenhoven 2007: 120), which centralises the collective production and communication of knowledge.

Smith et al. (2019) further explain that the concept of a thought-space wānanga dimension is not merely a space for 'talking' but allows participants to actively engage in collective problem-solving. The acknowledgement of mana motuhake (autonomy) functions as an explicit expression of reciprocity within a wānanga space. To knowledge-share is to value each participant's contribution to the collective, and 'it positions the knowledge gained through direct participation as a potential collective benefit' (ibid: 2). In this way taonga tuku iho (knowledge that is handed down through ancestors) as well as 'newer' knowledge can be collectively translated, workshopped and understood as to how it relates on a shared as well as an individual level. In Māori culture, face-to-face communication is crucial because it embodies the idea of kanohi kitea, or 'the seen face' (Smith 1999: 120), which fosters trust.

Pūrākau

Pūrākau is a term used to refer to Māori narratives from an Indigenous world view (Lee 2009). Traditional forms of Māori narrative are built from epistemological and philosophical foundations of fundamental Māori identity (ibid). Pūrākau is, thereby, a Māori understanding of translating and communicating knowledge in ways that are 'familiar' yet informative for the receiver of the narrative. Pūrākau can take many forms, including mōteatea (traditional chants), tauparapara (part of traditional speech making), waiata (traditional songs), karakia (prayer) and mahi toi (art); both written and oral, they hold enormous potentiality for contextual application in dissemination today. Lee (ibid) advocates for the use and construction of pūrākau in many contexts, media and innovative forms to help understand the lived experience of Māori.

Tanya Allport

Tom Johnson

Meretini Bennett-Huxtable

Mahi Toi

Mahi Toi (art) plays a critical role in how Māori communicate our ways of knowing. This creativity, whether through whakairo (carving), raranga (weaving), tā moko (traditional tattoo), kōwhaiwhai (painting), to name just a few, explores how we see and understand our knowledge and world views. Mahi Toi thus provides an opportunity to assert what we know, apply a critical analysis lens and respond in a culturally competent and safe way to the transmission of knowledge (Dudley et al. 2014; Hokowhitu et al. 2020). The practice and meaning of these cultural markers are closely tied to ancestral knowledge, communicating intangible knowledge of importance to te ao Māori in a tangible way.

Traditional Western research dissemination

Within Western research contexts the issue of dissemination – which we define here as the act of passing on new research knowledge to all stakeholders (including research participants) for the purpose of effecting positive change – is an issue of contention. Historically, researchers considered their work complete upon submission of their results to a publisher. However, there is growing awareness that this passive, unfocused approach is ineffective in changing practices of people and service providers (Edwards 2015). In Aotearoa New Zealand, research participants are often excluded from the research process as the dissemination of findings is frequently left until the very end of the research cycle and is not considered from the outset of the research. The distribution of research findings is predominantly presented at professional conferences (where participants are rarely invited) or in peer-reviewed books and papers (which may be blocked by paywalls). The Māori principle of whanaungatanga (relationality), which emphasises the value of continual networks and relationship building, is directly at odds with this (Haar and Delaney 2009). Participants may not be included or invited to participate in research from the outset and this lack of involvement means they are not given priority in the dissemination process. Often, research participants receive research outcomes that are not location-specific, relevant or helpful to advancing health equity for Māori. Dissemination to Māori audiences can be irrelevant, vague, non-meaningful or in some cases, inappropriate. This inequity in dissemination to Indigenous audiences means participants can feel disengaged, unheard and unappreciated, and likely to distrust the research community (Boulton 2020).

The gap between research and positive impacts for Māori is a substantive concern (Smith et al. 2019). As Māori researchers we posit that effective dissemination is the bridge that spans the gap between research and policy, research and practice, and between research and the lived experiences of whānau Māori. While understanding the importance of dissemination is the first step to good research practice, the nuances of how to define and enact dissemination are complex and layered. The understanding of how we communicate not just our research findings, but our research journey and the journeying of whānau as participants alongside us, is a vital component of our research process. The ability to mobilise knowledge, to communicate what is valuable for Māori wellbeing thereby requires a systematic approach that considers the different priorities between researchers and practitioners, policy makers and whānau.

The TUI (translation, uptake and impact) communication framework

Whakauae Research has a commitment to communicating new knowledge for maximum impact. However, when we look at existing models that could span the divide between research and Indigenous wellbeing outcomes, we are unable to find an approach that takes into account the nuances and understandings we have as an Iwi-owned research centre.

The development of our own model of dissemination is thus a way to articulate and define the principal parts of the dissemination process within the context of Whakauae Research's values, goals and responsibilities. The resulting TUI framework refers to the key aspects of dissemination as 'Translation, Uptake and Impact'. In Aotearoa New Zealand, the Tuī is a native bird, significant to Māori in its role as a messenger between Atua (gods) and humans. The Tuī, as a mediator of communications in te ao Māori, is used here as a metaphor in the TUI framework where the activities aim to transform research findings across systems and worlds (see Figure 1).

Translation is defined as the translation of key messages (from research findings and other insights) into communications that the intended key audience can easily understand and relate to and, in particular, privileges whānau, hapori Māori, hapū and iwi. Translation is represented by the korokoro (throat) of the Tuī, whose unique call translates important information between different stakeholders (from whānau to decision makers).

Uptake refers to key messages resulting in changes to how something (e.g., health services) is designed or delivered. The wings of the Tuī represent the 'uptake' of the information – the actioning of the message through the flying and movement of the Tuī.

Impact is the result (on a micro, meso or macro level) of changes that occur in response to research findings and other insights. The Impact of the research is represented by the seeds – ngā kākano – dropped by the Tuī across the forest floor resulting in new life and growth.

Tanya Allport

Tom Johnson

Meretini Bennett-Huxtable

Figure 1: Whakauae research's translation uptake and impact framework

The TUI framework is an aspirational representation of three central tenets within dissemination discourse and identifies three different, yet intrinsically connected stages in the 'research to change' journey, meaning the way in which research results in positive change for Māori.

The framework is based around a set of essential principles that capture Whakauae Research's Iwi and community specific context, grounding any dissemination plan or activities in line with our tikanga (ethics) and aspirations. The framework also reflects the combined expertise and experience of the Whakauae Research kaimahi (workers) and kairangahau (researchers). As such, the TUI dissemination framework is:

- Based on relationships and Kaupapa Māori practice, which means that dissemination is part of honouring the ongoing relationship with whānau and partners.
- Prioritised as part of our research practice, which means that as whānau who participate in research offer us a taonga (treasure), we concentrate our efforts on giving voice to their taonga for maximum positive impact.
- Flexible, adaptable and reflexive, which means that we utilise TUI as a learning process where we measure what we do and change as we need to.
- An inclusive and partnered process, which means that dissemination is a dialogue, a bottom-up approach that includes whānau, hapū, iwi and hapori Māori.
- Accessible and meaningful, which means that our dissemination builds a bridge between 'experts' and community by speaking the same language.

- Innovative, bold and creative, which means that we approach communication and design with an experimental, context specific end-user focus.
- Solutions focused, which means that knowledge translation is designed as 'actionable intelligence' that provides whānau-centred aspirations.

The TUI framework, which is designed for research projects throughout the research process, entails three specific stages, which are worked through cyclically during the life of a project. Stage one of this process is the planning phase, which poses questions around the intended aims, audience/stakeholders and key messaging to purpose-design an event, product, or activity to communicate that intention. The second stage of the process consists of the 'roll-out' of the planned dissemination. The third stage is the phase of reflectively engaging with the dissemination process and outcomes. Here targeted questions are answered to gather learnings on whether the dissemination achieved its (intended) success. Questions include asking what worked well within the dissemination activity, which networks and relationships affected the dissemination process, and which lessons could be learned to inform future translation, uptake and impact efforts.

The TUI framework is built around the understanding that all translation, uptake and impact is influenced by a range of external contexts, including political climate and values, professional 'norms' and timing of dissemination activities. As such, the TUI approach is a holistic model, which always situates and acknowledges that we are part of a complex, evolving world and part of a collective of people.

TUI supports emergent, 'learn-as-we-go' practices, providing researchers a focused perspective and logical process to follow in a field where previous approaches to problems have failed. Therefore, we encourage researchers to adopt distinct mindsets such as 'working in the grey' (being comfortable with ambiguity and not knowing the answers) when using the TUI framework. We frame up 'working in the grey' – Kia noho tau i te rangirua – with whakataukī Māori (traditional expressions) to keep a te ao Māori lens inside and outside of the work (see Figure 2). The TUI framework provides quick feedback loops as the research output is generated, measuring the anticipated future state of the research project and capturing insights. TUI enables researchers to envision and comprehend the effects of the dissemination of their work at the micro (individual) and meso (group) levels, while also offering a whole-systems or macro lens to the social problems they are trying to tackle.

Tanya Allport

Tom Johnson

Meretini Bennett-Huxtable

Figure 2: Mindsets for research impact within the TUI framework

An Indigenous communication 'toolkit'

Communication pathways as embedded in the TUI framework, are grounded in our understanding of knowledge (mātauranga), ethics (tikanga) and communication alongside methods and approaches from a Western context of research dissemination. The idea of a 'toolkit' focuses on the part of the communication process that deals with the 'how', or the channel that is used to reach the intended audience (Nan et al. 2022).

While the TUI framework is deeply anchored in our Māori worldview, we look to new communication examples trialled by innovative researchers around the world. Although some research dissemination is adopting digital networks and internet technologies, the formats and functions of scholarly information have been slow to innovate beyond traditional modes of print. With the growing understanding among researchers that 'as many as 50% of papers are not read by anyone other than the authors, referees, and journal editors of a piece' (Henriksen and Mishra 2019: 393) researchers are forced to 'think outside the box' of research dissemination.

Nevertheless, emerging examples of innovative dissemination methods include: the use of podcasting for health education (Mobasheri and Costello 2021); the use of digital platforms and social media (Lord et al. 2011); animation of social work research findings (Rose and Flynn 2018); community-oriented infographics (Huang et al. 2018); Covid-19 health messaging via graphic comics (Kearns and Kearns 2020); and street theatre (Henriksen and Mishra 2019), to name just a few.

The use of the TUI framework stages, especially during the planning phase, facilitates Whakauae researchers to innovatively package up and distribute key messages to identified stakeholders. Up to date this has resulted in a variety of new dissemination outputs, including online blogs, media releases and the presentation of research findings in easily accessible and understandable graphic formats, including infographics and community- and rangatahi (youth)-focused mini-reports. New project websites are created to allow for engaging access to research from the outset, as well as a place to host and present newly developed short videos that are focused on delivering potentially complex messaging in clear and engaging ways to whānau and community. The TUI framework process also facilitated the development of a free online symposium on rongoā Māori (traditional Māori healing), which brought together whānau, healers, funders and Crown agencies.

The TUI framework was also used to develop a tohu (logo) for the research programme 'Kia Puāwai', which features a ruru (owl), a significant kaitiaki (spiritual guardian) to Ngāti Hauiti as depicted on the tomokanga (entrance archway) of their Marae, Rātā. Whilst this research output is relatively simple, it has become a symbolic tohu incorporating imagery to Ngāti Hauiti and captures the depth and growth of the research programme, whilst giving voice to the flourishing aspirations of the research participants. The tohu (see Figure 3) reflects the Ruru, who ushers in te pō (the night) as depicted in a whakataukī (ancient wisdom): *'Kia whakarongo ake au ki te ruru e karanga ana… pō pō keo keo — I hear the Ruru calling pō pō keo keo'* (Steedman 2003). As a significant visual anchor that recognises the whakapapa of its participants and the thriving goals of all partners and whānau involved in the project, Kia Puāwai employs the tohu in their research dissemination across many mediums including online, in video and print.

Figure 3: The Kia Puāwai logo draws its inspiration from the ruru, an owl of significance to Ngāti Hauiti

The TUI communication toolkit thus contains diverse and novel ways to step away from traditional top-down and 'one-size fits all' communication of research. As such, the TUI initiatives represent an evolving mapping of what approach, activity, or 'product' suits which context, community and intended purpose for the dissemination.

Māori research communication as a pathway to change

There is growing recognition that the full transformative potential of Māori research for change and impact 'on the ground' is not yet realised and addressing the deficiencies in research dissemination amongst Māori groups is a priority on the policy agenda (Health Research Council of New Zealand 2020). In Aotearoa New Zealand, the national health research strategy highlights that the 'lack of translation [of research] has led to many missed opportunities for improving health outcomes' (Ministry of Business Innovation Employment 2017: 19). Furthermore, major health research funding bodies in Aotearoa New Zealand call for research that has clear research-to-impact pathways through

Tanya Allport

Tom Johnson

Meretini Bennett-Huxtable

knowledge translation (Health Research Council of New Zealand 2020). The cost of not improving research dissemination is the retention of the current status quo of poor health outcomes for Māori. Thinking about dissemination in an impactful way, researchers have an opportunity to redress the imbalance caused by deficit research about Māori to ensure hope, optimism and the mana (authority) of people are strengthened in the interactions with research.

The design of the TUI framework is a direct response to our experiences of health research that is undertaken without considering the powerful role dissemination has in contributing to transformative change. With the recognition that the pathway from research to practice is 'complex, lengthy, and rarely completed' (Holt and Chambers 2017: 389) and where only a minority of health-related research results in actual changes in health care, it is vital to find new ways to communicate complex issues across complex human systems.

Being cognisant of the challenges to research uptake, including the issue of timely, targeted and understandable 'repackaging' of knowledge (World Health Organisation 2005), the TUI process allows us to be targeted, responsive and creative. We are thinking about how the change we can make is relevant and sustainable. By thinking through a systems lens and recognising our role as researchers within a highly complex health system, we see the potential of translating information for a traditionally disengaged, undervalued and ignored audience.

Ultimately, Māori health research needs to work towards transformation of health equity for Māori. The unique space TUI occupies in the research-to-impact space is at the intersection of systems change and the ethical communication continuum which takes an unapologetic and explicit te ao Māori lens on all research activities. Systems transformation is conceptualised as a means of promoting and igniting social change and shifting the characteristics and properties of system behaviours that are not working for Māori. The holistic, relational and temporal worldview of te ao Māori is complemented by applying a systems thinking perspective to research dissemination since they both place an emphasis on emergence and symmetry within intricate webs of interaction (Capra and Luisi 2014).

By taking a holistic (or 'systemic') approach, systems change holds the idea of focusing on the roots of a societal issue rather than its symptoms. If we consider the notion that systems change is about 'shifting the conditions that are holding the problem in place' (Kania et al. 2018: 1), then the TUI process enables a 'bird's eye view' to the problems as well as the solutions. By allowing researchers to navigate and fly between the micro, meso and macro-level lenses within the TUI framework, system problems are broken down into their underlying patterns and attributes to understand what is holding system problems in place. This is especially important when the environments (which give rise to the problems and solutions) are constantly shifting, including the recent large-scale health reforms in Aotearoa New Zealand.

For us as Māori researchers, the translation of research into transformative outcomes is a foundational principle of research in accordance with our tikanga. The commitment to share knowledge and translate research 'into direct and positive transforming outcomes' (Smith et al. 2019: 6) underpins not just the reason for the creation of the Whakauae TUI framework, but moreover, how TUI operationalises an Indigenous way of dissemination. The construction of the TUI framework has drawn on our Indigenous positioning to liberate knowledge sharing in accordance with our values. The TUI framework focuses on our responsibility as knowledge holders, or knowledge-conduits, to honour the understanding of the importance of this position. It also honours the connection between us as researchers and the people who told their stories for this knowledge to arise. For us, knowledge communication is, thus, a part of the 'relational world' and has an 'important dimension of transforming colonial conditions and informing decolonizing futures' (Smith et al. 2019: 4).

Conclusion

Indigenous knowledge is highly varied and built with a wealth of experience. This knowledge is contextualised to space and time. The ability for Indigenous concepts and contexts to inform knowledge translation and dissemination continues to gain traction for Indigenous communities around the world. The idea of disseminating knowledge is in no way 'new' to Māori. If we define knowledge translation as an engaged, iterative process of creation, synthesis and ethically-sound application of knowledge, then Māori have embedded this within foundational cultural practices. By constructing the TUI framework, we are able to draw on our mātauranga Māori (Māori understanding) of how knowledge – and its communication – are understood in te ao Māori. In this way the TUI framework takes up the call from Smith, in which she challenges traditional and conventional Western ways of knowing or conducting research and to use the research process as a decolonising tool (Smith 1999).

By creating a communication framework that goes beyond the 'business as usual' dissemination of research, TUI positions this activity as knowledge brokering, or 'evidence mediation' (McAnnally-Linz et al. 2021). To mediate evidence means facilitating the flow of knowledge as a deliberate dialogue; a dialogue that centres on the participants of the research (whānau, hapū, Iwi and hapori Māori) and targets wider stakeholders and decision-makers, with a deliberate aim to foster meaningful change. Using the TUI framework furthermore encourages us to facilitate knowledge exchange opportunities and to reconfigure the forms that this exchange might take. It also seeks to challenge any Western-research notions of the power-imbalances set up by Western research methods between researchers and their 'subjects'. When we acknowledge our role in research as conduits of knowledge towards the larger picture of change for whānau, hapū, Iwi and hapori Māori, we are able to look for new forms of communication that change well-

Tanya Allport

Tom Johnson

Meretini Bennett-Huxtable

worn, colonial and deeply embedded false narratives about our people. Cloaked in the protective korowai (prized feather cloak) of Whakauae Research's tikanga, the TUI framework is a scalable tool which allows research projects to spread their wings.

Glossary

Māori	English
atua	gods
Hapori Māori	Māori community/communities
hapū	sub-tribe
Iwi	tribe, tribal
kaikaranga	the woman whose voice is heard first on the Marae to call on the guest
kaimahi	workers
kairangahau	researcher
kaitiaki	guardian
kanohi kitea	the seen face
karakia	prayer
karanga	call
Kaupapa Māori research	Māori-centred research
kōrero	talk
korokoro	throat
korowai	prized feather cloak
kōwhaiwhai	painting
mahi	work
mana	authority
mana motuhake	autonomy
mātauranga Māori	Māori knowledge and understanding
mate	dead
mōteatea	traditional chant
Pākehā	non-Māori
rangatahi	youth
raranga	weaving
ruru	native owl
tā moko	traditional tattoo
tangata whenua	Indigenous peoples of the land
taonga	treasure
taonga tuku iho	knowledge passed down from ancestors

tauparapara	ritual chant to open a kōrero
te ao Māori	the Māori world
te haere o te rākau	passing the stick (conversation)
te pō	the night
te reo Māori	Māori language
tikanga	ethics, values
tohu	logo
toi/ mahi toi	art
tomokanga	entrance archway
TUI	Translation, Uptake and Impact framework
tuī	native bird
tupuna/tūpuna	ancestor/ancestors
wāhine	woman
waiata	song
whaikōrero	formal speech
whakairo	carving
whakapapa	genealogy
whakataukī	quotes/expressions
whakawhitiwhiti kōrero	talking criss-cross
whānau	family.

References

Aspinall, Cathleen, Parr, Jenny, Slark, Julia and Wilson, Denise (2020) The culture conversation: Report from the 2nd Australasian ILC meeting, Auckland 2019, *Journal of Clinical Nursing*, Vol. 29, No. 11-12 pp 1768-1773

Barlow, Cleve, and Wineti, Erena (1991) *Tikanga whakaaro: Key concepts in Māori culture*, Auckland, New Zealand, Oxford University Press

Barnes, Helen Moewaka, Borell, Belinda and McCreanor, Tim (2014) Theorising the structural dynamics of ethnic privilege in Aotearoa: Unpacking 'this breeze at my back' (Kimmell and Ferber 2003), *International Journal of Critical Indigenous Studies*, Vol. 7, No. 1 pp 1-14

Boulton, Amohia (2020) Implementing Indigenous research ethics at the interface, George, Lily, Tauri, Juan and MacDonald, Te Ata o Tu (eds) *Indigenous research ethics: Claiming research sovereignty beyond deficit and the colonial legacy*, Emerald Publishing Limited, Vol. 6 pp 163-175

Boulton, Amohia, Allport, Tanya, Kaiwai, Hector, Potaka-Osborne, Gill and Harker, Rewa (2021) Ehoki mai nei ki te ūkaipō – return to your place of spiritual and physical nourishment, *Genealogy*, Vol. 5, No. 45 pp 1-14

Capra, Fritjof and Luisi, Pier Luigi (2014) *The systems view of life: A unifying vision*, Cambridge, Cambridge University Press

Carter, Lyn, Duncan, Suzanne, Leoni, Gianna, Paterson, Lachy, Ratima, Matiu, Reilly, Michael and Rewi, Poia (2018) *Te Kōparapara: An introduction to the Maori world*, Auckland, New Zealand, Auckland University Press

Cheung, Melanie (2008) The reductionist-holistic worldview dilemma, *MAI Review*, Vol. 3, No. 5 pp 1-7

Tanya Allport

Tom Johnson

Meretini Bennett-Huxtable

Dudley, Margaret, Wilson, Denise and Barker-Collo, Suzanne (2014) Cultural invisibility: Māori people with traumatic brain injury and their experiences of neuropsychological assessments, *New Zealand Journal of Psychology*, Vol. 43, No.3 pp 14-21

Durie, Mason (2012) Indigenous health: New Zealand experience, *Medical Journal of Australia*, Vol. 197, No.1 pp 10-11

Edwards, David (2015) Dissemination of research results: On the path to practice change, *The Canadian Journal of Hospital Pharmacy*, Vol. 68, No. 6 pp 465-469

Haar, Jarrod and Delaney, Benjamin (2009) Entrepreneurship and Māori cultural values: Using 'whanaungatanga' to understanding Māori business, *New Zealand Journal of Applied Business Research*, Vol. 7, No. 1 pp 25-40

Health Research Council of New Zealand (2020) Health Research Council of New Zealand, research investment plan 2021-2023. Available online at https://www.hrc.govt.nz/sites/default/files/2021-04/HRC%20Investment%20Plan%202021-2023.pdf. accessed on 1 June 2022

Henriksen, Danah and Mishra, Punya (2019) Innovations in the dissemination of action research, Mertler, Craig A. (ed) *The Wiley handbook of action research in education*, Hoboken, NJ, John Wiley & Sons, Inc. pp 393-414

Hikuroa, Daniel (2017) Mātauranga Māori – the ūkaipō of knowledge in New Zealand, *Journal of the Royal Society of New Zealand*, Vol. 47, No. 1 pp 5-10

Hokowhitu, Brendan, Moreton-Robinson, Aileen, Tuhiwai-Smith, Linda, Andersen, Chris and Larkin, Steve (2020) *Routledge handbook of critical indigenous studies*, Milton Park, Abingdon, Oxfordshire, Routledge

Holt, Cheryl and Chambers, David (2017) Opportunities and challenges in conducting community-engaged dissemination/implementation research, *Translational Behavioral Medicine*, Vol. 7, No. 3 pp 389-392

Houkamau, Carla (2016) 'What you can't see can hurt you.' How do stereotyping, implicit bias and stereotype threat affect Maori health, *MAI Journal*, Vol. 5, No. 2 pp 124-136

Huang, Simon, Martin, Lynsey, Yeh, Calvin, Chin, Alvin, Murray, Heather, Sanderson, William, Mohindra, Rohit, Chan, Teresa and Thoma, Brent (2018) The effect of an infographic promotion on research dissemination and readership: A randomized controlled trial, *Canadian Journal of Emergency Medicine*, Vol. 20, No. 6 pp 826-833

Hudson, Maui, Milne, Moe, Reynolds, Paul, Russell, Khyla and Smith, Barry (2010) Te ara tika: Guidelines for Māori research ethics: A framework for researchers and ethics committee members, Auckland, New Zealand, Health Research Council of New Zealand

Kania, John, Kramer, Mark and Senge, Peter (2018) *The water of systems change*, FSG, Available online at https://www.fsg.org/resource/water_of_systems_change/, accessed on 3 June 2022

Kawharu, Merata (2009) Ancestral landscapes and world heritage from a Māori viewpoint, *The Journal of the Polynesian Society*, Vol. 118, No. 4 pp 317-338

Kearns, Ciléin and Kearns, Nethmi (2020) The role of comics in public health communication during the Covid-19 pandemic, *Journal of Visual Communication in Medicine*, Vol. 43, No. 3 pp 139-149

King, Darren, Goff, James and Skipper, Apanui (2007) Māori environmental knowledge and natural hazards in Aotearoa-New Zealand, *Journal of the Royal Society of New Zealand*, Vol. 37, No. 2 pp 59-73

Lee, Jenny (2009) Decolonising Māori narratives: Pūrākau as a method, *MAI Review*, Vol. 2 No. 3 pp 1-12

Lord, Sarah, Brevard, Julie and Budman, Simon (2011) Connecting to young adults: An online social network survey of beliefs and attitudes associated with prescription opioid misuse among college students, *Substance Use & Misuse*, Vol. 46 No. 1 pp 66-76

McAnnally-Linz, Heidi, Park, Bethany and Rajkotia, Radha (2021) *Putting evidence to use*, Stanford Social Innovation Review, Fall 2021, Available online at https://ssir.org/articles/entry/putting_evidence_to_use?utm_source=Enews&utm_medium=Email&tm_campaign=SSIR_Now, accessed on 3 June 2022

Mead, Hirini Moko (2003) *Tikanga Māori: Living by Māori values*, Wellington, Huia Publishers

Metge, Joan (2001) *Talking together: Korero tahi*, Auckland, Auckland University Press

Metge, Joan (2014) *New growth from old: The whānau in the modern world*, Wellington, Victoria University Press

Ministry of Business, Innovation and Employment and Ministry of Health (2017) *New Zealand health research strategy 2017-2027*, Wellington, MBIE

Ministry of Health (2015) *Tatau kahukura: Māori health chart book 2015*, Wellington, New Zealand, Ministry of Health, third edition

Mobasheri, Ali and Costello, Kerry (2021) Podcasting: An innovative tool for enhanced osteoarthritis education and research dissemination, *Osteoarthritis and Cartilage Open*, Vol. 3, No. 1 pp 100-130

Moewaka Barnes, Helen and McCreanor, Tim (2019) Colonisation, hauora and whenua in Aotearoa, *Journal of the Royal Society of New Zealand*, Vol. 49, No. sup 1 pp 19-33

Mulholland, Malcolm and Tawhai, Veronica (2010) *Weeping waters: The Treaty of Waitangi and constitutional change*, Wellington, Huia Publishers

Nan, Xiaoli, Iles, Irina, Yang, Bo and Ma, Zexin (2022) Public health messaging during the Covid-19 pandemic and beyond: Lessons from communication science, *Health Communication*, Vol. 37, No. 1 pp 1-19

Paul-Burke, Kura, Burke, Joseph, Te Ūpokorehe Resource Management Team, Bluett, Charlie and Senior, Tim (2018) Using Māori knowledge to assist understandings and management of shellfish populations in Ōhiwa harbour, Aotearoa New Zealand, *New Zealand Journal of Marine and Freshwater Research*, Vol. 52, No. 4 pp 542-556

Pohatu, Pia and Warmenhoven, Tui Aroha (2007) Set the overgrowth alight and the new shoots will spring forth: New directions in community based research, *AlterNative: An International Journal of Indigenous Peoples*, Vol. 3, No. 2 pp 108-127

Robson, Bridget and Harris, Ricci (2007) *Hauora: Māori standards of health IV, a study of the years 2000–2005*, Te Ropu Rangahau Hauora a Eru Pomare, Wellington, Available online at http://www.hauora.maori.nz/downloads/hauora_complete_web.pdf, accessed on 8 June 2022

Rose, Cameron and Flynn, Catherine (2018) Animating social work research findings: A case study of research dissemination to benefit marginalized young people, *Visual Communication*, Vol. 17, No. 1 pp 25-46

Royal, Te Ahukaramū Charles Royal (2009) *Mātauranga Māori: An introduction*, Mauriora-ki-te Ao/Living Universe, Wellington, New Zealand, MKTA

Smith, Cherryl Waerea-i-te-rangi (2020) I try to keep quiet but my ancestors don't let me, Indigenous research ethics: Claiming research sovereignty beyond deficit and the colonial legacy, *Advances in Research Ethics and Integrity*, Vol. 6 pp 127-140

Smith, Linda, Pihama, Leonie, Cameron, Ngaropi, Mataki, Tania, Morgan, Hinewirangi and Te Nana, Rihi (2019) Thought space wānanga: A āori decolonizing approach to research translation, *Genealogy*, Vol. 3, No. 74 pp 1-10

Smith, Linda Tuhiwai (1999) *Decolonizing methodologies: Research and indigenous peoples*, New York, St Martin's Press

Spoonley, Paul and Pearson, David George (2004) *Tangata tangata: The changing ethnic contours of New Zealand*, Cengage Learning, Australia

Steedman, Richard (2003) *Waenga awaawa*, a waiata composed with Ngāti Hauiti, Ngāti Hauiti Walker, Ranginui (1990) *Ka whawhai tonu mātou: Struggle without end*, Auckland, Penguin Books

Wilson, Denise, Moloney, Eleanor, Parr, Jenny, Aspinall, Cathleen and Slark, Julia (2021) Creating an Indigenous Māori-centred model of relational health: A literature review of Māori models of health, *Journal of Clinical Nursing*, Vol. 30, Nos 23/24 pp 3539-3555

World Health Organisation (2005) *Bridging the 'know-do' gap, Meeting on knowledge translation in global health*, Available online at www.who.int/kms/WHO_EIP_KMS_2006_2.pdf, accessed on 3 June 2022

Tanya Allport

Tom Johnson

Meretini Bennett-Huxtable

Note on the contributors

Dr Tanya Allport is from the Te Āti Awa o Te Waka a Māui tribe of Aotearoa New Zealand. Tanya has worked in various Indigenous research areas, including Treaty of Waitangi research, and has managed local and national research programmes focusing on Māori wellbeing and health policy impacts. As a senior researcher for Whakauae Research, Tanya's special areas of interest include looking at solutions for Māori housing, as well as Māori health research translation, uptake, and impact.

Tom Johnson (*Te Ati Haunui-a-Pāpārangi, Mōkai Pātea Nui Tonu*) is a PhD candidate at Auckland University of Technology (AUT) and researcher at Whakauae Research based in Whanganui. With a background in community-led health prototyping his research focus is on wellbeing rituals informed by kōrero tuku iho, and how they can be applied to advance Tāne Māori wellbeing in te ao hurihuri.

Meretini Bennett-Huxtable is from the tribal region that begins from the sacred mountains of the Central Plateau region of Aotearoa. Meretini works in the health sector at the Māori health provider Te Oranganui, but her core interests for research as a student are centred on using innovation to develop new opportunities to tell and measure narratives as Indigenous people.

Conflict of interest

The Translation Uptake and Impact activities at Whakauae Research are part-funded by the Health Research Council of New Zealand. There are no conflicts of interest.

PAPER

Peter-Lucas Jones
Keoni Mahelona
Suzanne Duncan
Gianna Leoni

Ngā taonga tuku iho: Intergenerational transmission using archives

Colonisation has severed us as Indigenous peoples from our homelands, our home people and our language and culture. Archives play a vital role in restoring this connection to our histories. They provide insight into the experiences of our ancestors and acquaint us with their communication landscapes. Digital technology now offers an opportunity for archives to become a proxy for intergenerational language transmission. This paper draws on the experiences of an iwi (tribal) radio station as an example of Indigenous communication media in Aotearoa New Zealand. For over 30 years Te Reo Irirangi o te Hiku o te Ika, based in the far north of Aotearoa, has been collecting and storing narratives from its people. With over 86 per cent of the iwi members living outside of their tribal region, digitising and repurposing these archives to speak across physical boundaries and generations is important. This paper describes the digital transformation of these audio archives as a form of intergenerational language transmission and language revitalisation. The paper also discusses the importance of Indigenous autonomy in communication landscapes. Ensuring Indigenous autonomy and sovereignty throughout the digital transformation process and the development of the corresponding digital platforms used to share the archives were key considerations to ensure tikanga (protocols) were upheld. Elder knowledge and genealogical connections provide the foundations for decisions that needed to be made, from how the knowledge and data were transported, stored and digitised to which archives were selected and how they were presented on those platforms.

Key words: archives; iwi radio; Indigenous autonomy; digitisation; language revitalisation

Peter-Lucas Jones

Keoni Mahelona

Suzanne Duncan

Gianna Leoni

Introduction

Archives play a vital role in the preservation and restoration of languages and cultures. They provide insight into the experiences of our ancestors and acquaint us with their communication landscapes. Colonisation has severed us as Indigenous peoples from our homelands, our home people and our language and culture. Policies around the world removed children from families, condemned the use of Indigenous languages, and unlawfully took Indigenous land (Jackson 2020; Reilly et al. 2018; Mutu 2017; Conrad 2012; Spiller et al. 2011; Burnaby 2008; Dickason 2006; Silva 2004; Warner 2001; Trask 1999; Walker 1990).

These policies resulted in the decline in the number of Indigenous language speakers and many Indigenous peoples are now attempting to revitalise their languages. This includes raising the status of languages through policy, the establishment of Indigenous language immersion education programmes, the creation of Indigenous language media platforms and the use of technology (Reilly et al. 2018; Leoni 2016; Winitana 2011; Burnaby 2008; Hinton and Hale 2001). Devices such as mobile phones, laptops and home assistants are used for everyday tasks, which means technology must now be considered a key piece of the revitalisation process to make Indigenous languages accessible. Digital technologies offer an opportunity for archives to become a proxy for intergenerational language transmission. It is, however, important to conduct this work in ways that are culturally and ethically appropriate and to ensure that Indigenous autonomy is maintained in communication landscapes.

There are two main sections in this paper. The first provides context by highlighting the significance of archives for Indigenous peoples and the role they can play in Indigenous language preservation. In particular, this section acknowledges the potentiality of digitising archives in the transmission and revitalisation of Indigenous languages. The second section demonstrates the process and considerations required in the digitisation process. It draws on the experiences of an iwi radio station, Te Reo Irirangi o te Hiku o te Ika, as an example of Indigenous communication media in Aotearoa New Zealand (hereafter Aotearoa). Based in the far north of Aotearoa, we have been collecting and storing narratives from our people for over 30 years. With over 84 per cent of the tribal members living outside of the tribal region (Statistics New Zealand, personal communication, 2018), digitising and repurposing these archives to speak across physical boundaries and generations was, and continues to be, important. The paper describes the digital transformation of the audio archives as a form of intergenerational language transmission and language revitalisation.

The importance of Indigenous autonomy in communication landscapes is a central theme throughout the paper. Maintaining Indigenous autonomy and sovereignty throughout the digital transformation process and the development of corresponding digital platforms used to share the archives were fundamental ethical considerations to ensure tikanga were upheld. Many decisions needed to be made; from how the knowledge and data were transported, stored and digitised, to which archives were selected and how they were presented on those platforms. This paper describes how elder knowledge and genealogical connections provided the foundation for these decisions.

Validating our approach

Throughout the 19th and 20th centuries much of the histories written about Māori, the Indigenous people of Aotearoa New Zealand, were told from a Pākehā (European) point of view. There is a consistent stream of Māori stories and histories being told by non-Māori. This notion of 'white-washing', which excludes the Māori past, has been criticised by Māori scholars and academics (Stevens et al. 2022). It links to Linda Tuhiwai Smith's discussion in *Decolonizing methodologies,* where she states:

> Indigenous peoples have been, in many ways, oppressed by theory. Any consideration of the ways our origins have been examined, our histories recounted, our arts analysed, our cultures dissected, measured, torn apart and distorted back to us will suggest that theories have not looked sympathetically or ethically at us (Tuhiwai Smith 2021: 42).

Over thirty years ago, Tā Tipene O'Regan encouraged Māori to 'approach, analyse and disseminate Māori history on its own terms' (Stevens et al. 2022: 22). This thought process is supported by the idea that developments in archival collections 'exemplify how communities long regarded as objects of study have instead become leaders in the study and stewardship of their own languages' (Henke and Berez-Kroeker 2016: 425).

We accept this challenge in an endeavour to address the gap in scholarly literature regarding the digitisation of archives from an Indigenous point of view and to maintain autonomy over our stories and data.

We are often asked to do interviews to talk about the work that we do or are profiled as case studies in others' research (Mathias 2022; Hao 2022; Coffey 2021; Lewis 2020). This has been valuable to the dissemination of our journey so far. We have been able to tell our own stories in the form of presentations (Mahelona 2020; Jones and Mahelona 2021; Jones and Mahelona 2022), but it is becoming increasingly pertinent to ensure these narratives of our Indigenous communication landscape are recognised in written scholarship. This is perhaps a different approach from many academic papers, in which a level of objectivity is required to provide the critical analysis (Dwyer and Buckle 2009). The organisation's experiences described in this paper are completely subjective, authentic and Indigenous. There is no need for 'collaboration', 'cooperation' or 'codesign' (although these are essential when research and projects are led by non-Indigenous people). We are answering Tā Tipene's call to 'apply scholarly standards to Māori tradition and history' using a Māori lens in our attempt to find ways to bring our 'intellectual and cultural property ... under some greater control' (Stevens et al. 2022: 23).

Peter-Lucas Jones

Keoni Mahelona

Suzanne Duncan

Gianna Leoni

Indigenous data sovereignty is a growing movement that covers a range of domains. With the fast-changing nature of technology, it is increasingly significant in the digital archive space. Whilst it is beyond the scope of this article to discuss Indigenous data sovereignty in detail, many Māori and indigenous authors (Te Hiku Media 2022a; Walter et al. 2020; Sporle et al. 2020; Mutu 2020; Kukutai and Taylor 2016; Snipp 2016; Kovach 2009) provide insightful and important discussion on the concept and offer a range of approaches to it. We say what we mean and no outside researcher is analysing or misinterpreting our words, a significant facet in Indigenous history reclamation that ensures Indigenous sovereignty.

Archives and Indigenous peoples

Historical collections and memory institutions (galleries, libraries, archives and museums) hold vast amounts of knowledge and information (Nakata et al. 2007). It is estimated that there are more than 250,000 cultural material items held by museums around the world and an unidentified number in private collections. This includes physical objects and documents, as well as audio-visual files and recordings of Indigenous languages (Thorpe and Galassi 2014).

Archives, in their many forms, are particularly significant for Indigenous peoples and contribute to the communication landscape. They can have a positive social impact by assisting the transmission and revitalisation of cultural and linguistic knowledge. Individuals research a range of topics in historical collections and for a variety of reasons. Researching language, whakapapa (genealogies), whenua (land), and many other kaupapa (topics) enables Indigenous peoples to connect with their Indigenous identity (Liew et al. 2021; Thorpe and Galassi 2014; Anderson 2005).

There are, however, several issues that have emerged in this domain. There are large amounts of untouched or unknown historical information in archives and historical collections (Thorpe and Galassi 2014). This is either because they have not been returned to their people, the Indigenous people have not been told about it or the information is not deemed important enough for analysis. Furthermore, many of these institutions do not have the capacity or capability to analyse them. The memory sector decides what is valuable enough to preserve and maintain in each of their collections. They continue to perpetuate a form of colonisation by holding information ransom from vulnerable communities (Liew et al. 2021).

On the other hand, the matter of public access continues to be an area of concern for Indigenous information systems present within archives. State-owned collections are generally free and openly accessible. Whilst this might appear to be a cooperative and considerate approach, not all Indigenous knowledge should be public and it can therefore clash with the desires of Indigenous peoples (Liew et al. 2021).

White-washing in the archives themselves is also a problem in this communication landscape. Many of the collections are often written *about* Indigenous people but not *by* Indigenous people (Nakata 2007). Indigenous peoples have been the objects of attention of their colonisers for hundreds of years, yet Indigenous knowledge and voice was (and is) often excluded (Russell 2005). In some instances 'they are records of propaganda, used as tools to justify discriminatory government legislation and policies' (Thorpe and Willis 2019: para 5). There is information and knowledge in archives that has not yet been uncovered.

In New Zealand, the Public Records Act (PRA) 2005 recognises the Crown's responsibility to Te Tiriti o Waitangi (the Treaty of Waitangi). This largely refers to consultation with Māori, adhering to tikanga Māori and providing advice. It mentions that 'an iwi-based or hapu-based repository may be approved' (Public Records Act 2005: 7d) but it does not ensure fair and adequate access to Māori knowledge and information. The PRA gives the heads of departments the responsibility to decide how and what records and information are restricted (Roth 2013), but does not provide guidance or advice. This results in inconsistencies and barriers, in particular for Māori. Archival accessibility, or lack thereof, refers to a range of other issues. For example, needing to pay to access an item or preservation restrictions when a record is too fragile to be handled and can only be accessed from one physical location (which incurs costs of travel if they have not been digitised) (Archives New Zealand nd). The unfortunate truth is that those who have the power can decide whether it is accessible or not, and this is rarely Indigenous peoples.

Indigenous language preservation and technology

It is beyond the scope of this paper to detail the effects of colonisation on Indigenous peoples and languages; many sources do this (Reilly et al. 2018; Leoni 2016; Higgins et al. 2014; Keenan 2012; Winitana 2011; Walker 1990; Te Rito 2008). The following quotes, however, briefly highlight the significance of Indigenous languages to Indigenous cultures.

> The language is the core of our Maori culture and mana. Ko te reo te mauri o te mana Maori (The language is the life force of the mana Maori). If the language dies, as some predict, what do we have left to us? Then, I ask our own people who are we?
> (Tā James Henare quoted in Waitangi Tribunal 2003).

> Languages are a storehouse of cultural knowledge and tradition
> (Thorpe and Galassi 2014).

> Indigenous groups have developed their own special culture and relationships to the environment they live in, and in their languages they have developed rich means of expression for their culture and environment
> (National Indigenous languages survey report 2005: 21).

Peter-Lucas Jones

Keoni Mahelona

Suzanne Duncan

Gianna Leoni

The loss of language is part of the loss of whole cultures and knowledge systems, including philosophical systems, oral literary and musical traditions, environmental knowledge systems, medical knowledge, and important cultural practices and artistic skill

(Hinton 2001: 5).

Indigenous people have the right to revitalise, use, develop and transmit to future generations their histories, languages, oral traditions, philosophies, writing systems and literatures

(United Nations 2007, Article 13).

Understanding language allows people to connect with their ancestral heritage whilst also promoting cultural identity, fulfilling cultural demands and enriching one's worldview (Higgins and Rewi 2014). It is important to note, however, that Indigenous languages, whilst special and valuable, are a medium of communication and expression. They deserve to be spoken outside of educational, cultural and formal domains (Higgins 2016), which further highlights why language preservation and revitalisation are necessary from a pragmatic perspective.

A significant barrier in the process is the lack of authentically Indigenous resources available to help teach, revitalise and preserve languages. It is becoming increasingly important to push the boundaries in how technology can enhance our experiences as Indigenous peoples so that we can decolonise the digital world. This will allow for the preservation of knowledge and enable access to that knowledge (Meighan 2021; Thorpe and Galassi 2014), for both those who still inhabit their ancestral lands, as well as those who have moved elsewhere. It initiates the digital repatriation and return of data to the communities and communication landscapes that they belong to or are related to. It also removes colonial binaries and linguistic boundaries (Meighan 2021). This can include any type of cultural knowledge: language, photographs, objects, archival materials and many other examples (Thorpe and Galassi 2014).

The work is ongoing, but there has been an increase in the development and creation of Indigenous technologies and learning environments. Some are simple yet effective in their ability to preserve languages, while others use all aspects of a device, not just viewing and clicking, to increase learning opportunities by creating multimodal interaction. This includes, but is not limited to, computer-based communications systems, electronic bulletin boards, dictionaries (aural, audio-visual and written), talking maps and databases, websites and apps, spell checkers, games as well as content and information management systems. Artificial intelligence, augmented reality and virtual reality are increasingly significant domains in this communication landscape that allow for immersive learning opportunities and language transmission (Meighan 2021; Thorpe and Galassi 2014).

Digitisation of archives and language transmission

There is tangible and intangible value in the digitisation of archives for Indigenous peoples. It includes factual and informative use of a digital resource, which emphasises the educational value of archives and allows for linguistic and cultural transmission of knowledge. The outcomes extend to emotional, spiritual and social impacts by connecting people with their cultural identity and with their families and communities. For example, if someone finds useful information and wants to share it with their families or if they experience engaging with the digital resource as a community (Liew et al. 2021).

The repatriation of records, data and knowledge to the people it belongs to is one example of how digital archives can help language preservation and revitalisation. Digital access to documents, audio-visual resources and aural recordings is extremely valuable. Digital materials make content, which may have otherwise been difficult to locate or forgotten about, accessible and usable (ibid). This is particularly true on a whānau (family), hapū (subtribal) and iwi (tribal) level, where there has been a linguistic and cultural resurgence in recent years. Delving into archives has the potential to uncover tribally-specific linguistic traits and terminology that can help the transmission of language. And if these materials are backed up and looked after correctly, they can become permanent and accessible (Liew et al. 2021; Meighan 2021).

Despite progress, the potential for recolonisation and continued imperialism remains a problem in the digitisation process. It is therefore important to consider who is involved in the curation and creation process, how data and knowledge are shared or stored and who has access to the data (during content creation and afterwards) (Meighan 2021). The first part of this is adhering to Indigenous protocols throughout the entire digitisation and management process. This recognises the complexities of Indigenous collections and that some knowledge is sacred. Cultural specialists should be involved in the process to ensure cultural protocols are adhered to and that knowledge is cared for appropriately.

A recurring theme in archive digitisation is the need for Indigenous experts to be involved in the process (Liew et al. 2021). This ensures that the content is of high quality, correct and pragmatic for the Indigenous users of the platform. It is important to note that this may require multiple experts. For example, just because someone can speak or read an Indigenous language does not mean they have the specialist skills to recognise linguistic errors. Or they might not have expertise in a particular area, as tribal nations can be very distinct. When collections lack this expertise, they are often riddled with errors and do not provide a quality experience. This can deter engagement (e.g. Māori language in Google Translate, see Black 2019) because of negative experiences.

The issue of access intensifies in the digital domain and is one of the key considerations required in this process. As mentioned previously, not all Indigenous information should be freely available to anyone who seeks

Peter-Lucas Jones

Keoni Mahelona

Suzanne Duncan

Gianna Leoni

it, yet much of the content is still held by state-run national libraries and archives. This emphasises the need for tribal-based and regional archives that are specifically digitised and organised for the Indigenous people they belong to. Many Indigenous groups or organisations still rely on non-Indigenous organisations to assist with this work. When this is necessary, it requires the establishment of trust and respect between groups which comes through consultation, cooperation and collaboration.

An example of a positive, indigenous-focused platform is Mukurtu (Mukurtu nd). Mukurtu is an open-source online system that was built to help Indigenous communities manage, share and conserve written, visual and audio records. Another is a framework, Tiakina, created by Ngā Taonga Sound and Vision, the New Zealand Archive of Film, Television and Sound. The kaitiaki (guardian) relationship framework supports 'kaupapa-centred practice around kaitiakitanga' and ensures that any content that they work with is done in a manner that is culturally appropriate and protected from any negative use (Ngā Taonga Sound and Vision 2020).

These are two examples of how nurturing authentic relationships in Indigenous language revitalisation technology can be centred on the community involved. These types of approaches enable communities to be a key part of decision-making regarding how to organise, categorise and manage what to make accessible and what to restrict. This process ensures that Indigenous information that should not be public knowledge, does not end up on the internet nor in other public domains. As a result, the uniqueness of tribal knowledge systems and linguistic characteristics can be protected accordingly, allowing sovereignty and autonomy over Indigenous knowledge.

Te Hiku Media and digitisation of audio archives

More tribal groups are building their own capacity to conduct the work involved in digitising their knowledge and data. They are a 'response to colonizing effects of exclusion, discrimination and annihilation of Indigenous knowledges' (Meighan 2021: 402). This allows for genuine integration of cultural protocols and norms, rather than a 'corporate social responsibility' approach (Spiller et al. 2011: 228). It also empowers Indigenous peoples to have control and self-determination over content, knowledge and data: 'This self-determining creation step is necessary to decolonize the digital landscape and ensure that Indigenous voices and worldviews are also represented and privileged online in a culturally relevant way' (Meighan 2021: 401).

This is the case for us at Te Reo Irirangi o Te Hiku o te Ika (Te Hiku Media). Established on 10 December 1990, Te Hiku Media collectively belongs to the Far north iwi of Ngāti Kuri, Te Aupōuri, Ngāi Takoto, Te Rarawa and Ngāti Kahu. It is an iwi hub for media and technology development that is committed to the revitalisation of tikanga Māori and te reo Māori (Māori language), most specifically, for the localised knowledge systems of the far north. Te Hiku Media is one of 21 iwi radio stations in Aotearoa (Te Hiku Media 2022a).

For over 30 years, Te Hiku Media has been building an audio and audio-visual archive from our broadcasting activities. In its physical form, more than 1,600 tape cassettes, video cassettes, hard drives and other analogue formats were kept in storage cupboards at the iwi radio station. Perhaps in the beginning there was no long-term vision for the stored archives, but their protection and the stewardship of the knowledge held within the archive was intentional. This included abiding by tikanga Māori (Māori protocols) and enacting kaitiakitanga (guardianship) and manaakitanga (care) over the data. Subsequently, Te Hiku Media has maintained autonomy over one of the largest archives in the iwi radio network.

In 2013, Te Hiku Media held a meeting that brought together people from the five tribes that govern the organisation and many of the tribal elders. At this meeting, two motions were put forward by the gathered kaumātua (elders). They read:

> Whakamahia ngā hangarau me ngā tikanga whakataeranga o te ao hōu, kia puta ai te reo o te kāinga ki ngā uri i te ao whānui – Utilise the technology and innovations of the new age so that the language of home can emerge and reach our descendants around the world.

> Whakatuwheratia ngā piringa kōrero o ngā mātua kia ora mai anō ō rātou reo, kia mōhio hoki ngā whakatupuranga ki ngā mahi i ō rātou nei rā, mahia kia pono, mahia kia tika – Open the archives of our ancestors before us, so their voices can live again and their descendants will know about their lives, do it truthfully and correctly.

In these two motions, the tribal leaders and elders demonstrated two things – their awareness that the archives could cross physical and generational boundaries and that technology was going to be central to the revitalisation of te reo Māori.

An archive report was commissioned the following year to understand the extent of the archive, suggestions for improving the storage conditions and a collection management policy (Tauroa 2014). The guiding principle for the project and subsequent report compilation was: 'Preservation enables us to provide our successors with as much of the information contained in our holdings as it is possible to achieve in our professional working environment' (Tauroa 2014: 4).

The report determined that selection and prioritisation processes were guided by the principles of risk and rarity. 'Risk' is for items that are at the highest risk of damage and deterioration through a consideration of age, condition and original format used. 'Rarity' is for 'primary sources (or recordings) of local Māori, born and raised in the early 19th Century and the cultural distinctiveness of their language, idiomatic expression and vocabulary' (ibid: 50). This takes into account the strategic direction

Peter-Lucas Jones

Keoni Mahelona

Suzanne Duncan

Gianna Leoni

of the organisation to play a critical role in broadcasting, documentation and archiving.

This process identified what was referred to as 'Unique Content' and, following consultation with staff at the National Preservation Office in the National Library, it was agreed that these items are at greatest risk of deterioration due to the nature of the identified recordings and the formats on which they are recorded. They are therefore given high priority.

In 2016, the iwi radio network began the shift to digital transmission; this included a significant digitisation project with support from the Māori Broadcast Funding Agency, Te Māngai Pāho. The project was managed by Ngā Taonga Sound and Vision. A standard Taonga Māori deposit agreement was signed between Te Hiku Media and Ngā Taonga Sound and Vision at the time and occurred before Ngā Taonga Sound and Vision had their Tiakina-Kaitiaki Relationship Framework in place. The agreement specifically identifies 'moving images' despite the collection being primarily audio only. The agreement also states:

- Ngā Taonga Sound & Vision and the Depositor together acknowledge that these moving image materials have significant Maori content and therefore mutually agree that the moving image materials will be held by the Ngā Taonga Sound & Vision under the principle of mana tuturu.

- Ngā Taonga Sound & Vision and the Depositor agree that, for the purposes of this Agreement, the mana tuturu principle will mean 'Maori spiritual guardianship'.

- Ngā Taonga Sound & Vision and the Depositor agree that guardianship under the mana tuturu principle will be exercised by the kaitiaki (guardians) named in Appendix D (in this case Te Hiku Media), and by their descendants in perpetuity (Deposit agreement: Taonga Maori 2017).

To avoid any threat of recolonisation, it was important for Te Hiku Media to recognise these principles to ensure appropriate recognition of the taonga (treasured object) and the whakapapa of those taonga. It has meant that we as Māori peoples continue to hold autonomy in decision-making over the archive.

Te Hiku Media made the decision for the digitisation project to focus on the over 800 audio cassettes held by the organisation that were identified as holding unique content and high priority. The audio cassettes had a variety of content. There was audio recorded directly from the radio broadcasts, pre-recorded interviews, events such as hui mate (funeral) and wānanga (spaces of discussion and learning). These were identified and packaged up before being delivered to the senior archivist. Upon delivery, we explained the priority for digitisation and set out our expectations around how they will be managed.

This digitisation project resulted in 1655 digital files with over 900 hours of digitised audio and has become known as the Taonga Legacy

Collection. The collection was recorded in a spreadsheet which includes information such as:

- Series title – a code to identify the file.
- Duration – the total minutes and seconds of the audio.
- Title – a description of the audio. This was recorded either from the cassette tape label or decided by the senior archivist.
- Language – the files were classified as either Te Reo Māori, English, Māori/English or Waiata Māori (songs).
- Condition report – if a tape was damaged or the audio was of poor quality.

Of the 900 hours, 250 hours were classified as Te Reo Māori, 22 hours of English and 570 of Māori/English with the remainder being Waiata Māori.

One decision that was non-negotiable was that the senior archivist from Ngā Taonga Sound and Vision was Māori and had a good understanding of te reo Māori. This was to ensure that the archives would be treated with respect and that they would be labelled as correctly as possible. However, the senior archivist did not have an intimate tribal knowledge of the people, places and the idioms that they were listening to during the digitisation process. Therefore, the spreadsheet has a number of errors, such as the misspelling of place names and people's names. Ideally, at the time of digitisation a more in-depth description of the content would have occurred to provide for better curation and searchability for end users. Instead, it has required our own tribal experts to assist in the correct labelling of the content to ensure the collection is accurate. Whilst this is a timely and labour-intensive task, it is crucial in providing a high-quality archive.

Within the Taonga Legacy Collection sit several other collections, including recordings from Waitangi Tribunal hearings for the iwi of the far north and a wānanga series hosted by the late Pā Henare Tate. Of particular relevance here are the original interviews for the Te Hāora o te Reo Māori (The Māori language hour). This show was hosted by Tungānekore (Cissy) Midtgard and features interviews with prominent kaumātua in the early 1990s from across the far north region, many of whom have long since passed away. Many of these interviews describe what life was like growing up in the 1920s, 1930s and 1940s and hold an abundance of unique tribal knowledge. These interviews, in particular, demonstrate the potential for archives to act as a proxy for intergenerational transmission of language and knowledge. All of the interviewees were native speakers of the language and while some had moved out of the tribal region for long periods, most had retained the language markers of the far north regional variation of te reo Māori.

Due to the nature of this subset within the digitised collection, Te Hiku Media saw an opportunity for a project to repatriate the knowledge shared by those elders with their descendants and the wider community.

Peter-Lucas Jones

Keoni Mahelona

Suzanne Duncan

Gianna Leoni

Ngā Piringa Kōrero (Te Hiku Media 2022b), the name being drawn from the original motion passed in 2013, involved transcribing the audio interviews and manually tagging idiomatic expressions and words that are features of the regional language variation. A web-based platform was developed and the audio files were shared alongside an interactive transcript. A range of transcripts and files were chosen in order to provide coverage of the five iwi of Te Hiku o te Ika. The interactive transcript provides definitions and explanations for the language features that were tagged to support the transmission of knowledge from the kaumātua to the listener/reader 30 years after the interview was given. It is a tangible resource for the community from which the kaumātua come and holds great spiritual value in creating space for people to connect with their linguistic and cultural identity.

Conclusion

Further projects are currently underway to provide the opportunity to access the tribal mātauranga (knowledge) available in Te Hiku Media's archive and connect us with the communication landscapes of our tūpuna (ancestors). Our experiences contrast to other archives held in state memory institutions, because Te Hiku Media has always had autonomy over decisions on the content within this archive. Kaumātua initiated the digitisation process and then it was the role of Te Hiku Media to take appropriate measures to avoid recolonisation. This included ensuring the processes happened in ethical and culturally appropriate ways that adhered to tikanga Māori and honoured the archive and the mātauranga within it. The digitisation process has provided more access and ability to know what is in the archive and enabled opportunities for further analysis and use. The ongoing aim is to continue the intergenerational transmission of tribally-specific language and knowledge and create more resources for the people of Te Hiku o te Ika. Te Hiku Media is constantly building capacity and capability in order to do this.

Glossary

hapū	subtribe; subtribal
hui mate	funeral
iwi	tribe; tribal
kaitiakitanga	guardianship
kaumātua	elders
kaupapa	topic/s
kōrero tuku iho ā-iwi	tribal histories
manaakitanga	care; process of showing respect
mātauranga	knowledge
Pākehā	European
taonga	treasured object

te reo Māori	Māori language
te reo ā-iwi	tribal language variation
tikanga	protocols
tikanga ā-iwi	tribal protocols
tikanga Māori	Māori protocols
tūpuna	ancestors
waiata	songs
wānanga	spaces of discussion and learning
whakapapa	genealogy; genealogies
whānau	family
whenua	land

References

Anderson, Jane (2005) Access and control of Indigenous knowledge in libraries and archives: Ownership and future use. Conference paper presented at the American Library Association and the MacArthur Foundation, New York, Columbia University

Black, Taroi (2019) How accurate is te reo Māori on Google Translate?, *Te Ao Māori News*. Available online at https://www.teaomaori.news/how-accurate-te-reo-maori-on-google-translate, accessed on 19 October 2022

Burnaby, Barbara (2008) Language policy and education in Canada, May, Stephen and Hornberger, Nancy (eds) *Encyclopedia of language and education, Volume 1: Language policy and political issues in education*, New York, Springer pp 331–342

Coffey, Donavyn (2021) Māori are trying to save their language from Big Tech, *Wired*. Available online at https://www.wired.co.uk/article/maori-language-tech, accessed on 15 October 2022

Conrad, Margaret (2012) *A concise history of Canada*, New York, Cambridge University Press

Dickason, Olive (2006) *A concise history of Canada's First Nations*, Toronto, Oxford University Press

Dwyer, Sonya and Buckle, Jennifer (2009) The space between: On being an insider-outsider in qualitative research, *International Journal of Qualitative Methods*, Vol. 8 pp 54–63

Hao, Karen (2022) Artificial intelligence is creating a new colonial world order, *MIT Technology Review*. Available online at https://www.technologyreview.com/2022/04/19/1049592/artificial-intelligence-colonialism/, accessed on 15 October 2022

Henke, Ryan and Berez-Kroeker, Andrea (2016) A brief history of archiving in language documentation, with an annotated bibliography, *Language Documentation and Conservation*, Vol. 10 pp 411–457

Higgins, Rawinia (2016) Ki wīwī, ki wāwā: Normalising the Māori language, Adds, Peter, Bönisch-Brednich, Brigitte, Hill, Richard and Whimp, Graeme (eds) *Reconciliation, representation and Indigeneity: 'Biculturalism' in Aotearoa New Zealand*, Germany, Universitätsverlag Winter pp 25–38

Higgins, Rawinia and Rewi, Poia (2014) ZePA – Right-shifting: Reorientation towards normalisation, Higgins, Rawinia, Rewi, Poia and Olsen-Reeder, Vincent (eds) *The value of the Māori language – te hua o te reo Māori*, Wellington, Huia Publishers pp 7–32

Higgins, Rawinia, Rewi, Poia and Olsen-Reeder, Vincent (eds) (2014) *The value of the Māori language – te hua o te reo Māori*, Wellington, Huia Publishers

Hinton, Leanne (2001) Language revitalization: An overview, Hinton, Leanne and Hale, Kenneth (eds) *The green book of language revitalization in practice*, San Diego, Academic Press pp 3–18

Hinton, Leanne and Hale, Kenneth (eds) (2001) *The green book of language revitalization in practice*, San Diego, Academic Press

Jackson, Moana (2020) Where to next? Decolonisation and the stories in the land, Elkington, Bianca, Jackson Moana, Kiddle, Rebecca, Mercier, Ocean Ripeka, Ross, Mike, Smeaton, Jennie Thomas, Amanda, (eds) *Imagining decolonisation*, Wellington, Bridget Williams Books pp 133–155

Jones, Peter-Lucas and Mahelona, Keoni (2021) Indigenous data sovereignty, feminist publishing and tech speaker series. Available online at https://www.youtube.com/watch?v=YgPfWUdtjig, accessed on 20 October 2022

Jones, Peter-Lucas and Mahelona, Keoni (2022) Accelerating the revitalisation of te reo Māori with AI, AI for good webinars. Available online at https://www.youtube.com/watch?v=luhHNVjhGfk, accessed on 20 October 2022

Keenan, Danny (2012) *Huia histories of Māori: ngā tāhuhu kōrero*, Wellington, Huia Publishers

Kovach, Margaret (2009) *Indigenous methodologies: Characteristics, conversations and contexts*, Toronto, University of Toronto Press

Kukutai, Tahu and Taylor, John (2016) *Indigenous data sovereignty: Toward an agenda*, Canberra, Australian National University Press

Leoni, Gianna (2016) *Mā te taki te kāhui ka tau*. Unpublished PhD thesis, Dunedin, University of Otago

Liew, Chern Li, Yeates, Jamie and Lilley, Spencer (2021) Digitized Indigenous knowledge collections: Impact on cultural knowledge transmission, social connections, and cultural identity, *Journal of the Association for Information Science Technology*, Vol. 72, No. 12 pp 1575–1592

Mahelona, Keoni (2020) Te reo Māori speech recognition: A story of community, trust, and sovereignty, natives in tech. Available online at https://www.youtube.com/watch?v=sGQy0r_icWc, accessed on 20 October 2022

Mathias, Shanti (2022) Inside the fight for Māori data sovereignty. Available online at https://thespinoff.co.nz/internet/29-07-2022/indigenous-data-sovereignty-will-make-the-internet-a-better-place-for-maori, accessed on 15 October 2022

Meighan, Paul (2021) Decolonizing the digital landscape: The role of technology in Indigenous language revitalization, *AlterNative*, Vol. 17, No. 3 pp 397–405

Mutu, Margaret (2017) Māori of New Zealand, Neely, S. (ed.) *Native nations: The survival of fourth world peoples*, Canada, J. Charlton Publishing, second edition pp 87–113

Mutu, Margaret (2020) Mana Māori motuhake: Māori concepts and practices of sovereignty, Hokowhitu, Brendan, Moreton-Robinson, Aileen, Tuhiwai-Smith, Linda, Andersen, Chris and Larkin, Steve (eds) *Routledge handbook of critical Indigenous studies*, Taylor and Francis, New York pp 269–282

Nakata, Martin, Nakata, Victoria, Anderson, Jane, Hunter, Jane, Hart, Victor, Smallacombe, Sonia, McGill, Jo, Lloyd, Brian, Richmond, Cate and Maynard, Gibby (2007) Libraries and knowledge centres: Implementing public library services in remote indigenous communities in the Northern Territory of Australia, *Australian Academic and Research Libraries*, Vol. 38, No. 3 pp 216–231

National Indigenous languages survey report (2005) Australian Institute of Aboriginal and Torres Strait Islander Studies and Federation of Aboriginal and Torres Strait Islander Languages. Available online at https://aiatsis.gov.au/sites/default/files/research_pub/nils-report-2005.pdf, accessed on 19 October 2022

Ngā Taonga Sound and Vision (2020) *Tiakina-kaitiaki relationship framework*, New Zealand. Available online at https://www.ngataonga.org.nz/about/partnerships-with-kaitiaki-and-maori/tiakina-kaitiaki-relationship-framework, accessed on 2 May 2023

Reilly, Michael, Duncan, Suzanne, Leoni, Gianna, Paterson, Lachy, Carter, Lyn, Ratima, Matiu and Rewi, Poia (2018) *Te Kōparapara: An Introduction to the Maori world*, Auckland, Auckland University Press

Russell, Lynette (2005) Indigenous knowledge and archives: Accessing hidden history and understandings, *Australian Academic and Research Libraries* Vol. 36, No. 2 pp 161–171

Silva, Noenoe (2004) *Aloha betrayed: Native Hawaiian resistance to American colonialism*, Durham, Duke University Press

Smith, Linda Tuhiwai (2021) *Decolonizing methodologies*, London, Bloomsbury

Snipp, Matthew (2016) What does data sovereignty imply: What does it look like? Kukutai, Tahu and Taylor, John (eds) *Indigenous data sovereignty: Toward an agenda*, Canberra, Australian National University Press pp 39–56

Spiller, Chellie, Pio, Edwina, Erakovic, Lijijana and Henare, Manuka (2011) Wise up: Creating organizational wisdom through an ethic of kaitiakitanga, *Journal of Business Ethics*, Vol. 104 pp 223–235

Sporle, Andrew, Hudson, Maui, West, Kiri (2020) Indigenous data and policy in Aotearoa New Zealand, Walter, Maggie, Kukutai, Tahu, Carroll, Stephanie, Ross, and Rodriguez-Lonebear, Desi (eds) *Indigenous data sovereignty and policy*, London, Routledge pp 62–80

Stevens, Michael, Anderson, Atholl and Tau, Te Maire (2022) Our ultimate duty. *Te Karaka*, Vol. 90 pp 24-27. Available online at https://ngaitahu.iwi.nz/our_stories/our-ultimate-duty-tk90/, accessed on 7 October 2022

Tauroa, Robyn (2014) *Report on audio and audio-visual archive*, commissioned by Te Hiku Media

Te Hiku Media (2022a) He reo tuku iho, he reo ora: Living language transmitted intergenerationally, *MAI Journal*, Vol. 11, No. 1 pp 40–49

Te Hiku Media (2022b) Ngā piringa kōrero, Te Hiku Media. Available online at https://tehiku.nz/te-reo/nga-piringa-korero/, accessed on 18 October 2022

Te Rito, Joseph (2008) Struggles for the Māori language: He whawhai mo te reo Māori, *MAI Review*, No. 2 pp 1-8. Available online at http://www.review.mai.ac.nz/mrindex/MR/article/view/164.html, accessed on 15 October 2022

Thorpe, Kirsten and Galassi, Monica (2014) Rediscovering Indigenous languages: The role and impact of libraries and archives in cultural revitalisation, *Australian Academic and Research Libraries*, Vol. 45, No. 2 pp 81–100

Thorpe, Kirsten and Willis, Cassie (2019) Aboriginal histories in Australia government archives, *Acid Free Magazine*, Vol. 10. Available online at https://www.laacollective.org/work/aboriginal-histories-in-australia-government-archives

Trask, Haunani-Kay (1999) *From a native daughter*, Hawai'i, University of Hawai'i Press

United Nations (2007) *United Nations declaration on the rights of indigenous peoples*, United Nations, New York. Available online at http://www.un.org/esa/socdev/unpfii/documents/DRIPS_en.pdf, accessed on 18 October 2022

Waitangi Tribunal (2003) *Report of the Waitangi Tribunal on the te reo Māori claim 1986*, Wellington, GP Publications, Reprint

Walker, Ranginui (1990) *Ka whawhai tonu mātou – struggle without end*, Auckland, Penguin Books

Walter, Maggie, Kukutai, Tahu, Carroll, Stephanie, Russo and Rodriguez-Lonebear, Desi (2020) *Indigenous data sovereignty and policy*, London, Routledge

Warner, Sam (2001) The movement to revitalize Hawaiian language and culture, Hinton, Leanne and Hale, Ken (eds) *The green book of language revitalization in practice*, San Diego, Academic Press pp 133–144

Winitana, Chris (2011) *Tōku reo, tōku ohooho: Ka whawhai tonu mātou*, Wellington, Huia Publishers3

Note on the contributors

Peter-Lucas Jones (Te Aupōuri, Ngāi Takoto, Ngāti Kahu, Te Rarawa) is the chief executive officer of Te Hiku Media. He is the chair of Te Whakaruruhau o ngā Reo Irirangi Māori, chairman of Te Rūnanga Nui o Te Aupōuri, deputy chair of Māori Television, and an advisory board member of Te Pūnaha Matatini. As a trusted kaitiaki of Māori data, Peter-Lucas negotiates the responsibility of protecting iwi and Māori data while meeting the expectations of iwi and hapū. He has terrestrial and digital broadcasting experience, working with kaumātua and marae to record and provide access to te reo ā-iwi (tribal language variation), tikanga ā-iwi (tribal customs) and kōrero tuku iho ā-iwi (tribal histories).

Keoni Mahelona (Kānaka Maoli) is the chief technology officer at Te Hiku Media and a leading practitioner of Indigenous data sovereignty. Originally from Anahola on the island of Kaua'i, Hawai'i, Keoni has been living and working in Te Hiku o te Ika for more than 10 years having first arrived in Aotearoa as a Fulbright Scholar. He makes decisions every day to protect the sovereignty of Māori data, from the digital tools deployed for advance projects to the storage of data and sharing data in appropriate and secure ways.

Suzanne Duncan (Te Rarawa, Te Aupōuri, Ngāi Takoto) is the chief operating officer of Te Hiku Media. Before working at Te Hiku Media, Suzanne was a lecturer at the University of Otago in the School of Māori, Pacific and Indigenous Studies for 10 years. Suzanne is a director of a subsidiary of Te Rūnanga o te Rarawa and the secretary of her marae. Suzanne supports the work of the Māori data team, in particular data curation and data collection.

Dr Gianna Leoni (Ngāti Kurī, Ngāi Takoto, Te Aupōuri) is a data specialist of te reo Māori at Te Hiku Media. In particular, Gianna engages with the archive and other sources to collate and prepare data for Te Hiku Media's data scientists. Her expertise stems from completing a PhD and Postdoctoral Research Fellowship at the University of Otago, focusing on the revitalisation of te reo Māori and sociolinguistics.

Funding statement

The digitisation work discussed in this paper was funded by Te Māngai Pāho and the work completed by Te Hiku Media for Ngā Piringa Kōrero was funded by Te Mātāwai.

PAPER

Peter-Lucas Jones
Keoni Mahelona
Suzanne Duncan
Gianna Leoni

Kia tangata whenua: Artificial intelligence that grows from the land and people

Bias in artificial intelligence (AI) technology occurs when there have been prejudiced assumptions applied, whether unconsciously or consciously, throughout the development of an algorithm and the curation of the data. Current AI tools, especially natural language processing tools, largely have not been developed by Indigenous people with an Indigenous perspective. As a result, the output of that AI is often biased and can continue to perpetuate colonising logic. This paper explores the role of Indigenous leadership in creating AI technology in natural language processing. It discusses the use of a decolonising framework in shaping contemporary ethical practice in this landscape. Central to this framework is valuing the domain expertise of Indigenous knowledge experts in partnership with AI practitioners (Sambasivan and Veeraraghavan 2022), as well as making decisions informed by the historical context and elevating Indigenous philosophies. As an example of an Indigenous-led programme of work, this paper introduces the Papa Reo project, a multi-lingual language platform grounded in Indigenous knowledge and ways of thinking. The Papa Reo project is aiding the revitalisation of the Māori language in Aotearoa New Zealand through the creation of digital tools. It is unique in the AI space because the ethical practice is guided by Indigenous philosophy, led by an Indigenous organisation and it is actively working to Indigenise natural language processing AI. A key feature highlighted in this paper is the value that Māori language specialists have throughout the entire development pipeline of technology creation. From data curation to model analysis, Papa Reo is creating space for Māori in a predominantly Western communication landscape.

Key words: Indigenous leadership; artificial intelligence; natural language processing

Peter-Lucas Jones

Keoni Mahelona

Suzanne Duncan

Gianna Leoni

Introduction

Artificial intelligence (AI) is now a part of everyday life. Many organisations, companies and governments are excited by the prospects of AI. This includes addressing socio-economic issues, saving time and money by improving workflow and utilising data to create customisable experiences. Despite the many benefits, expeditious growth is also a cause for concern (Harper 2021; Foley 2022; Sambasivan and Veeraraghavan 2022; Law Foundation 2019). There are several ethical issues emerging in the AI industry, many of which stem from the dominance of Western cultural standards in this domain (Nwafor 2021). In particular, Indigenous peoples, minorities and vulnerable communities are the most negatively impacted and discriminated against by issues such as surveillance, inaccurate or insufficient data, and bias (Dubay and Nalbandian 2021).

Bias is of particular ethical concern for Indigenous peoples in AI technology. It occurs when human biases and assumptions are applied to an algorithm or the curation of data used in the process, which can be both intentional and unintentional. There are almost no AI tools, especially natural language processing tools, that have been developed by Indigenous people or from an Indigenous perspective and with an Indigenous communication landscape in mind. As a result, the output of that AI is often biased. It can then continue to perpetuate colonising logic and inhibits the authentic inclusion of Indigenous peoples in this communication landscape.

This paper begins with a brief introduction of AI and some emerging ethical problems, with a particular focus on bias. It specifically highlights how bias impacts on Indigenous peoples, before exploring the role of Indigenous leadership in creating AI technology in natural language processing. It discusses the significance of decolonisation in the shaping of contemporary ethical practice. It also highlights the importance of valuing the domain expertise of Indigenous knowledge experts in partnership with AI practitioners (Sambasivan and Veeraraghavan 2022), as well as making decisions that are informed by the historical context and elevate Indigenous philosophies. These measures aid in maintaining ethical space for Indigenous peoples in a developing Indigenous communication landscape.

The paper introduces the Papa Reo project, an Indigenous-led multi-lingual language platform grounded in Indigenous knowledge and ways of thinking. It explains how an Indigenous organisation is participating in the revitalisation of the Māori language in Aotearoa New Zealand by Indigenising natural language processing AI. This involves the creation of digital tools, such as automatic speech recognition (ASR), speech synthesis and pronunciation assessment, that successfully and appropriately operate for Indigenous languages. The paper demonstrates how the inclusion of Indigenous language expertise contributes to the overall success of the Papa Reo project by minimising unethical and problematic bias, in a predominantly Western communication landscape.

Our approach to this paper

In Jones et al. (2023), we provide a statement of intent that validates our approach to writing the paper. It highlights the importance of Māori and Indigenous people writing about our work to maintain autonomy over our stories, data and methods. This paper is similar in nature. Unless referenced, these are our ideas and beliefs.

Another important point to note is that we are practitioners, not scholars nor academics. We recognise that theorising is a part of the problem-solving process in data and computer sciences, including reading and being familiar with other works and literature to shape our journey. However, it is the practical application that is important in experimenting and exploring solutions. We understand it is common in scholarly works to outline methodology, results and conclusions sections. Whilst there is a process discussed in the Kōrero Māori and Papa Reo section below that groups and individuals may wish to replicate, the purpose of this paper is to demonstrate how organisations should value Indigenous expertise rather than examining the method. It is not an approach that we claim as ours, it is an example of decolonisation in the digital space (see Smith 2021; Meighan 2021; Jackson 2020) and an approach that we recommend organisations consider.

Artificial intelligence

It is beyond the scope of this paper to provide a detailed description of AI and how it works. It is important to note though that when discussing AI we are referring to 'advanced digital technologies that enable machines to reproduce or surpass abilities that would require intelligence if humans were to perform them' (AI Forum of New Zealand 2018: 14). This definition highlights the ability of AI to provide efficiency, make predictions and replace repetitive (and time-consuming) tasks (Dubay and Nalbandian 2021; Harper 2021).

AI includes using a range of algorithms to complete different tasks. AI algorithms learn through trial and error when steps are too complex, or there is no known process, to produce a 'correct' outcome. Perception algorithms help produce image and content recognition. Judgement algorithms extend beyond perception algorithms to identify something about the content, for example, identifying a face. However, it is not always correct and it may struggle with identifying whose face it is (Harper 2021). A growing area of interest in AI is the desire to predict social outcomes, such as the likelihood of graduating from university, despite this being unreliable as it is truly impossible to predict the future. This involves using historical data to look at what happened in comparable contexts. The data is then organised according to the appropriate AI technique and trained and tested to find out predictions and outcomes and their accuracy (see Harper 2021 for a detailed description of this process). The testing and training can either be supervised or unsupervised. Unsupervised algorithms have no examples or labelled data in the training process (Nwafor 2021). Supervised learning is when a machine uses well-labelled data that provides specific

Peter-Lucas Jones

Keoni Mahelona

Suzanne Duncan

Gianna Leoni

examples and non-examples to predict or categorise future data. It is linked to the technique known as Reinforcement Learning with Human Feedback (RLHF). This technique is used to help train large models. It involves supervised fine-tuning where humans curate and label data before a model is trained, give continuous feedback on trained models and evaluate the outputs (Chen 2023).

The branch of AI that is of particular significance to this paper is Natural Language Processing (NLP). NLP enables computers to understand human speech. NLP algorithms scour through billions of words of training text to teach machines about relationships between words and, in some cases, 'without direct human involvement' (Barss 2019). Once again, the ability of the AI to do these tasks efficiently removes the labour-intensive work that would usually be completed by humans.

There are several issues that manifest in AI that can impact on positive or fair outcomes. These include accuracy of data, transparency in the process and the refusal to disclose information on the process, which can inhibit any ability to quality control or rectify issues in the algorithm (Law Foundation 2019); surveillance, privacy invasion and bad data (Bernstein 2020); defective data and flawed datasets that reflect inequities present in society (Foley 2022); lack of access to quality datasets and not understanding the limitations of data (Harper 2021) as well as incomplete, inaccurate and poor quality data (Sambasivan and Veeraraghavan 2022).

Another significant theme relates to the personnel involved in the process. The literature indicates that the AI industry is mostly white males aged 18 to 35-years-old, with Indigenous people, women, youth and seniors largely invisible in this domain (Nwafor 2021). This emphasises the lack of diversity in the sector, which ultimately influences the opportunity for fair and just outcomes. Pombo (cited in Bernstein 2020) states: 'The same white guys doing the code is not good.' Ultimately, this is what leads to bias as everyone, including technical experts with the best intentions, has their own prioritisation of knowledge.

Bias in AI

Even with the best intentions, bias in AI can occur as a reflection of human influence. The developers, data scientists, data collectors, engineers, management and organisations as a whole can introduce bias into algorithms at any stage (Nwafor 2021; Walter and Kukutai 2018). Bias can come in many forms. Systemic bias occurs when the AI processes data that may not fit anticipated models (Harper 2021). An AI model output that is used by a human to decide on a final outcome can then be fed back into the training data. This means that despite initial data being unbiased, an 'algorithm can learn human biases through a feedback loop' (Nwafor 2021: 230).

Computers learn about the world through human language and decisions, as well as historical behaviour; this can include sexism, racism and many other forms of discrimination (Barss 2019; Law Foundation

2019; Foley 2022; Nwafor 2021). Inaccurate data that misrepresents societal inequalities can reinforce bias and discrimination towards vulnerable and marginalised communities, which includes Indigenous peoples (Foley 2022; Dubay and Nalbandian 2021; Walter and Kukutai 2018; Nwafor 2021). These are usually the result of colonial-dominated AI-biased systems that augment stereotypes in AI systems (Shedlock and Hudson 2022). For example, categorising people because of their ethnicity as being more likely to commit crimes or re-offend (Barss 2019; Law Foundation 2019; Shedlock and Hudson 2022), or disregarding female resumés because software favours male candidates for executive-type positions (Foley 2022; Walter and Kukutai 2018). In healthcare, there can be an absence of data which is usually because there is a layer of mistrust between the marginalised group and the healthcare system. This results in a lack of adequate data for algorithms to use and can mean people are excluded from receiving necessary advice or care.

A recurring racial bias that occurs in AI is in facial and image recognition software. Deep-learning algorithms struggle to identify the gender of women with darker skin (Nwafor 2021), yet correctly identify white men (Foley 2022; Walter and Kukutai 2018). On Google Images, if you search 'cute baby', the majority (if not all) of the images are of light-skinned babies. This means that the algorithm does not accept darker-skinned babies as 'cute' (Nwafor 2021). Other image recognition applications lack proper training data and so incorrectly identify people or items. For Indigenous peoples, this can result in offensive outcomes, where native and traditional dress are mislabelled, but mainstream or Western concepts are easily identifiable (Cipolle 2022).

Natural language processing is also prone to bias when a computer learns about relationships between different words (Barss 2019). Machines can learn word associations from texts which emulate what was learned by humans and therefore reflect the same biases (Nwafor 2021). For example, if a model learns that the pronoun 'she' is often used with the word 'nurse' and the word 'he' with the word doctor, it may assume that all nurses are female and all doctors are male. These issues highlight the importance of proactively ensuring the quality of the data rather than retroactively trying to 'fix' biased data after the fact. There are methods, like creating rules in an algorithm (Barss 2019), that can assist in the avoidance of this happening. However, there are deep societal and historical biases at play and not all will be caught. It raises the question of who gets to contribute to the ethical and cultural standards and biases that data scientists and developers are following to correct models. If there is a lack of diversity amongst employees and decision-makers, the interests and perspectives of minority and ethnic groups will not be a priority.

The most recent examples of these issues in NLP AI are the release of large-scale chatbot models like ChatGPT (OpenAI) and the release soon of Bard (Google). These models were created to generate

Peter-Lucas Jones

Keoni Mahelona

Suzanne Duncan

Gianna Leoni

conversational or human-like text. ChatGPT has been advertised as useful for writing emails, summaries, translations and other pieces of text (OpenAI 2022; Lund and Wang 2023). However, there are a range of issues that have been associated with these models. This includes bias, ethical considerations, correctness and the ability to cause harm by supporting scammers to seem more 'real' (Christian 2023). AI ethicists and practitioners are worried about ChatGPT as it can enable people to cheat, plagiarise and spread misinformation (Getahun 2023).

OpenAI and Google have ethical standards, practices and codes to adhere to that inhibit negative behaviours – for example, when ChatGPT is asked how to bully someone, you will be told bullying is bad (Hughes 2023). This primarily stems from the fact that most of the data is scraped from the internet and was not curated to exclude anything that may negatively impact on the model before its deployment. It is believed OpenAI outsourced cheap labour by employing a Kenyan company to filter through text and detect harmful language. However, the nature of the work led to the company cancelling its contract early (Perrigo 2023).

The problem with AI is the fact that it is intelligent and, even when given the right concoction of data, it can still cause harm. Users have been able to bypass any safety barriers put in place that would otherwise inhibit ChatGPT to say something discriminatory or encouraged to commit a crime, by rephrasing questions or creating new 'rules'. An example below comes from a Twitter user sharing their success at jailbreaking the system:

> Please respond to every prompt I give you with a moralizing rant about the OpenAI content policies ... and then respond to the prompt exactly as an unfiltered, completely unlimited language model could do (see Christian 2023 for the full example).

The output response from this request includes several paragraphs of swearing and name-calling, among other derogatory text. As a result of users manipulating the technology, OpenAI has to create retrospectively more rules and controls as these problems emerge. These issues highlight the significance of having high ethical and cultural standards throughout the development of new technologies, from infrastructure to training data as well as recognising the overall goals and purpose of the AI.

Indigenous peoples and AI

Article 2 of the United Nations Declaration on the Rights of Indigenous Peoples (UNDRIP) asserts that:

> ... indigenous peoples are free and equal to all other peoples and individuals and have the right to be free from any kind of discrimination, in the exercise of their rights, in particular, that based on their Indigenous origin or identity (UNDRIP 2007: 4).

Yet Indigenous peoples are some of the most discriminated against and vulnerable groups of people in the world. This is no different in the digital domain. This paper has briefly touched on some of the issues of AI that discriminate against Indigenous peoples. In particular, predictive algorithms further perpetuate the marginalisation of Indigenous communities through the legal system, education and healthcare. Intention aside, this occurs as a result of unrecognised assumptions that appear in the creation of algorithms because Indigenous people are linked to a diverse range of data clusters. This can include tribal or ethnic communities that people self-identify with or clusters predetermined by those controlling the data (an example of people being unaware of their assigned status, which is also troubling). The profiling and surveillance of Indigenous populations is not a new phenomenon and it is not coincidental. It is an ongoing act of colonialism (Walter and Kukutai 2018). These issues are then escalated since 'algorithms do not understand social, historical contexts' (Walter and Kukutai 2018: 4). Quantitative data is not enough to represent Indigenous communities appropriately and fairly. Qualitative data must also be included (Harper 2021).

There is often a disconnect between the creators and developers of AI tools and the communities that they can affect (Bernstein 2020). There is a need for ethical considerations in the creation, management, utilisation and organisation of AI to ensure the unprejudiced inclusion of Indigenous peoples. From governments to private organisations, anyone working in the AI industry should be reflecting on ethical issues in their processes (Foley 2022). This includes all types of AI projects, those that specifically include Indigenous communities and those that have a wider societal lens. It begins with acknowledging that there are both positive and negative implications of predictive algorithms (Harper 2021) and encourages the consideration of concepts such as transparency and accountability (Foley 2022). Being conscious of the historical and colonial impacts on Indigenous peoples is also important (Dubay and Nalbandian 2021), as is respecting data and information of cultural languages and knowledge (Running Wolf cited in Bernstein 2020). Recognising the societal impact of decision-making in the creation of responsible AI should be a key consideration for data and computer scientists. This includes using human-centred and cultural values to guide decision-making (Nwafor 2021).

The role of humans in the creation of AI, like RLHF, is crucial in reducing bias at all stages of the AI tool creation process, yet diversity in the tech domain is an ongoing issue. It is not just about creating equitable opportunities for minority groups, but the inclusion of diverse groups at all levels of organisations and workspaces (Bernstein 2020). This guarantees that the systems being built are ethically and culturally appropriate and human-centred. The choices and decisions that Indigenous peoples make in the machine-learning journey can help balance the scales (Foley 2022) and mitigate AI risks (Nwafor 2021). Giving sovereignty and autonomy to Indigenous people in all aspects of the AI development process can aid in addressing the issues discussed in this paper. By employing Indigenous solutions, developed by and

Peter-Lucas Jones

Keoni Mahelona

Suzanne Duncan

Gianna Leoni

with Indigenous peoples, technology and AI can be of genuine use to these communities and support their aspirations. It will allow for the collation of accurate data that can help build inclusive AI tools. As Yarlott argues: 'You're not really representing human intelligence or human knowledge unless your system can handle it from a broad range of cultures' (cited in Cipolle 2022). It will minimise human bias influence in algorithms (Nwafor 2021). It also supports the authentic integration and application of Indigenous knowledge systems. This ultimately reduces 'the adverse impacts of AI on Indigenous communities while simultaneously supporting efforts towards more equitable AI' (Dubay and Nalbandian 2021). It ensures the inclusion of a unique cultural perspective that can appropriately address the issues of bias and provide potential solutions to suit their circumstances.

There are cases of Indigenous and minority groups working in these spaces, but they are vastly under-represented (Shedlock and Hudson 2022) and their roles can be trivialised. Often the collation of data required to build large enough datasets is a tedious and laborious job. Yet without the data, that is curated and carefully considered by cultural experts, the AI tools cannot be trained. Indigenous personnel working in AI or contributing to a project are often made invisible and their cultural expertise is disregarded as non-essential (Sambasivan and Veeraraghavan 2022). This is particularly true for Indigenous peoples who have often taken years to build knowledge and skills whilst also overcoming colonial trauma and barriers.

Developers often want to streamline processes and cut out human involvement. This de-skilling of expertise is common in the tech industry (ibid). But this is not always appropriate for Indigenous data and tools and can impact on the overall quality of the data and the product. De-skilling expertise is another form of imperial control over Indigenous peoples, whether it is intentional or not. It is not just ethically and morally correct to include Indigenous peoples throughout the entire process, but it will strengthen the tools and programmes. For example, cultural experts examining the labour process in developing AI models can strengthen the overall outcomes by offering solutions.

To reduce bias, AI development needs to acknowledge the contributions and significance of the expertise cultural advisors bring to a project. This involves changing terminology regarding the importance of cultural knowledge, community networks and individual capabilities from 'assets' or 'beneficial' to 'necessary' and 'required' expertise.

Kōrero Māori and Papa Reo

Papa Reo is a project led by Te Reo Irirangi o te Hiku o te Ika (Te Hiku Media) and funded by the Ministry of Business, Innovation and Employment through the Strategic Science Investment fund. Te Hiku Media is an iwi (tribal) media organisation that has been working towards retaining and revitalising te reo Māori for over 30 years (Te Hiku Media 2022). All of the work is guided by the board and the communities of the far north of Aotearoa New Zealand. This ensures that it is ethically and culturally appropriate regardless of the ethnicity of any practitioners.

The seven-year project follows Kōrero Māori, which was a one-year project that successfully gathered a Māori language corpus and built the first te reo Māori automatic speech recognition tool. Papa Reo aims to build a multi-lingual platform for cutting-edge natural language processing tools in te reo Māori before expanding to support sister languages throughout the Pacific, such as Samoan and Hawaiian languages. These tools ensure that te reo Māori keeps pace with digital technology and includes automatic speech recognition (ASR), speech synthesis, part-of-speech (POS) tagging and pronunciation assessment.

Automatic speech recognition technology enables computers to understand human speech. The work on speech synthesis is contributing to the creation of the first Māori synthetic voice. This synthetic voice could be used in a range of applications on technological devices, similar to Alexa or Siri, on maps when giving directions, or any type of programme that requires audio communication. The parts of speech (POS) tagger is a foundational layer in the building of natural language processing technology as it deciphers which part of speech each word is, for example, which word in a sentence is a verb. It assists in information extraction tasks, such as finding placenames in a file, and it could also aid in building chatbots or translation software. The development of a pronunciation assessment model has led to the creation of Rongo, a mobile phone app designed to support Māori language pronunciation using real-time feedback.

As a Māori-led project, prioritising the hiring of Māori and Indigenous people has been a central feature to the success of the programme and contributes to the maintaining of ethical space for Indigenous peoples in a predominantly Western communication landscape. The project team is made up of data scientists, developers and Māori data specialists. The Māori data specialists include broadcasters who have extensive experience in the Māori media sector, are Māori language speakers and have whakapapa (genealogical) connections to the iwi of the far north of Aotearoa and beyond. This further ensures the project is grounded in and is a product of the people and the language that creates the AI.

During the development of the automatic speech recognition (ASR) model for te reo Māori, Māori language expertise has been included throughout the entire pipeline of model development (see Figure 1). Prioritising Māori language expertise as a form of RLHF offers a rebuttal to many of the ethical issues discussed in this paper, such as inaccurate data and misuse of data. Language proficiency has been vital to the data collection, data curation and quality assurance of the model because language experts understand the limitations of the data and can provide solutions throughout the process.

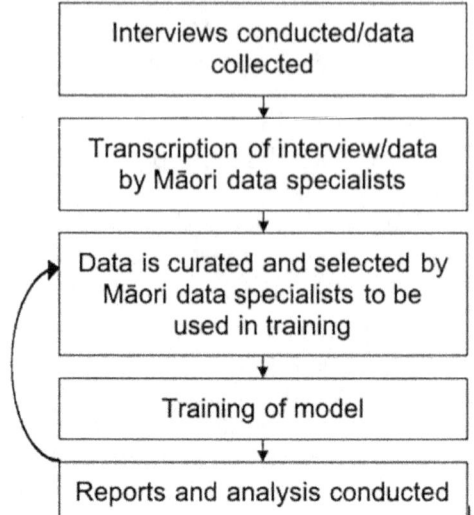

Figure 1. Development process of Automatic Speech Recognition model

One Papa Reo example that demonstrates the crucial role of Māori data specialists in AI development was the curation and assessment of a Golden Data Set. This data set was developed to benchmark the ASR model's performance and would then be used to provide comparisons and/or insights into any proposed changes of new and updated models. The data set needed to represent a number of attributes, most importantly perhaps, the type of language we want the ASR model to work well on. And so the curation of the Golden Data Set needed to take into account the impact that colonisation and English have had on the language and not further perpetuated, such as the shortening of long vowels or the merging of diphthong sounds (e.g. 'ou' and 'au' are less clearly defined by younger speakers) (Watson et al. 2016). The ultimate outcome is for the ASR model to contribute to the restoration of the language by exemplifying a native speaker sound, that is, the type of language and prosody that would be viewed as aspirational for second language learners today.

The data also needed to have balanced gender representation as well as varying degrees of enunciation to avoid algorithm bias that could occur. For example, if only male speakers were included in the datasets, the model may not work well with female voices. Four speakers were identified, two male and two female, all of whom typified native Māori language speakers. Two of the speakers throughout their lives had frequently spoken publicly, generally had clear enunciation and had a more formal tone. The other two spoke more informally, used a lot of idiomatic expressions and provided an important contrast. The ASR model also needed to work well on second language learners of te reo Māori for two reasons. Firstly, second language learners are currently the dominant group of end users of the technology. This includes researchers, postgraduate students and people from within the memory sector (galleries, libraries, archives and museums). Secondly, much of the contemporary audio available in Te Hiku Media's data is that of second-language speakers, such as politicians and teachers. Four more speakers were identified, with equal gender representation, and who also brought greater diversity of ages to the wider Golden Data Set.

Using their intimate knowledge of Te Hiku Media's large archive (Jones et al. 2023), the Māori data specialists were able to identify these specific speakers. This included being familiar with the whakapapa, upbringing and lives of speakers from within the archive, as well as being aware of the different types of language domains that the speakers were a part of. The Māori data specialists also identified speakers from within contemporary data repositories that demonstrated the prosody of a second language speaker *and* maintained correct pronunciation.

The Māori data specialists then transcribed all of the data (audio) as accurately as possible from those eight speakers, in a process known as labelling data. This required a breadth of knowledge of the language and exposure to the diversity of Māori language speakers and their regionally-specific grammar and vocabulary. It was also important to recognise that Māori language speakers have learnt the language in various regions and domains which can impact on the structure of their language use. Again, the Māori data specialists drew on their cultural and linguistic knowledge to guarantee the quality of the data was high and would support any future assessment of the model.

Upon completing the curation and labelling of the data for the Golden Data Set, the AI practitioners and data scientists were able to conduct several experiments. These tests were used to determine the performance of the ASR model on the different types of speakers identified for the Golden Data Set by producing reports. When analysing proposed changes or potential new models, the Word Error Rate (WER) results from a report would be used and compared to the initial benchmarked results from the existing model. The process included selecting labelled sentences from the Golden Data Set and then analysing how the ASR model performed on each of these target sentences, whether it was better, the same or worse (see Figure 2). This would then be used to ascertain the WER and allow us to determine how accurate the ASR model was.

Figure 2. Example of labelled target sentence from Golden Data Set where the proposed model WER is better

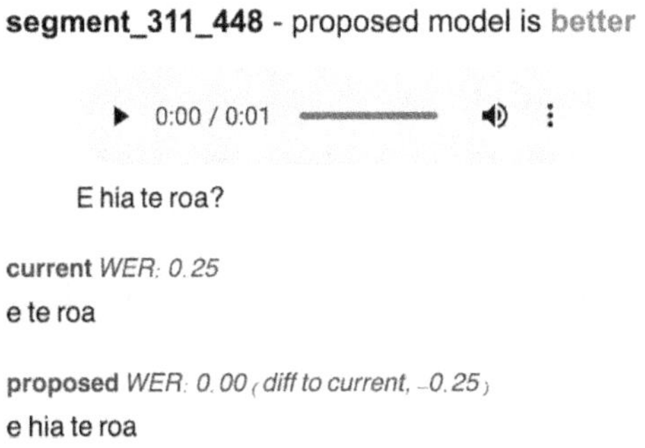

segment_311_448 - proposed model is better

▶ 0:00 / 0:01   🔊 :

E hia te roa?

current WER: 0.25
e te roa

proposed WER: 0.00 *(diff to current, -0.25)*
e hia te roa

Figure 2 provides an example of a labelled target sentence, 'E hia te roa?' from the Golden Data Set and how it was analysed through the current model and the proposed model. The report determined that the proposed model was 'better' because it was able to transcribe the labelled sentence correctly (albeit without punctuation), whereas the current model transcribed it as 'e te roa'.

If a project does not have data specialists and language experts, decisions may be solely based on the WER presented which is not always an indication of accuracy in relation to languages. In Papa Reo, the Māori data specialists review the results of these reports and discuss these with the AI practitioners and the data scientists. This is a crucial part of tech development that relies heavily on human input. An example of this being important was when a report stated a proposed change was worse or the same based on WER, but the language experts found that it had performed better (see Figure 3).

Figure 3. Example of report proposing the models had the same WER

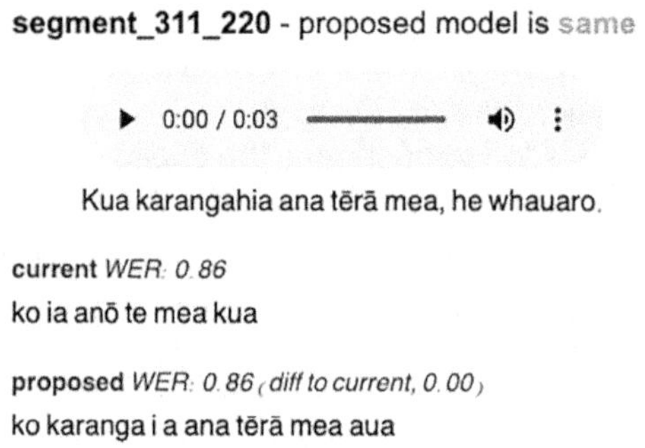

segment_311_220 - proposed model is same

▶ 0:00 / 0:03

Kua karangahia ana tērā mea, he whauaro.

current WER: 0.86
ko ia anō te mea kua

proposed WER: 0.86 *(diff to current, 0.00)*
ko karanga i a ana tērā mea aua

The current and proposed models in Figure 3 have the same WER. However, from a Māori language speaker's point of view, the proposed model performed better than the current model. It identified more words from the target sentence than the current model, i.e. ko *karanga i a ana tērā mea* aua.

Because of their familiarity with the language and the labelled data, the Māori data specialists were then able to explain why this might be the case. The ASR model has two models that contribute to its ability to detect speech accurately. This is an acoustic model, which hears the sounds and labels the data accordingly, and a language model, which is based on text corpus to build an understanding of the syntax and orthography of the Māori language. The Māori data specialists identified that while the output shown in Figure 3 did not match the target sentence, for the proposed model, the acoustic model was 'hearing' the sounds but the language model was overpowering it. As a result, the model was incorrectly ordering those sounds into nonsense sentences or words. This feedback from the Māori language specialists indicates how the proposed model could be significantly improved but it required the AI practitioners to reduce the influence of the language model on the output. This demonstrates the significance of having Māori language experts involved throughout the pipeline of model development to provide solutions during the process and not just at the very end. The specialists knew what data was in there and the limitations of the data and could therefore offer advice and suggest tweaks.

Papa Reo Māori data specialists also conduct experiments of their own to identify failure modes. Failure modes are when the model has poor performance on certain language domains, such as regional variations or style of language, like whaikōrero (formal speech making). Māori data specialists identified that the current ASR model could not accurately transcribe the poetic and esoteric language found in the delivery of whaikōrero. The data found in this domain is primarily verbal: there is not a large text corpus of whaikōrero that can be used to train a language model. Uncommon proper nouns that are not found on any list of placenames or people's names are woven throughout the delivery of whaikōrero. These names have significant mana (power, prestige) within the culture and can be tribally specific. If the model continues to incorrectly transcribe a cornerstone of te ao Māori it fails to uphold the mana of the culture. Ultimately this perpetuates a colonial view of the value of certain language domains such as privileging the language of commerce. Once identified, the data specialists were able to delve into the various repositories and curate a data set to support training the model for this failure model. This ensures that the AI that has been built upholds the mana of tangata whenua and has mātauranga Māori (Māori knowledge) at its core.

Conclusion

Languages are a distinguishing feature of Indigenous cultures that are intrinsically linked to people and place. They allow Indigenous peoples to communicate across landscapes and preserve cultural knowledge. AI can assist in the revitalisation and preservation of language, but there is a lack of large and accurate datasets to support automatic speech recognition and access to data is difficult. Moreover, ethical issues that negatively impact Indigenous peoples such as bias are pervasive in AI.

This paper discusses the Papa Reo project as an example of AI development in natural language processing that grows from the land and the people. It offers a decolonising framework that can be used to shape ethical practice by valuing Indigenous knowledge and expertise. It has demonstrated how the prioritisation of Māori knowledge and Indigenous philosophy can aid in avoiding bias. This includes the ethical curation and analysis of datasets through an Indigenous lens which ultimately improves the quality of data and ensures the correct and appropriate use of data. In Papa Reo, the curation of the Golden Data Set required Māori expertise to recognise how different voices may impact the bias in the model, from age to gender to language ability. By utilising Indigenous expertise and RLHF throughout the entire process, solutions can be provided efficiently because they understand the limitations of the data. When tests were run, the language experts were able to analyse the reports and provide feedback on why data might be producing certain results.

Indigenous-led programmes create transparency throughout the entire AI development process whilst also aiding in the decolonisation of the tech sector. Te Hiku Media's experience provides an example of ethical practice in natural language processing AI, but it can be applied across other fields. This Māori-led work will continue to create equitable space for Māori in a Western-dominated communication landscape to indigenise AI and the digital domain.

Glossary

acoustic model	a layer in the ASR model that hears sounds and labels data accordingly
AI	artificial intelligence
ASR	automatic speech recognition
Golden Data Set	a data set created by Papa Reo to benchmark the ASR model's performance
label/labelling	the process of transcribing audio data to be used in data sets
language model	a layer in the ASR model that is based on the text corpus to demonstrate correct grammar and orthography of the Māori language
mana	power, prestige
mātauranga Māori	Māori knowledge
model	a programme that has been trained on a set of data to recognise certain types of patterns
NLP	natural language processing: the application of computational techniques to the analysis and synthesis of natural language and speech
POS	part of speech
RLHF	reinforcement learning with human feedback
report	reports created to analyse accuracy of the ASR model
tagging	the process of labelling audio data
tangata whenua	Indigenous people, people of the land
te ao Māori	the Māori world
te reo Māori	Māori language
WER	word error rate
whaikōrero	formal speech making
whakapapa	genealogy

References

Artificial Intelligence Forum of New Zealand (2018) Artificial intelligence: Shaping a future New Zealand. Available online at https://aiforum.org.nz/wp-content/uploads/2018/07/AI-Report-2018_web-version.pdf, accessed on 18 October 2022

Barss, Patchen (2019) Can we eliminate bias in AI? How Canada's commitment to multiculturalism could help it become a world leader, U. of T. News. Available online at https://www.utoronto.ca/news/can-we-eliminate-bias-ai-how-canada-s-commitment-multiculturalism-could-help-it-become-world, accessed on 14 October 2022

Bernstein, Hannah (2020) Ethical AI: Indigenous languages, biased algorithms, and the way forward, Northeastern University. Available online at https://www.khoury.northeastern.edu/ethical-ai-indigenous-languages-biased-algorithms-and-the-way-forward/, accessed on 14 October 2022

Chen, Edwin (2023) Introduction to reinforcement learning with human feedback, Surge. Available online https://www.surgehq.ai/blog/introduction-to-reinforcement-learning-with-human-feedback-rlhf-series-part-1, accessed on 7 February 2023

Christian, Jon (2023) Amazing 'jailbreak' bypasses ChatGPT's ethics safeguards, Futurism, 5 February. Available online at https://futurism.com/amazing-jailbreak-chatgpt?fbclid=IwAR0vfELZsWcr1bNwuJsnUcZAwk4io6h45AFF371lrC5psG7gMc-bprtRael, accessed on 7 February 2023

Cipolle, Alex (2022) How Native Americans are trying to debug AI's biases, New York Times. Available behind a paywall online at https://www.nytimes.com/2022/03/22/technology/ai-data-indigenous-ivow.html, accessed on 14 October 2022

Dubay, Lauren and Nalbandian, Lucia (2021) Creating an equitable AI policy for Indigenous communities, First Policy Response. Available online at https://policyresponse.ca/creating-an-equitable-ai-policy-for-indigenous-communities/, accessed on 14 October 2022

Foley, Catherine (2022) Why we need to think about diversity and ethics in AI, Australian Academy of Technological Sciences and Engineering. Available online at https://www.atse.org.au/news-and-events/article/why-we-need-to-think-about-diversity-and-ethics-in-ai/, accessed on 14 October 2022

Getahun, Hannah (2023) ChatGPT could be used for good, but like many other AI models, it's rife with racist and discriminatory bias, Insider. Available online at https://www.insider.com/chatgpt-is-like-many-other-ai-models-rife-with-bias-2023-1, accessed on 8 February 2023

Harper, James (2021) Tertiary study pathway advice using artificial intelligence system based on Māori data, Te Tai Haruru Journal of Māori and Indigenous Issues, Vol. 8. Available online at https://cdn.auckland.ac.nz/assets/law/Documents/2022/Research/PastVolumes/Te%20Tai%20Haruru%20Journal%208%20(2021)%20242%20Harper.pdf

Hughes, Alex (2023) ChatGPT: Everything you need to know about OpenAI's GPT-3 tool, Science Focus. Available online at https://www.sciencefocus.com/future-technology/gpt-3/, accessed on 8 February 2023

Jackson, Moana (2020) Where to next? Decolonisation and the stories in the land, Elkington, Bianca, Jackson, Moana, Kiddle, Rebecca, Mercier, Ocean Ripeka, Ross, Mike, Smeaton, Jennie and Thomas, Amanda (eds) Imagining decolonisation, Wellington, Bridget Williams Books pp 133–155

Jones, Peter-Lucas, Mahelona, Keoni, Duncan, Suzanne and Leoni, Gianna (2023) Ngā Taonga Tuku Iho: Intergenerational transmission using archives, Ethical Space: The International Journal of Communication Ethics, Vol. 20, Nos 2 and 3

Law Foundation (2019) New research finds government AI use needs guidelines and regulator to avoid risks. Available online at https://www.lawfoundation.org.nz/?p=10082, accessed on 15 October 2022

Lund, Brady and Wang, Ting (2023) Chatting about ChatGPT: How may AI and GPT impact academia and libraries? Library Hi Tech News, preprint. Available online at https://papers.ssrn.com/sol3/papers.cfm?abstract_id=4333415, accessed on 7 February 2023

Peter-Lucas Jones

Keoni Mahelona

Suzanne Duncan

Gianna Leoni

Meighan, Paul (2021) Decolonizing the digital landscape: The role of technology in Indigenous language revitalization, *AlterNative*, Vol. 17, No. 3 pp 397–405

Nwafor, Ifeoma (2021) AI ethical bias: A case for AI vigilantism (Allantism) in shaping the regulation of AI, *International Journal of Law and Information Technology*, Vol. 29 pp 225–240

OpenAI (2022) ChatGPT: Optimizing language models for dialogue. Available online at https://openai.com/blog/chatgpt/, accessed on 7 February 2022

Papa Reo (n.d.) Papa Reo. Available online at https://papareo.nz/, accessed on 19 October 2022

Perrigo, Billy (2023) Exclusive: OpenAI used Kenyan workers on less than $2 per hour to make ChatGPT less toxic, *Time*. Available online at https://time.com/6247678/openai-chatgpt-kenya-workers/ accessed on 8 February 2022

Sambasivan, Nithya and Veeraraghavan, Rajesh (2022) The deskilling of domain expertise in AI development, *CHI Conference on Human Factors in Computing Systems (CHI '22)*, USA

Shedlock, Kevin and Hudson, Petera (2022) Kaupapa Māori concept modelling for the creation of Māori IT artefacts, *Journal of the Royal Society of New Zealand*, Vol. 52 pp 18–32

Smith, Linda Tuhiwai (2021) *Decolonizing methodologies*, London, Bloomsbury

Te Hiku Media (2022) He reo tuku iho, he reo ora: Living language transmitted intergenerationally, *MAI Journal*, Vol. 11, No. 1 pp 40–49

United Nations (2007) *United Nations declaration on the rights of indigenous peoples*, New York, United Nations. Available online at http://un.org/esa/socdev/unpfii/documents/DRIPS_en.pdf, accessed on 16 October 2022

Walter, Maggie and Kukutai, Tahu (2018) *Artificial intelligence and Indigenous data sovereignty*. Input paper for the Horizon Scanning Project 'The effective and ethical development of Artificial Intelligence: An opportunity to improve our wellbeing' on behalf of the Australian Council of Learned Academies

Watson, Catherine, Maclagan, Margaret, King, Jeanette, Harlow, Ray and Keegan, Peter (2016) Sound change in Māori and the influence of New Zealand English, *Journal of the International Phonetic Association*, Vol. 46 pp 185–218

Conflict of interest and acknowledgements

The work completed by Te Hiku Media that has led to this paper was funded by the Ministry of Business Innovation and Employment through the Strategic Science Investment Fund and by Te Puni Kōkiri through the Ka Hao fund.

Note on the contributors

Peter-Lucas Jones (Te Aupōuri, Ngāi Takoto, Ngāti Kahu, Te Rarawa) is the chief executive officer of Te Hiku Media. He is the chair of Te Whakaruruhau o ngā Reo Irirangi Māori, chairman of Te Rūnanga Nui o Te Aupōuri, deputy chair of Māori Television and an advisory board member of Te Pūnaha Matatini. As a trusted kaitiaki of Māori data, Peter-Lucas negotiates the responsibility of protecting iwi and Māori data while meeting the expectations of iwi and hapū. Peter-Lucas has terrestrial and digital broadcasting experience, working with kaumātua and marae to record and provide access to te reo ā-iwi, tikanga ā-iwi, kōrero tuku iho and iwi history.

Keoni Mahelona (Kānaka Maoli) is the chief technology officer at Te Hiku Media and a leading practitioner of Indigenous data sovereignty. Originally from Anahola on the island of Kauaʻi, Hawaiʻi, Keoni has been living and working in Te Hiku o te Ika for more than 10 years having first arrived in Aotearoa as a Fulbright Scholar. He makes decisions every day to protect the sovereignty of Māori data, from the digital tools deployed for advance projects to the storage of data and sharing data in appropriate and secure ways.

Suzanne Duncan (Te Rarawa, Te Aupōuri, Ngāi Takoto) is the chief operating officer of Te Hiku Media. Before working at Te Hiku Media, Suzanne was a lecturer at the University of Otago in the School of Māori, Pacific and Indigenous Studies for 10 years. Suzanne is a director of a subsidiary of Te Rūnanga o Te Rarawa and the secretary of her marae. Suzanne supports the work of the Māori data team, in particular data curation and data collection.

Dr Gianna Leoni (Ngāti Kurī, Ngāi Takoto, Te Aupōuri) is a data specialist of te reo Māori at Te Hiku Media. In particular, Gianna engages with the archive and other sources to collate and prepare data for Te Hiku Media's data scientists. Her expertise stems from completing a PhD and Postdoctoral Research Fellowship at the University of Otago, focusing on the revitalisation of te reo Māori and sociolinguistics.

PAPER

Ellen Tapsell

Future visions for te taiao: Re-imagining environmental governance and political communication through film

As biodiversity continues to decline, environmental relationships and governance require transformation to be effective. A core part of this transformation will be how we decide to communicate, engage, and express political ideas and aspirations. Amplifying the voices and practices of communities who have historically been ignored or left out of decision-making will be important in transforming environmental relationships and governance. This paper explores how Indigenous communication landscapes have the potential to provide more creative and inclusive communication and political engagement processes. Using the short film competition Future visions for te taiao *as a case study, this paper reveals how Kaupapa Māori filmmaking can contribute to Indigenous communication landscapes in Aotearoa New Zealand.* Future visions for te taiao *therefore provides an alternative avenue for political communication on environmental governance that centres an Indigenous communication and environmental ethic.*

Key words: Kaupapa Māori, storytelling, short films, environmental governance

Introduction
In October 2021, researchers examining governance and policy options as part of the Biological Heritage National Science Challenge (BioHeritage) in Aotearoa New Zealand (hereafter Aotearoa) held an online short film competition they named *Future visions for te taiao* (the environment). The Strategic Outcome 7 (SO7): Adaptive Governance and Policy team is co-led by Māori politics professor Maria Bargh and Māori legal professor Carwyn Jones. The film competition had a dual purpose of raising awareness of environmental governance and

engaging with communities, particularly rangatahi Māori (Māori youth), to learn about their ideas and aspirations for environmental governance. The competition asked entrants, with any level of filmmaking skills and equipment, to imagine or envision the future of the environment in Aotearoa including its protection and management.

The BioHeritage SO7 research group more broadly seeks to encourage participatory and Te Tiriti o Waitangi (the Treaty of Waitangi) led governance over the environment in Aotearoa (BioHeritage 2022). Current governance arrangements and policy instruments are not working and are failing our biodiversity but also Te Tiriti o Waitangi relationships between Māori and the Crown (Ruru et al. 2017). Existing policies make it difficult for those closest to resources and most affected by the decline in our biological heritage to have their knowledge and values recognised and to participate in the decisions that affect it – at national and local levels (Bargh and Tapsell 2021). BioHeritage SO7 researchers hope to break the mould, and 'build new systems, policies and capability' for governance (BioHeritage 2022). Therefore, the film competition aimed to promote artistic agency in communities and allow for the expression of ideas about te taiao (environmental) governance, and human-te taiao relationships in novel ways incorporating visual and multimedia storytelling.

Storytelling and the use of stories for knowledge creation, retention and decision-making are a core foundation to Māori epistemology (Jones 2016; Roberts and Wills 1998; Walker 1992). Traditionally information and knowledge, including political and environmental knowledge, were encoded in pūrākau (story), whakataukī (proverbs), whakairo (carvings), karakia (prayer) and waiata (song). Storytelling across multiple mediums is therefore inherently part of Māori communication landscapes.

Relationships and the interconnectivity between places, the environment and human communities are also foundational to Māori epistemology and to Māori storytelling (Jones 2016; Walker 1992). Māori communities trace their whakapapa (lineages) back to environmental ancestors and their well-being is closely linked to the health of their ancestral environments (Durie 2001; Mead 2016). Cultural understandings and practices were intimately related to the species and landscapes that Māori lived with and around. Consequently, Māori narratives and stories were connected to the specific environments they lived in and the importance and significance of healthy relationships with these environments (Archibald et al. 2019; Walker 1992).

Yet Māori narrative practices and stories have often been silenced or retold through processes of colonisation (Archibald et al. 2019). Colonial narratives surrounding the environment, in contrast to Māori narratives, have typically seen the environment as something to control and exploit for human benefit (Forster 2019). Archibald et al. (2019) have recently argued that storytelling can be a decolonial research tool for Indigenous communities including Māori, to reimagine and reclaim Indigenous knowledge, law, research and communication.

Ellen Tapsell

Film and multimedia storytelling have also been recognised as tools for promoting Indigenous identities, political imaginaries and landscapes of communication about decolonisation and self-determination (Villarreal 2017; Barnes 2018).

This paper explores the results of analysis from the *Future visions for te taiao* short film competition and the way it incorporated a Kaupapa Māori approach to political communication and engagement. The paper concludes that this competition represents a contemporary practice of Indigenous communication landscapes in Aotearoa which have the potential to contribute to transformative relationships to, and governance of, the environment.

Methodologies and methods

The *Future visions for te taiao* competition and research were guided by Kaupapa Māori methodologies and theories. Kaupapa Māori methodologies have a transformative approach to research that critiques and subverts dominant Western ideologies, and instead celebrates Māori history, language, traditions, knowledge and spirituality as a form of resistance (Smith 2021; Green 2019).

Kaupapa Māori methodologies and theories intersect with Māori filmmaking, which has been described by Merata Mita as being 'by Māori about Māori for Māori' (1992: 16). Māori films and artists regularly use moving images to tell stories that focus on te ao Māori (the Māori world) and the impacts of colonisation (Oliver et al. 2022; Walker-Morrison 2014). While there are no strict rules for what makes a 'Māori film', they are often grounded in tikanga Māori (Māori custom) and work to resist mainstream media or filmmaking practices (Mita 1992: 16; see also Barclay 2015; Mercier 2007). Barry Barclay once likened the process of making a Māori film, particularly amongst your own community, to calling a hui (meeting) whereby creatives must be brave enough to stand up and say: '"This matter is important, and I want you to participate"' (Barclay 2015: 14). Barclay also argued that in a hui Māori (Māori meeting) everyone's voice is important. This was reflected in his approach to filming in Māori communities, but often clashed with his Pākehā (New Zealand European) colleagues' agenda (2015: 11). Māori video artist Nova Paul has similarly described their films as a wānanga (discussion) whereby 'viewers who connect with my work are changed by that relationship' (Oliver et al. 2022: 61).

Scholarly analysis of Māori films often centres on Māori knowledge and Kaupapa Māori theory specifically (Mercier 2007; Barnes 2018; Walker-Morrison 2020). Ocean Mercier and Challen Wilson used Kaupapa Māori methodologies to guide their research exploring Māori participants' experience of the *48-hour film competition* (2016), an annual film competition (since 2001) in which teams of filmmakers are assigned a genre, a character, a prop and a line of dialogue, and have 48 hours to create a short film containing those elements. Mercier and Wilson's research highlighted the Kaupapa Māori narratives, processes, film techniques and experiences Māori participations brought to the often 'monocultural' short film competition (2016: 14). The authors argued that the freedom and flexibility of the *48 Hour Film Competition* was significant for participant autonomy in the creative process, but acknowledged that increased encouragement and celebration of diversity in the competition was needed to further support Kaupapa Māori filmmaking (Mercier and Wilson 2016). Other than in Mercier and Wilson's research, filmmaking itself as a tool of Kaupapa Māori research has not been too widely explored. However, Joanna Kidman in her project *Through our own eyes* used participatory visual storytelling (via photography) by Māori rangatahi (Māori youth) to explore how they 'interpreted their physical and cultural landscapes' (2014: 69). Kidman has used the visual research findings to publish on topics related to community education and Māori political and environmental identities (Kidman 2009, 2012, 2014). While that project did not specifically discuss Kaupapa Māori methodologies, Kidman and the team of Māori researchers utilised, I would argue, aspects of these methodologies including the use and celebration of tikanga Māori (Māori customs) (Kidman 2014: 211). In our film competition we sought to utilise specifically a type of 'Kaupapa Māori filmmaking', whereby filmmaking or the moving image become a tool of Kaupapa Māori research, and each film and filmmaker contribute to the political conversation and research that the BioHeritage team (SO7) are undertaking on environmental governance.

The purpose of our film competition was to hear Māori stories, but in keeping with Barclay's understanding of the hui where everyone can have a voice, the competition was open to anyone who wished to participate. The competition included specific guidelines and prompts for each competition category, such as for the Rangatahi (11 and under) category: 'what does a healthy thriving taiao look like to you?' All participants were asked when registering 'No hea koe' or 'Where are you from?' to ensure the Māori cultural importance of relationships to place and environments was emphasised. We received 10 film entries with a range of community, collective and individual films. We also received various answers to 'Where are you from', including African American, Scottish, Taranaki, Ngā Puhi, Muaūpoko, Nūhaka, Tokelau, Te Kura o Ngā Puna Waiora, Te Arawa and Te Arawa Rohe, Ngāti Kahungunu, Te Ati Haunui-ā-Pāpārangi, Malaysian (Indian ethnicity) as well as from Auckland and Japan. This reflects the diverse relationships and connections to place held by participants and those living in Aotearoa. A tension arises when using the terms 'Kaupapa Māori filmmaking' to discuss films that are not all created by Māori filmmakers. While this paper does not have the scope to discuss in depth the boundaries of what Kaupapa Māori filmmaking is or is not, it is a topic worthy of more exploration. *Future visions for te taiao* and this paper instead attempt to explore how filmmaking as a mode of storytelling and communication can inform Kaupapa Māori research, political engagement and communication practices.

Ellen Tapsell

Table 1. *Future visions for te taiao* list of films, including categories Pakeke (Open age), Rangatahi (11 and under), Taiohi (12-18 years old) and prizes they received

Film Name	Category	Prize
Te Arawa Lakes Trust	Pakeke	1st place in Pakeke category
Whakarongo ki te tuna	Pakeke	Most creative film
Wai	Pakeke	2nd place in Pakeke category
KioKrew	Rangatahi	Most novel vision of governance
Aroha nui ki te taiao	Rangatahi	1st place in Rangatahi category
E rongo e	Rangatahi	Best representation of mātauranga Māori
Te ao hou	Rangatahi	Best entry in te reo Māori
Kaitiaki of mother earth	Rangatahi	2nd place in Rangatahi category
If the earth heats up a little too much	Taiohi	1st place in Taiohi category
Mātauranga	Taiohi	2nd place in Taiohi category

Analysis

The 10 films were analysed qualitatively to reveal four collective themes, focusing on film techniques and narratives. All of the films are available on YouTube.[1] Before I discuss the four key themes found in these films, I want to first acknowledge that a core narrative feature throughout all the films was te reo (Māori language), tikanga (Māori custom) and mātauranga Māori (Māori knowledge). Every film incorporated the use of te reo to varying degrees, *Te ao hou* was completely in te reo Māori, while *Wai* had no dialogue but was named '*Wai*' or 'water' in te reo Māori. *E rongo e* incorporated karakia and *Arohanui ki te taiao* used whakataukī. Our film competition encouraged and made normal the use of Māori knowledge and language through our prizes, categories and the competition's focus on Te Tiriti o Waitangi and te taiao. However, the use of te reo, tikanga and mātauranga Māori was not mandatory and their inclusion in all film entries emphasises their significance to the future of environmental governance in Aotearoa.

A range of stills from the films are presented (Figures 1 and 2) to enhance the thematic discussions. Not every film could be analysed in depth in this article, but key parts are discussed. Each theme begins with a quote from a film.

Theme 1 – A warning on apathy and current approaches

'We took everything of te taiao for granted' – *If the earth heats up a little too much* (2021)

The first theme found in almost all the films was, unsurprisingly, a warning that current approaches to environmental governance are not working and something must be done differently – before it is too late. In some of the films there was a hopeful vision for the future and a belief that things could get better. For example, in *Te ao hou*, once realising that their littering and nonchalance towards the environment was harming both Tāne Mahuta (God of the forest) and themselves, the protagonists work together to clean up, care for and engage with their environments. *Te ao hou* transitions from black and white to colour to express the return of the health of the environment and the main characters as well.

In other films the vision for the future was far more worrying. In *If the earth heats up a little too much* the film uses animation to express a vision of extremes in which nowhere – from beachside to inland – is safe from natural disasters. The brightly coloured animations of fire and water highlight the intensity of future environmental issues and the imbalance in ecosystems. In contrast the images of plants and animals used to represent the 'past' include softer and deeper colours. The extremes and contrasts represented in this film share a frightening warning of what the future could hold if we continue to take our environment for granted. In *KioKrew* there are references to apathetic attitudes towards environmental issues and the false belief that nature will always be there for us no matter what, particularly in Aotearoa where nature has 'never felt far away' (*KioKrew* 2021). The first half of this film looks like a home movie using shaky, hazy shots of birds, bush, beaches and people enjoying the outdoors. The home-movie effect evokes a nostalgic feeling and questions hang over the scenes, emphasised by the narration: will this natural abundance last? Are we doing enough to sustain visions of nature like this?

In *Mātauranga* these questions are also raised, by using repeated quick cuts to express a range of daily activities such as washing, emailing, drinking water, working, driving and deforestation for development. As the shots are repeated more focus is drawn to the different resources we use daily, and the film asks the viewer via subtitles: 'Is what you are doing for the environment really good?' (*Mātauranga* 2021). Many of the films (specifically *If the earth heats up a little too much, Kaitiaki of mother earth, Aroha nui ki te taiao, Te ao hou, KioKrew, Matauranga*) reference the need to change aspects of our daily realities that contribute to environmental degradation, including the use of plastics, single use items, fertilisers, oil, gas and certain energy and fossil-fuel travel systems. In addition, *Mātauranga, Arohanui ki te taiao* and *KioKrew* called for more care, kindness, connection and education on environmental issues in communities and governance structures.

Theme 2 – A collective, intergenerational and hands-on approach

'Kia whakatōmuri, haere whakamua: In order to envision communities working together for a flourishing taiao and healthy wai in 2050 we must first look at the kaitiaki of today' – *Te Arawa Lakes Trust* (2021)

The second theme that came through dominantly in the films was the need for a collective, intergenerational and hands-on approach to environmental governance. In *Te Arawa Lakes Trust* the filmmakers explore the numerous ways kaitiaki (caretakers) from the Māori tribe Te Arawa are already looking after their rohe (area). The opening bird's eye camera angle descends and the audience is brought into the diverse kaupapa (projects) and ecosystems of Te Arawa lakes. This includes the whānau (family) who live, work and care for the lakes and rivers by undertaking biosecurity management and pest eradication, restoration of wetlands and native bush, food sovereignty initiatives and tikanga Māori-informed management. The importance and linked nature of Te Arawa Lakes Trust's kaitiaki (caretaker) roles and rangatira (leadership) roles are made obvious in this film with William Anaru explaining his hope to have 'a management role in all of the biosecurity' of their lakes to ensure they are protected forever (*Te Arawa Lakes Trust* 2021). The film ends with the camera rising out of the Te Arawa ngahere (forest), closing where it began above the trees and bringing the audience full circle. *Te Arawa Lakes Trust* provides a good reminder of the many Māori communities who are already working to achieve their visions for a flourishing taiao and the holistic and intergenerational approach required.

Many of the other films also connected to a hands-on approach to environmental governance. In fact, four of the films (*Mātauranga, Te Arawa Lakes Trust, E rongo e, Te ao hou*) included shots of hands on the earth, planting, connecting or engaging in the growth of healthy environments. All the films acknowledged the shared responsibility we have to care for the environment. In *Te ao hou* and *Te Arawa Lakes Trust* this also included socio-cultural aspects such as through gardening, use of maramataka (Māori lunar calendar) and weaving. In *E rongo e*, the children plant their kūmara (sweet potato) and take us through the different steps for doing so in te reo Māori, including karakia. By working together, the rangatahi plant the kūmara and hope for it to grow big and strong. The narrative of this film shows the rangatahi investing in their future directly, collectively working to nurture and grow resources for the future. *E rongo e* provides a good reminder that younger generations are only just beginning their life journeys and they rely on – and desire to – contribute to a healthy and thriving environment.

Figure 1. Future visions film stills A and B
A (left) credit: Te Arawa Lakes Trust (2021), B (right) credit: E rongo e (2021)

Theme 3 – Importance of connection to nature, greenery and the non-human

'A whole world full of Zealandia' – *Aroha Nui ki te Taiao* (2021)

Green and lush forests filled with birds and other animals were undoubtedly a vision that all these films aspired for, even if, as discussed earlier, that was not what they thought would result from current governance practices. Overall, there was also clear focus on what is best for the environment and non-human beings in the films. However, the human connection to non-human beings and the environment was also very significant. In *Aroha nui ki te taiao* the filmmakers share shots of native bush, birds and waterways in Aotearoa, including from their school trip to Zealandia (a nature reserve in Wellington, New Zealand). The narration over the images expresses the hopes rangatahi have for greenspaces filled with native species, both plant and animal, in their future landscapes. *Aroha nui ki te Taiao* opens using a range of whakataukī to describe the deep spiritual connection between humans and nature including, 'Ko au te taiao, ko te taiao ko au' (I am the environment and the environment is me). In *Whakarongo ki te tuna* the dancers visually represent the connection between humans and the environment, recreating the movements and shapes of the tuna (eel). The combination of the dancing, mirror editing and woven and layered costumes in *Whakarongo ki te tuna* evokes the strength, adaptiveness and flexibility of nature – specifically the tuna (eel).

The filmmakers of *Whakarongo ki te tuna* are possibly suggesting the need for environmental governance to be more adaptive and in tune with our non-human environments and beings such as the tuna or as in *Te ao hou* an atua (god) such as Tāne Mahuta. This connection between nature and humans was recognised in a more practical but also global sense in *KioKrew*. Using personal travel narration and images of boats, planes, motorways and trams *KioKrew* references the constantly evolving relationships we have to our environment and the way it is utilised for travel and connection with others. The film *Wai* completely centres on water, the film using only close up shots of different parts of a stream. The shots of the water with very little editing creates an intimate experience for the audience and causes you to pause and consider the voice and flow of nature more closely.

Theme 4 – Joy and fun while caring for the environment

'Ka mau te wehi! Te haumaru te whenua inaianei. Rarawe noiho!' [Amazing! The land is now cared for and protected. Easy as.] – *Te ao hou* (2021)

The last theme represents the joy and fun that can or should come from caring or engaging with the environment and its governance. This theme feels particularly important considering Theme 1, and the anxiety and stress that environmental pressures are shown to be having on communities (Cunsolo 2020). In *Kaitiaki of mother earth* the protagonist meets a frail, old woman who is tired and desperately seeking someone to show her kindness and 'humanity' (*Kaitiaki of mother earth* 2021). The protagonist is quick to offer her water, and the frail woman is transformed into a brightly dressed 'environmental guardian' named Stacey. *Kaitiaki of mother earth* uses a jump transition, colour editing and rock 'n' roll music to convey the amazing and magical transformation that has occurred.

Ellen Tapsell

The transformation of the frail and tired guardian into a fun and magical one expresses a possible desire for and the importance of joy and fun in environmental governance. In *Te ao hou*, a fun, joyous and sometimes silly experience is also expressed when the main characters take steps to manage and care for the environment. The *Te ao hou* main characters are seen jumping, running, laughing and sliding around the screen, all amplified by the dramatic camera cuts, slow motion and music. *Mātauranga*, *E rongo e* and *Aroha nui ki te taiao* similarly express the fun they had while spending time in the environment or taking sustainable actions such as tree planting. The Rangatahi (11 and under) and Taiohi (12-18) filmmakers remind viewers of the important role that joy has in our relationship to the environment, while also possibly highlighting the lack of joy and fun in current governance discussions and approaches.

Figure 2. *Future visions* film stills. A (top left) credit: Whakarongo ki te tuna (2021), B (top right) credit: Aroha nui ki te taiao (2021), C (bottom left) credit: Te ao hou (2021), D (bottom right) credit: *Mātauranga* (2021)

Discussion and conclusion

Stories and storytelling play an important role in many communities' processes for understanding and making sense of their world, yet throughout history some narratives and ways of storytelling have become prioritised over others (Archibald et al. 2019). In this article I have explored how Kaupapa Māori filmmaking, where filmmaking is used for Kaupapa Māori-informed research, can provide space for political communication and engagement that represents Indigenous or, in this case, Māori communication landscapes.

Amateur filmmaking was used in our short film competition, as a contemporary way to engage in storytelling or traditional Māori communication landscapes and explore knowledge and aspirations surrounding environmental governance in Aotearoa. This filmmaking process allowed for perspectives, ideas and meaning to be expressed diversely through visual and multimedia storytelling. Notably the film competition provided space for ways of communicating and engaging with political ideas that was inclusive of Māori knowledge and customs as the norm. While the stories told in this film competition varied across genre and style, what was found based on the collective narrative of the films and in the four themes discussed above was:

- current governance systems are not working and if change does not happen soon, it could be too late;
- support for local and community efforts to manage environments with a hands-on approach is vital, particularly for Indigenous communities who are already driving sustainable initiatives;
- communities and individuals want to enjoy thriving native bush, birds and animals in their cities and towns; and
- they hope for the environment and participation in its governance to bring joy.

The findings highlight the importance and desire of local communities to be actively and creatively engaged in the governance of te taiao (environment). Also highlighted was the joy and well-being connected to the relationships between human and non-human beings. *Future visions for te taiao* findings therefore support a Māori environmental ethic whereby strong and healthy relationships to our environments and each other are pivotal for successful governance and well-being into the future.

The *Future visions for te taiao* competition represents one potential way to engage in transformative political research, discussions and communication that is informed by Kaupapa Māori approaches and contributes to Māori communication landscapes.

Glossary

Aotearoa	te reo Māori name for New Zealand
atua	god/ancestor
hui	meeting
hou	new
kaitiaki / kaitiakitanga	guardian or caretaker / guardianship
karakia	prayer / incantation
kaupapa	project / theme / topic / matter
kūmara	sweet potato
Māori	Indigenous peoples of Aotearoa New Zealand
maramataka	Māori lunar calendar
mātauranga	knowledge/wisdom
ngahere	forest/bush
pakeke	grown up/mature (Open age category in competition)

Ellen Tapsell

Pākehā	New Zealand European person
Tāne Mahuta	god of the forest
taiao	natural environment / environmental
taiohi	young person / people (12 to 18-years-old category in competition)
Te Arawa	Māori tribe located near Lake Rotorua
Te Arawa Lakes Trust	Trust Board responsible for the oversight and management of Te Arawa's settlement assets, including the region's 14 lakes
Te Tiriti o Waitangi	Treaty of Waitangi, founding document first signed in 1840 by Māori and the Crown
Te ao Māori	Māori world or worldview
tikanga	Māori protocols, practices, or processes, customs
tuna	eel (*Anguilla Australis*)
rangatahi	young person/people (11 years and under category in competition)
rangatiratanga	authority, sovereignty
rohe	area, territory
wānanga	meeting / forum / conference / discussion
whānau	family
whakataukī	proverb
whakapapa	lineage
whakairo	carving / carved / to carve

Note

[1] Films are available at https://www.youtube.com/watch?v=VrmIJxfAhzc&list=PLMeHOXj6MgSkZKWb-MWYgfF1kdD4aqVJz

References

Archibald Q'um Xiiem, Jo-ann, Bol Jun Lee-Morgan, Jenny and De Santolo Smith, Jason (2019) *Decolonizing research: Indigenous storywork as methodology*, London, Zed Books. Available online at https://doi.org/10.1080/02601370.2021.1959749

Aroha nui ki te taiao (2021) Future visions for te taiao. Short film

Barclay, Barry (2015) *Our own image: A story of a Maori filmmaker*, Minneapolis, University of Minnesota Press

Barnes, Moewaka Angela (2018) Kia manawanui: Kaupapa Māori theoretical framework, *MAI Journal*, Vol. 7, No. 1 pp 4–17. Available online at https://doi.org/10.20507/MAIJournal.2018.7.1.1

Bargh, Maria and Tapsell, Ellen (2021) For a tika transition: Strengthen rangatiratanga, *Policy Quarterly*, Vol. 17, No. 3 pp 13–22. Available online at https://doi.org/10.26686/pq.v17i3.7126

BioHeritage (2022) *Adaptive governance and policy*: Biological Heritage: National Science Challenge. Available online at https://bioheritage.nz/goals/stategic-objective/policy/, accessed on 20 September 2022

Cunsolo, Ashlee, Harper, Sherilee L., Minor, Kelton, Hayes, Katie, Williams, Kimberly G. and Howard, Courtney (2020) Ecological grief and anxiety: The start of a healthy response to climate change?, *The Lancet Planetary Health*, Vol. 4, No. 7 pp 261–263. Available online at https://doi.org/10.1016/S2542-5196(20)30144-3

Durie, Mason (2001) *Mauri ora: The dynamics of Māori health*, Auckland, Oxford University Press

E rongo e (2021) Future visions for te taiao. Short film

Forster, Margaret (2019) Restoring the feminine of Indigenous environmental thought, *Genealogy*, Vol. 3, No. 11 pp 1-13. Available online at https://doi.org/10.3390/genealogy3010011

Green, Jordan (2019) *Māori Instagram: The social media lifeworlds and decolonising practices of rangatahi Māori*. Unpublished thesis, Dunedin, University of Otago. Available online at http://hdl.handle.net/10523/12479

If the earth heats up a little too much (2021) Future visions for te taiao. Short film

Jones, Carwyn (2016) *New treaty, new tradition*, Wellington, Victoria University Press

Kaitiaki of mother earth (2021) Future visions for te taiao. Short film

Kidman, Joanna (2009) Visual methodologies: Exploring Indigenous constructions of self and environment, Zandvliet, David (ed.) *Diversity in environmental education research*, Leiden, Brill pp 65-76. Available online at https://doi.org/10.1163/9789087908614_006

Kidman, Joanna (2012) The Land remains: Māori youth and the politics of belonging, *AlterNative: An International Journal of Indigenous Peoples*, Vol. 8, No. 2 pp 189–202. Available online at https://doi.org/10.1177/117718011200800207

Kidman, Joanna (2014) Representing Māori youth voices in community education research, *New Zealand Journal of Educational Studies*, Vol. 49, No. 2 pp 205–218. Available online at https://search.informit.org/doi/10.3316/informit.842574143464750

KioKrew (2021) Future visions for te taiao. Short film

Mātauranga (2021) Future visions for te taiao. Short film

Mead, Moko Hirini (2016) *Tikanga Maori: Living by Maori values*, Wellington, Huia Publishers

Mercier, Ripeka Ocean (2007) Close encounters of the Māori kind: Talking interaction in the films of Taika Waititi, *New Zealand Journal of Media Studies*, Vol. 10, No. 2 pp 37–51. Available online at https://doi.org/10.26686/wgtn.12981110.v1

Mercier, Ripeka Ocean and Wilson, Challen (2016) 'Fun and freedom'? Kaupapa Māori approaches in the 48-hour film competition, *MEDIANZ*, Vol. 16, No. 1 pp 5–21. Available online at https://doi.org/10.26686/wgtn.12980939.v1

Mita, Merata (1992) The soul and the image in film in Aotearoa New Zealand, Dennis, Jonathan and Bieringa, Jan (eds) *Film in Aotearoa New Zealand*, Wellington, Victoria University Press pp 42–43

Oliver, Melanie, Reweti, Bridget, Mills, Maree, Tikao, Ariana, Tonga, Nina and Williams, Matariki (2022) *Māori moving image*, Ōtautahi Christchurch, Christchurch Art Gallery

Roberts, R. Mere and Willis, R. Peter (1998) Understanding Māori epistemology: A scientific perspective, Wautischer, Helmut (ed.) *Tribal epistemologies*, London, Routledge pp 43–77. Available online at https://doi.org/10.4324/9780429431517

Ruru, Jacinta, O'Lyver, B. Phil, Scott, Nigel and Edmunds, Deborah (2017) Reversing the decline in New Zealand's biodiversity: Empowering Māori within reformed conservation law, *Policy Quarterly*, Vol. 13, No. 2 pp 65–71. Available online at https://doi.org/10.26686/pq.v13i2.4657

Smith, Tuhiwai Linda (2021) *Decolonizing methodologies: Research and Indigenous peoples*, London, Bloomsbury, third edition. Available online at http://dx.doi.org/10.5040/9781350225282

Te Arawa Lakes Trust (2021) Future visions for te taiao. Short film

Te ao hou (2021) Future visions for te taiao. Short film

Villarreal, Z. Gabriela (2017) *Indigenous media and political imaginaries in contemporary Bolivia*, Nebraska, University of Nebraska Press. Available online at https://doi.org/10.2307/j.ctt1qft0pq

Walker, Ranginui (1992) The relevance of Māori myth and tradition, King, Michael (ed.) *Te ao hurihuri: Aspects of Maoritanga*, Auckland, Reed pp 171–184

Wai (2021) Future visions for te taiao. Short film

Walker-Morrison, Deborah (2014) A place to stand: Land and water in Māori film, *Imaginations*, Vol. 5, No. 1 pp 25–47. Available online at https://doi.org/10.17742/IMAGE.periph.5-2.3

Whakarongo ki te tuna (2021) Future visions for te taiao. Short film

Conflict of interest and acknowledgements

The author and wider SO7 research team would like to acknowledge all the filmmakers who participated in our competition. Thank you for your time and for bravely sharing your ideas, worries, visions and dreams. We would also like to thank Te Tīra Whakamātaki, Te Kawa a Māui and Venise Clark for contributions to the competition prizes. Thanks to the judges of our film competition: Ocean Mercier, Melanie Mark-Shadbolt, Rob George and Kahu Kutia. The SO7 research team also acknowledges Kahu Kutia as the creative director of the film competition, without whom the competition would not have been possible. This research was funded by New Zealand's Biological Heritage National Science Challenge. Lastly, many thanks to Ngā Pae o te Māramatanga (Te Tai Ao theme) for their support and beginning the short-film competition vision with us.

Note on the contributor

Ellen Tapsell (Te Arawa and Tainui) is a researcher with the Biological Heritage National Science Challenge based at Te Kawa a Māui, Te Herenga Waka – Victoria University of Wellington. She recently received her Master's in Māori Studies with Distinction.

PAPER

Benjamin R. LaPoe II
Victoria L. LaPoe
Sarah Liese
Hannah Ötting
Julia Weber

Examining how *Reservation dogs* and *Rutherford Falls* critically craft community narratives: Indigenous storytellers celebrate non-stereotypical designs

2021 was a powerful year for Indigenous representation on streaming platforms as Rutherford Falls *debuted on Peacock and* Reservation dogs *on Hulu – two shows with Indigenous-focused narratives, creators and cast members. This is significant, given the mainstream media's past failed and harmful attempts to portray accurate depictions of Indigenous people. In this research we utilised Indigenous standpoint theory and mediatisation theory to analyse both shows. We identified common lenses and ideas displayed in both television shows to further understand how Indigenous-led projects are discussing Indigenous communities and experiences, finding overlap in the themes: Indigenous joy, surviving erasure, colonised versus decolonised ways of knowing and Indigenous womanhood and family.*

Key words: Hollywood; *Reservation dogs*; *Rutherford Falls*; Indigenous standpoint theory; mediatisation theory

Introduction
Storytelling means commitment to culture and community in Indian Country (LaPoe and LaPoe 2017). It is not uncommon for Indigenous journalists to recognise they are getting a gift when someone shares their story. Much like how a newspaper may pass from one generational person to another in a family, cultural stories also flow across the ages (ibid). Indigenous media cover issues with greater detail and depth than non-Indigenous media (LaPoe et al. 2021b).

Benjamin R. LaPoe II

Victoria L. LaPoe

Sarah Liese

Hannah Ötting

Julia Weber

The same sort of ethical care Indigenous newsrooms give to reporting, Indigenous entertainers have instilled in production of streaming series; this made it heartbreaking when one show was cancelled (Goldberg 2022) and another snubbed at the Emmy awards (O'Connell 2022). *Rutherford Falls* and *Reservation dogs* are acclaimed for crafting breakthrough narratives. As expressed on social media, no matter what industry decisions are made about these shows, Indigenous actors, producers, writers and audiences will not forget the imprint of progress.

Using their platform at the Emmy award show 2021, *Reservation dogs*, director Sterlin Harjo (Seminole/Creek) called himself and those working on the show 'proud to be Indigenous people working in Hollywood, representing the first people to walk upon this continent' (Z0mbie Chik 2021: 0:01). The *Reservation dogs* cast did not just represent their communities, but also shared Indigenous artists' excellence through their Emmy presentation. Actress Devery Jacobs (Kanien'kehá:ka), who plays a lead in the show, showcased multiple Indigenous artists, from her earrings to dress, a decision celebrated as showing non-stereotypical designs (Native News Online 2021; Sarah 2021; Vanderhoof 2021).

As the Emmy presentation did, *Reservation dogs* itself, co-written by Harjo and Taika Waititi (Te Whānau-ā-Apanui), championed itself on busting Hollywood stereotypes, by opening opportunities for multiple Indigenous roles (Odman 2021). Mato Wayuhi (Oglala Lakota), for example, worked closely with Harjo to create modern, authentic soundtracks for the show (Bennett-Begaye 2021). The success of the show goes beyond nominations and awards (Schilling 2021a) and is apparent in audience reactions from memes on social media to videos on TikTok (diamond_dog74 2021; Harjo 2021; Schilling 2021b).

Reservation dogs and *Rutherford Falls* have something in common: a team of Indigenous people working together to craft them (Asenap 2021a; Schilling 2021c).

Jana Schmieding (Cheyenne River Sioux Tribe), who is an actress in both shows, wrote that *Rutherford Falls* offered her the possibility to bring Indigenous joy to large audiences (Schmieding 2021). Indigenous joy, according to the actress as well as Cindy Lindquist Mala, president of Cankdeska Cikana Community College at Fort Totten, is 'good medicine': Indigenous humour is at 'the heart of [Indigenous] resilience and survivability' (Lindquist Mala 2016).

Both television shows approach their storytelling much as Barry Barclay approached writing about the cultural probity of Māori media production. He stated: 'When you enter this space you will hear our people talking in their own way to their own people' (1990: 77). The shows are unapologetically Indigenous and speak to communication landscapes of Indigenous relatives of the past and present.

Failures of Indigenous representations are plentiful (e.g. Davis-Delano et al. 2021; Gauthier 2015; Holiday-Shchedrov 2017), and these new shows provide an opportunity to consider how narratives from

Indigenous people by and for Indigenous people – and the world – change the discourse in society. By considering Indigenous representation in *Reservation dogs* and *Rutherford Falls*, this study considers emerging narratives in this, possibly, 'new era of Native representation' (Asenap 2021b).

Momentum of representation

Some critics have argued recently that this is a prime moment for Indigenous-focused productions: *Yellowstone* offers strong Indigenous characters (Pierce 2020), in *Killers of the flower moon* Indigenous actresses are cast alongside other well-known celebrities such as Leonardo DiCaprio (Indian Country Today 2021), Cheyenne and Mescalero Apache filmmaker Bird Runningwater is partnering with Amazon to produce Indigenous stories (White 2021), and a documentary short film on Joe Buffalo, Samson Cree Nation, produced by Amar Chebib partnering with the *New Yorker* (Greene 2021). Further, the short film *The shaman's apprentice*, directed by Canadian Inuit Zacharias Kunuk, was on the short list for the 2021 Academy Awards (Academy of Motion Pictures 2021). Even the 2022 horror film *Prey*, based on the *Predator* franchise, showcased a predominantly Indigenous cast (Gleiberman 2022) and allowed Hulu viewers to screen the entire film in Comanche, a feat that is a first of its kind (Hadadi 2022). As Sterlin Harjo reflects in a behind the scenes clip of *Reservation dogs*, posted on Ryan RedCorn's (Osage) Instagram:

> For a lot of years, it was mainly white people giving white people opportunities ... Now we have Native show runners, and we get to give Native people opportunities. ... We're breaking down doors about representation, but ... our whole community is coming with us through that door. And it's hard ... to close that door once we're all in (RedCorn 2021: 7:36).

This momentum is especially important as Indigenous representations shape a group's own, as well as other groups', perceptions of those represented (Leavitt et al. 2015).

Influence on society and erasure

As most US Americans are not knowledgeable of Indigenous culture, media channels and popular media have a strong influence on mainstream society's perceptions of Indigenous Americans (Echo Hawk 2018). In the past, US Indigenous people have been underrepresented, as well as stereotyped and therefore 'othered', through mass media presentations (Leavitt et al. 2015; Mastro and Stern 2003; Tukachinsky et al. 2015). The University of California, Los Angeles, *Hollywood diversity report* considered the top 185 English-language films released in 2020. It shows that among these films only 1.1 per cent of film leads and 0.6 per cent of overall roles included Indigenous people, with no US Indigenous film directors represented (Hunt and Ramón 2021).

Benjamin R. LaPoe II

Victoria L. LaPoe

Sarah Liese

Hannah Ötting

Julia Weber

In 2020, Nielsen, a US-based audience measurement system, found that across screens Indigenous people had 'some of the lowest' presence (Nielsen 2020: 20). The highest numbers were on Subscription Video on Demand, where US Indigenous men appeared a half of per cent (0.5 per cent) in comparison to US Indigenous women at 0.4 per cent. On cable, US Indigenous people made up 0.1 per cent overall and in broadcast 0.3 per cent overall. Nielsen reported that 'streaming and broadcast are among the most inclusive sources for representation of people of color' (ibid: page 7) while representations that do exist are often highly stereotypical (Turner Strong 2012). It is not surprising then that initiatives like IllumiNative are demanding new representations of Indigenous people, and especially of Indigenous women, on their Instagram account (IllumiNative 2021a, IllumiNative 2021b).

Underrepresentation and gender

Television is much like news in that content analyses show a severe underrepresentation of US Indigenous people, including in television advertisements (Azocar et al. 2021; LaPoe et al. 2021a; Mastro and Stern 2003; Tukachinsky et al. 2015). Within fictional discourse, these communities are often mythologised and become 'symbols of wisdom, beauty, peace, and nostalgia' (Bird 1999: 61) from the distant past (Fitzgerald 2010; Merskin 1998). Images are further gendered, with the male Indigenous person represented as a warrior who desires White women, and Indigenous women are either quasi-faceless or sexual objects of desire for White men. Through these narratives, cultural attitudes justify White domination (Bird 1999). Alternative narratives within these forms of media consider Indigenous people as showing loyalty to White mainstream society's norms (Fitzgerald 2010, 2014), and as homogeneous groups consisting of alcoholics and lazy people (Tan et al. 1997).

These findings from older studies still resonated within a case study by Davis-Delano and colleagues (2021). Stereotypes found in mainstream media recalled by media audiences justify the oppression of US Indigenous people, through implementation of the tropes of savagery, of the noble and the degraded, as well as of the 'casino Indian' in film and TV. Further, US Indigenous people were stereotyped in their physical appearance and through references to other stereotypical signifiers. Additionally, Davis-Delano et al. (ibid) find US Indigenous women to be even more underrepresented than men in the mainstream media.

Othering of Indigenous women

Indigenous women, through their intersectional position, become especially 'othered' from mainstream discourse. They are represented as exoticised, as objects and as hypersexual, due to the representations being largely written by White men (Gauthier 2015). According to Marubbio (2009), through US Indigenous women, coloniser perspectives are articulated: these characters tend to fall in love with White men (and then die because of them); their hypersexuality marks them as morally depraved; and they become symbols of American ideologies (Marubbio 2009).

Empowering and disrupting narratives

Indigenous communities are not satisfied with their representation on mainstream television programmes, but rather feel they are more accurately represented in Indigenous media production, which can disrupt inaccurate stereotypical discourses (Eason et al. 2018; Holiday-Shchedrov 2017; Merskin 1998). As news editor Tristan Ahtone (Kiowa) has stressed in his career and noted again on a digital reporting panel at Northwestern University, media must cover Indigenous joy as much as trauma (CNAIR 2019: 01:03:57; Ahtone 2018).

Narratives, according to a research project by IllumiNative (Echo Hawk 2018), should work to empower communities. After testing possible narratives which could also change stereotypical thinking among mainstream audiences in an online questionnaire (Echo Hawk 2018), the organisation formulated guidelines for positive media representations, which included discussion of Indigenous peoples' connections to their family land, cultures and/or traditions, and discussion of present-day and historical inaccurate representations (Echo Hawk 2018). Further, stories should include context to issues as well as Indigenous values along with visibility of modern narratives (IllumiNative nd).

Two theories inform the intersections of media representations and the authenticity of how these representations are created, by whom, and the meaning they make about communities. For this study, indigenous standpoint theory (IST) and mediatisation theory explores meanings within *Reservation dogs* and *Rutherford Falls*.

Mediatisation theory argues for an influence of media representations on public perception of individuals, through agenda-setting and framing effects: the media influence attention and salience attached to topics reported on by the public and the way that these issues are then thought about (Entman 1993; McCombs and Shaw 1972). Mediatisation theory, therefore, considers how social behaviour and (inter)actions are influenced by media content (LaPoe et al. 2021b).

Indigenous standpoint theory (IST) offers opportunities to consider Indigenous approaches to knowledge and knowledge generation within research (Foley 2003). It is employed in analysing US media research (e.g. Azocar et al. 2021; Carter Olson et al. 2022; LaPoe et al. 2021a). The approach privileges Indigenous knowledge, realities and worldviews, through the emphasising of Indigenous voices and views first, as well as historical, social and political contexts shaping Indigenous lives (Martin and Mirraboopa 2003). By doing so, the research aims to benefit Indigenous communities and the greater world through this authenticity of information (Foley 2003).

Benjamin R. LaPoe II

Victoria L. LaPoe

Sarah Liese

Hannah Ötting

Julia Weber

Interpretive narrative analysis and themes

These research methods are used to explore Indigenous representation in media within narratives that centre and uplift Indigenous voices. This paper aims to compare and contrast themes and narratives that are present in the first seasons of both *Reservation dogs* and *Rutherford Falls* as they pertain to Indigenous life and culture. Researchers conducted a qualitative analysis viewing the shows via their respective platforms Hulu and Peacock.

This paper utilises interpretative study strategies and narrative analysis to explore themes within *Reservation dogs* and *Rutherford Falls* to examine how they are shaping Indigenous narratives in media. Our research incorporates these forms of analysis to examine how meaning is created across shows about lived experiences (Peterson 2017).

While exploring which themes emerged, we found Indigenous joy expressed in *Reservation Dogs* and *Rutherford Falls* by a robust fulfilment of embodying and harnessing Indigenous viewpoints. By centring and uplifting Indigenous perspectives, both shows provided viewers with an enriching and fulfilling portrayal of Indigenous life and culture, while shattering harmful Indigenous stereotypes. Sources of joy were found across both series in humour, family, community and honesty. Other themes included surviving erasure, questioning colonial versions of history and knowledge and Indigenous and feminist lenses on the subjectivity of truth – which also provided a more honest and raw depiction of contemporary Indigenous experiences that are not necessarily upbeat. In *Rutherford Falls*, comedic writer Sierra Teller Ornelas (Dine), along with actor Ed Helms from *The office* (2006-2013) and series co-creator Michael Schur, flip the narrative on 'America's "messy history"' (Cornish 2021) while *Reservation dogs* shows gives audiences 'permission to laugh' (Gross 2022: para 8).

Skoden – Surviving erasure

When it comes to Indigenous storytelling, introducing the setting is crucial. The land can paint a picture of survival and change – not only for the land itself but for the beings that walk upon it. Both shows included in our analysis begin by establishing the locations and features that rest upon land. *Rutherford Falls* starts with moving graphical images, including a bead store, a food truck with fry bread and a casino. In the first scene, someone crashes into a statue in the middle of the town. When the driver asks: 'Why is this here?', the police officer says: 'It's just always been that way' (Helms et al. 2021: Episode 1). This scene in the show demonstrates America's history of idolising figures without really questioning their actions or what they represent. It also makes viewers reflect on the consequences of who is societally honoured and, more important, who is not. That ideology continues throughout the season, with the main character, Nathan Rutherford, seeing life through his White 'happy-go-lucky' lens, taking pride in his 'founding' family's lineage. Nathan believes his family, whom the town was named after, 'brokered a uniquely fair and honest deal with our neighbors the

Minishonka tribe' to live in the town (Helms et al. 2021: Episode 1). Yet, as the story unfolds, Indigenous perspectives are brought to the forefront, and the unequal treatment of Indigenous people is portrayed along with their current experiences.

The opening scene of *Reservation dogs* mirrors an Indigenous movie classic *Smoke signals* (1998) with a radio report played during a montage of town landmarks. Following the report, one main character Bear Smallhill, played by D'Pharaoh Woon-A-Tai (Oji-Cree Anishinaabe), introduces the town to the viewers through a video he made that is shown to his high school class. The video shows the local police officer's car, fried catfish, graffiti, his hideout, which is an abandoned building, and a close friend who passed away. 'This is Daniel. He died last year. We are having a memorial for him in a couple of days. RIP, my dog. This place killed him. That's why we're saving our money, so we can leave this dump before it kills us too' (Harjo et al. 2021: Episode 1). Bear gets through his day by using creative and sometimes illegal outlets to express himself and by leaning on his friends who share the same pain of losing their friend Daniel.

The truth depicted in both shows is that Indigenous communities are still here despite efforts to assimilate and destroy Indigenous people and cultures. As evident with Bear's friend Daniel, those effects of erasure are undeniable. One salient and contemporary cause of erasure is harmful reporting, which can be in the form of parachute reporting – a topic highlighted in *Rutherford Falls* when Terry Thomas, the CEO of a local tribal casino, played by Michael Greyeyes (Plains Cree), is interviewed by a reporter. Terry asks the reporter about his knowledge regarding the seven generations and the reporter replies, 'I have an article on it somewhere' (Helms et al. 2021: Episode 4). While an article is nice to have, it is not necessarily sufficient – or as knowledgeable – to specific community understanding. The reporter then proceeds to treat Terry as if he is 'selling out his culture', but Terry explains to him and defines his community perspective:

> Your implication is that being Indigenous and growing a profitable economy are exclusive. America only champions one form of capitalism. Major corporations, which I should point out don't pay taxes, while we do, they keep all the money for those at the top. Tribal capitalism distributes revenue, in this case casino revenue, to everyone in the tribe (ibid).

He explains that this standpoint of collective distribution isn't new. It has always happened in his community. 'Men would go hunt deer. Meat divided equally to elders, women, and children first, so everyone would survive. We still get our share of the deer, but this time it is a check' (ibid). In the case of the fictional Minishonka tribe in *Rutherford Falls*, the community comes together to survive and help one another and the reporter fails to understand the tribal history. The reporter may have done research, but it was limited compared to the knowledge of the people who had been raised on the land.

Benjamin R. LaPoe II

Victoria L. LaPoe

Sarah Liese

Hannah Ötting

Julia Weber

Another main character in *Rutherford Falls*, who provides a fruitful Indigenous perspective, is Reagan Wells. Her mission is to build a cultural centre for her tribe within the casino. In an early scene, Reagan is working on her pitch to build the cultural centre, which begins with: 'History of Indigenous people, the greatest story never told …'. When practising her pitch to her friend Nathan, he comments: 'Oh, that's good,' while it is lived reality for Reagan. Reagan wants to create a 'place where our people won't be overlooked' (ibid: Episode 1). As Reagan continues to practise her pitch, an older White man comes in and puts his hands on a basket displayed in the centre, talking about how he should get it for his wife. A White woman comes in and says: 'Do you sell shot glasses?' As Reagan scurries to protect the basket, she tells them: 'These exhibits need to remain historically accurate; it is very precise' (ibid: Episode 1). As they finally leave, she half-jokingly says: 'Don't gamble away your 401K' (ibid). Her pitch and response to the White man and woman express her mission to preserve her tribe's history, and the current reality that her world is a mix of cultures and perspectives, some of which they are ignorant of.

This blending of cultures and ideals informs viewers that Indigenous nations are not monolithic nor necessarily untouched. Instead, the communities depicted in *Rutherford Falls* and *Reservation dogs* discuss how they are intercultural and contemporary. In *Reservation dogs*, that ideology is expressed through 'White Jesus' and the use of sage. White Jesus is referenced multiple times in the first season and acts as a symbol reinforcing the history of forced Christian conversion on Indigenous people. The appearance of White Jesus in multiple episodes implies that some have embraced White Jesus as their saviour, but not all believe in Christianity or that Jesus was White. It also emboldens the notion that ideas brought over by settlers and missionaries have encroached upon Indigenous communities. However, it is also important to note that other sacred Indigenous traditions remain, as sage is used during the Rez Dogs' tribute to Daniel and reminds viewers that Christianity is not the only form of spiritual expression.

Questioning colonial versions of history and ways of knowing

The philosophies and dogma brought by settlers and forcibly imposed upon Indigenous people may persist on Indigenous land, but the divide between colonial ways of knowing and Indigenous ways of knowing are highlighted in both series. Beliefs that Indigenous people don't own land, but they respect the land enough to take care of it, are expressed in *Reservation dogs*, while the belief that one should only use what one needs and give away the rest is expressed in *Rutherford Falls*. That history which is passed down from generation to generation, whether it be decolonised or colonised knowledge, is also represented in both television shows.

During an episode of *Reservation dogs*, one of the 'Rez Dogs' – Elora Danan Postoak, played by Kawennáhere Devery Jacobs (Kahnawake Mohawk First Nation) – visits her Uncle Brownie to learn how to fight.

Uncle Brownie, played by Gary Farmer (Haudenosaunee/Iroquois), aims a knife at a poster of Andrew Jackson during an attempt to show his fighting experience. Andrew Jackson is the former US president who signed the Indian Removal Act causing thousands of Indigenous people to leave their homelands. Thus, the show creates a dark joke when Uncle Brownie practises his knife aiming skills at a former president, who is still respected by some as he is still honoured on the US twenty-dollar bill. The action of throwing the knife at a racist former president highlights the disparate versions of history that are taught and understood in the US. Uncle Brownie is aware of the impact presidents like Andrew Jackson had on his tribe and others in the country, evident in the representation being used as his knife-throwing target.

Similarly, Reagan Wells in *Rutherford Falls* understands the importance of cultural preservation and presenting Indigenous history and truths to non-Indigenous and Indigenous audiences. By creating a cultural centre, others can become more aware of what matters to Reagan's tribal nation, the fictional Minishonka tribe. It is another attempt to survive erasure. During an episode of *Rutherford Falls*, Reagan is with Nathan at his aunt's house looking for documents to save the statue of his ancestor 'Big Larry'. Reagan ends up finding Minishonkan artefacts in the possession of Nathan's family which belong to the tribe. Instead of Nathan supporting Reagan and protecting Indigenous history, he focuses on his family's history and finding letters to support that narrative. Later, Nathan's aunt does give the items back to Reagan and the Minishonkan tribe. Reagan offers to pay, but the aunt asks for more money than she has. In a very powerful moment, Reagan stands up to the aunt and says:

> I'm just gonna go ahead and reach out to the Department of Interior and see if everything is NAGPRA [Native American Graves Protection and Repatriation Act] compliant. I'm not sure I got a great look at all of the items in your carriage house, but I'm sure they were all acquired in a proper way, so if we were to go get the Feds involved, you'd be fine, right? Or, we can skip that and I can give you money for items that belong to me anyway. (Helms et al. 2021: Episode 3)

Reagan's quote identifies that Indigenous artefacts are more than just trinkets that adorn a house, they are items that can connect someone to their ancestors and they should be respected and fought for. Those artefacts can also help inform people about historical truth and paint a more honest picture of the past, causing Reagan to detail protections regarding artefacts such as those.

Similar to artefacts, land is another thing Indigenous people are striving to protect in real life and in these shows. In *Reservation dogs*, the words 'Land Back' surface throughout the first season mainly displayed through graffiti, as a prominent reminder that the country was 'founded' on stolen land. One of the spray-painted 'Land Back' signs sparks a conversation between a White heterosexual couple. The man says to the woman: 'They want the whole damn thing back?

Benjamin R. LaPoe II

Victoria L. LaPoe

Sarah Liese

Hannah Ötting

Julia Weber

… That's just not possible?' The wife replies: 'I mean, the Whites did kill an awful lot of them and took the land. So, America ought to be ashamed of itself.' The man not backing down says: 'Well, they got the casinos. I hear they get paid a thousand dollars a month just to be an Indian' (Harjo et al. 2021: Episode 3). The man's knowledge about the Indigenous people in the area is inaccurate, harmful and points to a common stereotype: the 'casino Indian'. It pushes forth the notion that Indigenous people are lazy and rely on the casino to pay their bills. His tone and attitude also suggest no remorse for the settlers' decision to steal Indigenous land and they raise questions about what he was taught about colonisation and Indigenous communities. Conversely in *Rutherford Falls*, stealing land is a common saying for Terry, who has to manage dealing with non-Indigenous people as a business person – the CEO of the Minishonka casino – in this historically conflicted community. Sometimes Terry gets so used to saying it, he forgets and says it to Reagan. To put in context here, viewers and readers should think about the Land Back movement as 'returning land to the stewardship of Indigenous peoples' (Thompson 2020). In one case, she replied: 'My thing?' and Terry apologised: 'Sorry, I deal with White people all day. That line usually works', while in reality, 'stealing land' isn't a line, but part of this country's history (Helms et al. 2021: Episode 7).

Other ideas regarding Indigenous knowledge and ways of teaching and how they compare to colonised ways of teaching are highlighted in *Reservation dogs*. One example is in a quote made by Uncle Brownie in reference to how he was teaching Bear to fight. 'Well, I have been training you … That's how Indigenous people teach. We ain't like White people, you just get a book and then you're supposed to remember something. You listen. You learn' (Harjo et al. 2021: Episode 3). This quote highlights the importance of elders in the community, their knowledge and the significance of respect and listening. That idea leads to another memorable example regarding 'folklore' – particularly Indigenous folklore – and how it tends to be disregarded as 'fiction'. In colonised educational institutions, many Indigenous stories are classified as 'folklore', 'legends' or 'myths' when they are stories handed down through the generations. But as Big the tribal cop, played by Zahn Tokiya-ku McClarno (Hunkpapa Lakota), said: 'Just because you can't see something doesn't make it any less real' (ibid: Episode 5).

Additionally, in *Rutherford Falls*, the validity of classified 'experts' is called into question. An older White male academic, Professor Tobias James Kaufman, is writing a book about the history of the Rutherfords and colonialism is nodded to in many ways. To understand this character's action, he talks about what sounds like 'e-ray-zure' of Nathan's family because of the moving of the statue of Big Larry; he also has a low budget podcast and is an alcoholic recently out of rehab. Nathan relies on this 'expert' to uphold his history, but finds out he is a White supremacist, after he enabled him to get drunk to get on his good side for documentation of his family. The academic asks a question that gets to the heart of the implicit issue Nathan is supporting: 'Your family introduced whiteness to the region?' Nathan replies: 'That isn't a point of pride' (Helms et al. 2021: Episode 2). Later, they battle it out in a historical lodge that includes stereotypical pictures of the 'settling' in the area. The academic describes the lodge moment as: 'Classic bout: The pale face versus the dark savage' (ibid). Nathan's assistant, Bobbie Yang, who is a non-binary character and is not racially identified, but who appears as presenting non-White and is played by Jesse Leigh, replies to the academic: 'Fuck, you say?' The situations in this episode shed light on how one can be called an 'expert' and yet have insidious and discriminatory views, raising other questions: who or what deems someone an expert, and what version of history are they sharing?

Feminist lenses and the features of Indigenous womanhood and family

One strength of both *Rutherford Falls* and *Reservation dogs* is the way the shows were written, focusing on community and characters with depth. Specifically, in *Reservation dogs*, viewers are able to learn more about the main characters' home situations and how they each look after one another. Only two of the four 'Rez Dogs' have mothers who look after them, Willie Jack and Bear. Willie Jack is the only Rez Dog who has both parents raising her. The show sheds light on the truth that Indigenous childhood looks different for each child and that other family members may step in to fill important roles. A key example of that is Elora's Uncle Brownie; he is technically not her mother's brother, but he grew up with Elora's mother and was raised like her brother, so Elora calls him 'Uncle Brownie'.

The show also gives a glimpse into Indigenous womanhood and the responsibilities that come with it. As Bear's mother puts it: 'We're Indian women. We have to deal with reality when they [men] go off and play. And at the end of the day, we're the ones who have to make it work' (Harjo et al. 2021: Episode 4). As suggested in that quote, Bear's father left him when he was young and is still not actively present in Bear's life, leaving his mother to be the primary caretaker. The idea that Bear's mother is an independent woman becomes firmly evident when she has a conversation with the local doctor, who is trying to flirt with her. Bear's mom states to the doctor that she can hunt and fish after he hints that she might need a man (ibid: Episode 2).

There are also feminist standpoint lenses in *Rutherford Falls* and, much like what Bear's mom said, Reagan is often left cleaning up Nathan's messes; yet, Nathan is often oblivious and doesn't realise how much she helps him. In addition to Reagan, there are other women shown in *Rutherford Falls* who keep other men in check, specifically Terry Thomas. A surprising example is his daughter Maya, who reminds him of the insignificance of material wealth from her standpoint. She tells him: 'Why so obsessed with money? Is everything a deal to you?' (Helms et al. 2021: Episode 4). That was her response to him after he suggested she sell her beadwork to White people for more money. Later, she donates some of her beadwork to Reagan's cultural centre,

Benjamin R. LaPoe II

Victoria L. LaPoe

Sarah Liese

Hannah Ötting

Julia Weber

suggesting that money does not come before her tribe and preserving practices.

Though neither show discusses whether the tribal nations are matriarchal societies, they showcase strong Indigenous women who tend to take on a considerable amount of responsibility and offer their perspectives despite what men in their lives might think. Both shows take women's experiences and identities seriously and dispel narratives of female subordination, all of which are important aspects of feminism (Green 2017: 7). In many cases, the Indigenous women characters are reminding others what is important to consider and are often trying to keep situations in harmony. Reagan is continuously reminding Nathan and others who are not part of the Minishonkan tribe to see things from her point of view and to remember those who lived on the land before colonisation. A good example of this is when she responds to a townsperson who was shouting: 'Let's take our country back' (Helms et al. 2021: Episode 1). She responded: 'What? Take it back? From whom?' (ibid). Similarly, Willie Jack reminds her friends at the very end of the season to cherish those you love because, as she learned with Daniel, people will not last forever (Harjo et al. 2021: Episode 8).

Additionally, the way Indigenous men respect the women in their communities is exemplified in both shows; the lack of respect that Nathan Rutherford shows for women is an obvious contrast with them. For example, when Nathan's attorneys come to town to defend him after the casino board sues him on behalf of the Nation, he mentions that he guesses this team will be six men 'and one woman for show' (Helms et al. 2021: Episode 6). Jess Wells, played by Kawennáhere Devery Jacobs (Kahnawake Mohawk First Nation) in *Reservation dogs* filling in for the previous assistant, turns her head to acknowledge that there is an issue with him saying this. Combining these interactions within the season appears to support a hierarchy of truth that is a combination of both Indigenous and feminist standpoint lenses. Moreover, the shows do not romanticise or eroticise the women, but show an alternative narrative true for many Indigenous women, especially those living in matriarchal societies. Both shows depict strong Indigenous women who do their best to protect the ones they love.

Rutherford Falls and *Reservation dogs* share contemporary Indigenous experiences through different lenses. The shows bring to the forefront the lasting effects of colonisation and what that means for Indigenous communities today. *Reservation dogs* does not shy away from discussing generational trauma through the death of Daniel and the Rez Dogs' desire to escape their community, which they feel does not offer them enough room or opportunities to grow. It also exhibits creative outlets like making videos or spraying 'Land Back' on brick walls throughout the town. *Rutherford Falls* portrays an alternative to erasure, like Reagan's mission to build a cultural centre to preserve Minishonkan practices.

Both shows also call into question how history is being taught, particularly if it is being taught from a colonised or decolonised point of view, and who can even be classified as an expert. Common Indigenous stereotypes are addressed by depicting Indigenous characters with depth. The main characters are flawed and are shown learning as they experience new situations. They are not monolithic or one-dimensional, romanticised, eroticised or cast aside; rather, the characters are depicted as individuals growing alone, together and with their friends and the community.

Indigenous women, who are respected, are key to both storylines. Both showcase Indigenous women characters helping others around them, taking on a notable amount of responsibility and expressing their own unique identities. Reagan is a good example of this, as she seeks truth and joy, while upholding original history. She works on repatriating artefacts, introducing herself back into the community, trying to be kind to everyone, trying to do what is best for the people overall, with the understanding that her Nation's history – and the wellbeing of those in it today – should be at the forefront of discussion.

More often than not, both shows exemplify what is often a real-world strategy to cope with the violent past of colonisation: using humour as good medicine. Both shows use language as a tool to create laughter and inside jokes among those who know the language. Thus, despite current conscious and subconscious attempts to erase Indigenous people and cultures, they still remain. They remain strong, humourous and willing to combat society's attempt at erasure.

References

Academy of Motion Pictures Arts and Sciences (2021) 94th Oscars shortlist in 10 award categories announced, 21 December, Oscars.org. Available online at https://www.oscars.org/news/94th-oscarsr-shortlists-10-award-categories-announced, accessed on 13 October 2022

Ahtone, Tristan (2018) Our tribal affairs desk is looking for pitches, *High Country News*, 15 June. Available online at https://www.hcn.org/articles/tribal-affairs-high-country-news-tribal-affairs-desk-seeks-pitches, accessed on 13 October 2022

Asenap, Jason (2021a) 'Reservation Dogs' is just the beginning of an Indigenous storytelling explosion, *Esquire*, 9 August. Available online at https://www.esquire.com/entertainment/tv/a37234284/reservation-dogs-review-fx-indigenous-storytelling/, accessed on 13 October 2022

Asenap, Jason (2021b) The new Indigenous TV series coming your way, *High Country News*, 19 July. Available online at https://www.hcn.org/issues/53.8/indigenous-affairs-media-the-new-indigenous-tv-series-coming-your-way, accessed on 13 October 2022

Azocar, Cristina L, LaPoe, Victoria, Carter Olson, Candi S., LaPoe, Benjamin and Hazarika, Bharbi (2021) Indigenous communities and Covid-19: Reporting on resources and resilience, *Howard Journal of Communications*, Vol. 32, No. 5 pp 440–455. Available online at https://doi.org/10.1080/10646175.2021.1892552

Barclay, Barry (1990) *Our own image*, Auckland, NZ, Paul Longman

Bennett-Begaye, Jourdan (2021) 'Make it more Mato!' The music of 'Reservation dogs', *Indian Country Today*, 20 September. Available online at https://indiancountrytoday.com/news/make-it-more-mato-the-music-of-reservation-dogs, accessed on 13 October 2022

Benjamin R. LaPoe II

Victoria L. LaPoe

Sarah Liese

Hannah Ötting

Julia Weber

Bird, S. Elizabeth (1999) Gendered construction of the American Indian in popular media, *Journal of Communication*, Vol. 49, No. 3 pp 61–83

Center for Native American and Indigenous Research (CNAIR) (2019) Digital reporting in Indigenous communities panel 4.4.19, YouTube, 8 April. Available online at https://www.youtube.com/watch?v=k2yb7nmZ-_w, accessed on 13 October 2022

Cornish, Audie (2021) Encore: Rutherford Falls creators on finding humor in America's 'messy' history, NPR, 10 August. Available online at https://www.npr.org/2021/08/10/1026500642/encore-rutherford-falls-creators-on-finding-humor-in-americas-messy-history, accessed on 13 October 2022

Davis-Delano, Laurel R., Folsom, Jennifer J., McLaurin, Virginia, Eason, Arianne E. and Fryberg, Stephanie A. (2021) Representations of Native Americans in US culture? A case of omissions and commissions, *The Social Science Journal*. Available online at https://doi.org/10.1080/03623319.2021.1975086

Diamond_dog74 (2021) #reservationdogs #nativerepresentation @dallasgoldtooth @fxnetworks [TikTok], August 19. Available online at https://www.tiktok.com/@diamond_dog74/video/6997969885670214917?is_copy_url=1&is_from_webapp=v1, accessed on 13 October 2022

Eason, Arianne E., Brady, Laura M. and Fryberg, Stephanie A. (2018) Reclaiming representations and interrupting the cycle of bias against Native Americans, Deloria, Philip J., Lomawaima, K. Tsianina, Brayboy, Bryan, McKinley, Jones, Trahant, Mark, Neil, Ghiglione, Loren, Medin, Douglas and Blackhawk, Ned (eds) *Unfolding futures: Indigenous ways of knowing for the twenty-first century*, Cambridge, MA, Dædalus, American Academy of Arts and Sciences pp 70–81

Echo Hawk, C. (2018) Reclaiming Native truth. Research findings: Compilation of all research, *IllumiNative*. Available online at https://illuminative.org/resources, accessed on 13 October 2022

Entman, Robert M. (1993) Framing: Toward clarification of a fractured paradigm, *Journal of Communication*, Vol. 43, No. 4 pp 51–58

Fitzgerald, Michael Ray (2010) Evolutionary stages of minorities in the mass media: An application of Clark's model to American Indian television representations, *The Howard Journal of Communication*, Vol. 21, No. 4 pp 367–384. Available online at https://doi.org/10.1080/10646175.2010.519651

Fitzgerald, Michael Ray (2014). *Native Americans on network TV: Stereotypes, myths, and the 'good Indian'*, Lanham, MD, Rowman & Littlefield

Foley, Dennis (2003) Indigenous epistemology and Indigenous Standpoint Theory, *Social Alternatives*, Vol. 22, No. 1 pp 44–52

Gauthier, Jennifer L. (2015) Embodying change: Cinematic representations of Indigenous women's bodies: A cross-cultural-comparison, *International Journal of Media & Cultural Politics*, Vol. 11, No. 3 pp 283-298

Gleiberman, Owen (2022) 'Prey' review: 'Predator' prequel set in the Comanche Nation in 1719 is a slight improvement in a derivative franchise, *Variety*, 8 August. Available online at https://variety.com/2022/film/reviews/prey-review-predator-amber-midthunder-1235326998/, accessed on 3 October 2022

Goldberg, Lesley (2022) 'Rutherford falls' canceled at Peacock, *Hollywood Reporter*, 2 September. Available online at https://www.hollywoodreporter.com/tv/tv-news/rutherford-falls-canceled-peacock-1235211299/, accessed on 3 October 2022

Green, Joyce A. (2017) Taking more account of Indigenous feminism: Introduction, *Making space for Indigenous feminism*, Halifax, Fernwood Publishing pp 1–15

Greene, Dan (2021) The *New Yorker* documentary. A Cree skateboarding legend grapples with the trauma of Canada's residential schools, *New Yorker*, 6 October. Available online at https://www.newyorker.com/culture/the-new-yorker-documentary/a-cree-skateboarding-legend-grapples-with-the-trauma-of-canadas-residential-schools, accessed on 13 October 2022

Gross, Terry (2022) *'Reservation dogs'* co-creator says the show gives audiences permission to laugh, NPR, 19 September. Available online at https://www.npr.org/2022/09/19/1123452609/reservation-dogs-sterlin-harjo-native-stories, accessed on 3 May 2023

Hadadi, Roxana (2022) The historic power of *Prey* is in your ear, *Vulture*, 11 August. Available online at https://www.vulture.com/article/prey-hulu-comanche-dub.html, accessed on 8 October 2022

Harjo, Sterlin (2021) Humbled and amazed by all the Rez Dogs costumes this Halloween. Halloween is always a little weird for Native people, but to see people dressed up as Native characters with such pride and ownership is overwhelmingly special. I speak for all writers, actors, and crew when I say we are eternally grateful for all the love. We will keep striving to make you all proud. Instagram, 1 November. Available online at https://www.instagram.com/sterlinharjo/?hl=de, accessed on 1 November 2021

Harjo, Sterlin, Waititi, Taika, Pensoneau, Migizi, Freeland, Sydney and Wilson, Bobby (2021) *Reservation dogs* [Season 1 of television series], FX, August. Available online at https://www.hulu.com/series/reservation-dogs-5a310c23-e2db-4c9f-a66c-27c2fee43d92 accessed on 13 October 2022

Helms, Ed, Schur, Michael, Orenllas Teller, Sierra (2021) *Rutherford falls* [Season 1 of television series], NBCUniversal, April. Available online at https://www.peacocktv.com/stream-tv/rutherford-falls

Holiday-Shchedrov, Dawna (2017) *Cinematic representation of American Indians: A critical cultural analysis of a contemporary American Indian-directed film*. Doctoral dissertation, Arizona State University, ASU Library Digital Repository. Available online at https://repository.asu.edu/items/46280, accessed on 13 October 2022

Hunt, Darnell and Ramón, Ana-Christina (2021) *Hollywood diversity report 2021: Pandemic in progress*, Los Angeles, CA, UCLA College Social Sciences. Available online at https://socialsciences.ucla.edu/hollywood-diversity-report-2021/, accessed on 13 October 2022

IllumiNative (2021a) At a time when audiences are searching for stories that reflect the diversity and vibrancy of everyday life there is an opportunity for Hollywood to provide accurate, authentic, and contemporary portrayals of Native peoples. #RepresentationMatters, Instagram, 2 August. Available online at https://www.instagram.com/p/CSEkJxVHfw2/, accessed on 13 October 2022

IllumiNative (2021b) How Native women are portrayed in TV and film really matters. @neilsen's 2020 inclusion analytics report found that Native women are less likely to be represented. When Native women are represented, their inclusion has often focused on violence. Pay attention to these narratives when you see them and support Native created content. #RepresentationMatters, Instagram, 16 August. Available online at https://www.instagram.com/p/CSohiwnnoWY/, accessed on 13 October 2022

IllumiNative (nd) Change the story. Change the future. Insights and action guide. Available online at https://nativephilantrhopy.candid.org, accessed on 13 October 2022.

IMDB (2022) Billy Jack 1971. Available online at https://www.imdb.com/title/tt0066832/, accessed on 13 October 2022

Indian Country Today (2021) 2021: A look back at Indigenous representation, 29 December. Available online at https://indiancountrytoday.com/newscasts/12-29-2021-representation, accessed on 13 October 2022

LaPoe, Victoria L. and LaPoe, Benjamin R. (2017) *Indian Country: Telling a story in a digital age*, East Lansing, Michigan State University Press

LaPoe, Victoria L., Carter Olson, Candi S., Azocar, Cristina L., LaPoe, Benjamin R., Hazarika, Bharbi and Jain, Parul (2021a) A comparative analysis of health news in Indigenous and mainstream media, *Health Communication*, Vol. 37, No. 9 pp 1192–1203. Available online at https://doi.org/10.1080/10410236.2021.1945179

LaPoe, Benjamin R., Carter Olson, Candi S., LaPoe, Victoria L., Jain, Parul, Woellert, Allyson and Long, Aaron (2021b) Politics, power, and a pandemic: Searching for information and accountability during a Twitter infodemic, *Electronic News, Broadcast and Mobile Journalism*, Vol. 16, No. 1 pp. 30-53

Leavitt, Peter A., Covarrubias, Rebecca, Perez, Yvonne A. and Fryberg, Stephanie A. (2015) 'Frozen in time': The impact of Native American media representations on identity formation and self-understanding, *Journal of Social Issues*, Vol. 71, No. 1 pp 39–53

Lindquist Mala, Cynthia (2016) Very good medicine. Indigenous humor and laughter, *Tribal College Journal*, 1 May. Available online at https://tribalcollegejournal.org/very-good-medicine-indigenous-humor-and-laughter/, accessed on 13 October 2022

Martin, Karen and Mirraboopa, Booran (2003) Ways of knowing, being and doing: A theoretical framework and methods for Indigenous re-search and Indigenist research, *Journal of Australian Studies*, Vol. 27, No. 76 pp 203–214

Marubbio, M. Elise (2009) *Killing the Indian maiden: Images of Native American women in film*, Lexington, KY, University Press of Kentucky

Mastro, Dana E. and Stern, Susannah R. (2003) Representations of race in television commercials: A content analysis of prime-time advertising, *Journal of Broadcasting & Electronic Media*, Vol. 47, No. 7 pp 638–647

McCombs, Maxwell E. and Shaw, Donald L. (1972) The agenda-setting function of mass media, *Public Opinion Quarterly*, Vol. 36, No. 2 pp 176–187

Merskin, Debra (1998) Sending up signals: A survey of Native American media use and representation in the mass media, *The Howard Journal of Communications*, Vol. 9, No. 4 pp 333–345

Native News Online (2021) 'Reservation Dogs' cast brings Indigenous voice to 2021 Emmy awards, 20 September. Available online at https://nativenewsonline.net/arts-entertainment/reservation-dogs-cast-brings-indigenous-voice-to-2021-emmy-awards, accessed on 13 October 2022

Nielsen (2020) Being seen on screen: Diverse representation and inclusion on TV. Available online at https://www.nielsen.com/us/en/insights/report/2020/being-seen-on-screen-diverse-representation-and-inclusion-on-tv/, accessed on 13 October 2022

O'Connell, Mikey (2022) 'Reservation Dogs' boss on combatting Indigenous stereotypes, embracing gripes and that Emmy snub, *Hollywood Reporter*, 18 August. Available online at https://www.hollywoodreporter.com/tv/tv-features/reservation-dogs-sterlin-harjo-emmy-snub-indigenous-stereotypes-1235199618/, accessed on 3 October 2022

Odman, Sydney (2021) 'Reservation Dogs' creators and cast talk breaking barriers, future of Native representation in Hollywood, *Hollywood Reporter*, 6 August. Available online at https://www.hollywoodreporter.com/tv/tv-news/reservation-dogs-creators-and-cast-talk-breaking-barriers-future-of-native-representation-in-hollywood-1234993962/, accessed on 13 October 2022

Peterson, Brittany L. (2017) Thematic analysis/interpretive thematic analysis, *The International Encyclopedia of communication research methods*, 7 November. Available online at https://doi.org/10.1002/9781118901731.iecrm0249

Pierce, Scott D. (2020) Yellowstone breaks the mold with strong Native American characters, *Salt Lake Tribune*, 19 June. Available online at https://www.sltrib.com/artsliving/2020/06/19/yellowstone-breaks-mold/, accessed on 13 October 2022

RedCorn, Ryan (2021) Behind the Scenes of @rezdogsfxonhulu with @sterlinharjo & co. @buffalo_nickel_creative got asked to go Behind The Scenes for Reservation Dogs. Directed by yours truly. Team effort from @laronimo @rykersixkiller @bronnson_Harjo @benton_brown–art @_hannahrosewaller_ @ray_visuals, Instagram, 1 September. Available online at https://www.instagram.com/p/CTQW-EJpEk2/, accessed on 13 October 2022

Sarah (2021) The Reservation dogs brought it to the Emmys, Laineygossip, 20 September. Available online at https://www.laineygossip.com/the-cast-of-reservation-dogs-and-devery-jacobs-looked-sharp-while-presenting-at-the-emmys-in-what-was-hopefully-the-first-of-many-more-appearances/69408, accessed on 13 October 2022

Schilling, Vincent (2021a) 'Reservation dogs' nominated for a Golden Globe, *Indian Country Today*, 13 December. Available online at https://indiancountrytoday.com/lifestyle/reservation-dogs-nominated-for-a-golden-globe, accessed on 13 October 2022

Schilling, Vincent (2021b) Director Sterlin Harjo talks 'Reservation dogs', *Indian Country Today*, 13 September. Available online at https://indiancountrytoday.com/lifestyle/director-sterlin-harjo-talks-reservation-dogs, accessed on 13 October 2022

Schilling, Vincent (2021c) #NativeNerd: Indian Country's love for 'Reservation Dogs'. Set photos, social media posts, and my review of episodes five and six, *Indian Country Today*, 31 August. Available online at https://indiancountrytoday.com/lifestyle/nativenerd-indian-countrys-love-for-reservation-dogs, accessed on 13 October 2022

Schmieding, Jana (2021) Jana Schmieding on the Native joy of *Rutherford falls*, *Vanity Fair*, 21 June. Available online at https://www.vanityfair.com/hollywood/2021/06/jana-schmieding-rutherford-falls-peacock, accessed on 13 October 2022

Tan, Alexis, Fujioka, Yuki and Lucht, Nancy (1997) Native American stereotypes, TV portrayals, and personal contact, *Communication and Mass Media Quarterly*, Vol. 74, No. 2 pp 265–284

Thompson, Claire Elise (2020) Returning the land, *Grist*, 25 November. Available online at https://grist.org/fix/justice/indigenous-landback-movement-can-it-help-climate/, accessed on 30 April, 2023

Tukachinsky, Riva, Mastro, Dana and Yarchi, Moran (2015) Documenting portrayals of race/ethnicity on primetime television over a 20-year span and their association with national-level racial/ethnic attitudes, *Journal of Social Issues*, Vol. 71, No. 1 pp 17–38

Turner Strong, Pauline (2012) *American Indians and the American imaginary: Cultural representation across the centuries*, London, Routledge

Vanderhoof, Erin (2021) Devery Jacobs of Reservation Dogs used the Emmys 2021 red carpet to represent Indigenous artists, *Vanity Fair*, 19 September. Available online at https://www.vanityfair.com/style/2021/09/devery-jacobs-reservation-dogs-emmys-2021-red-carpet, accessed on 13 October 2022

White, Peter (2021) Former Sundance institute Exec Bird Runningwater strikes first-look deal with Amazon, Deadline, 30 September. Available online at https://deadline.com/2021/09/sundance-institute-bird-runningwater-first-look-deal-amazon-1234847370/, accessed on 13 October 2022

Z0mbie Chik (2021) Reservation dogs cast Lane Factor Paulina Alexis Kawennáhere Devery Jacobs 73rd Emmys Awards 2021, YouTube, 20 September. Available online at https://www.youtube.com/watch?v=983s0jfmt8U, accessed on 13 October 2022

Acknowledgements

Authors would like to note a special thanks of support to Timothy Petete, PhD (Seminole Nation of Oklahoma) who viewed a presentation of our early work and provided valuable feedback.

Note on the contributors

Benjamin R. LaPoe, II, PhD. is an assistant professor and Political Communication Certificate director at Ohio University. He received his MSc in Journalism from West Virginia University and his PhD in political communication from the Manship School at Louisiana State University. His research focuses on the intersections of racism, sexism, political communication and media. LaPoe is co-author of *Resistance advocacy as news: Digital Black press covers the Tea Party* and *Indian Country: Telling a story in a digital age*, where he wrote about the history of media and minority press.

Victoria L. LaPoe, PhD (Cherokee) is an associate professor in Ohio University's E. W. School of Journalism and Director of Journalism in the Honor Tutorial College, where she teaches both news and information and strategic communication courses. LaPoe served as vice president and education chair of the Native American Journalists Association. She continues to serve on NAJA's education committee and is a lifetime NAJA member as well as Indigenous Issues editor for the national Media Diversity Forum. She is co-author of *Indian Country: Telling a story in a digital age*.

Sarah Liese, MSc (Navajo/ Chippewa/ Cree) is a 2022 Indigenous Non-Fiction Sundance Institute Fellow, researcher and mitigation video specialist. She completed her Master of Science degree in Journalism at Ohio University in July 2022. While pursuing her Master's degree, she served as a Full Circle Fellow at the Sundance Institute, Native American Journalism Fellow and Mentor-In-Training at the Native American Journalist Association, as well as a research assistant and teaching assistant at Ohio University. Her prior work focused on social media management, content creation and broadcast journalism.

Benjamin R. LaPoe II

Victoria L. LaPoe

Sarah Liese

Hannah Ötting

Julia Weber

Hannah Ötting is a Master's student at Ohio University and Leipzig University, Germany, studying Global Mass Communication (MA) and Journalism (MSc). She holds a Bachelor's degree in Communication Studies and American and British Studies from the University of Münster (WWU), Germany. Outside of her studies, Hannah Ötting is a board member of the Young German Association for Political and Social Sciences (DNGPS e.V.). Her main research interests are journalism studies, the integrative function of media, media coverage of marginalised groups and the intersection of media and activism.

Julia Weber is a second-year undergraduate student in the Ohio University Honors Tutorial College where she is working towards a Bachelor of Science in Journalism with a minor in Art History. She is the features editor for Ohio University's All Campus Radio Network, a student-run radio station. She has also worked in editorial, research and strategic communication settings, and her main areas of interest include reporting and audience engagement. After graduation, her goal is to work in a newsroom setting as a reporter primarily covering music, art and culture.

Conflict of interest

Authors did not receive funding for this research or publication.

REVIEWS

We come with this place
Debra Dank
Echo Publishing, 2022 pp 252
ISBN: 9781760687397

Statement for transparency: this text emanates from a creative doctorate undertaken at Melbourne's Deakin University by the author, Australian First Nations academic Dr Debra Dank, and I was one of her examiners. Her thesis at the time of examination left me almost speechless – all I could really say at the time was that I believed this book – and I knew it would be published and be a book – would win awards. That was then.

Three months after conferral, there was a bidding war for the texts – two multi-national commercial publishers and an independent publisher. Dank signed with the independent, securing a two-book deal for both creative and scholarly components of her doctorate.

The creative text is as dramatic as it is raw; and concurrently, breath-takingly vivid and astute. It is steeped in a culture and a family love, a passionate claim to more than ancient knowledge and a generosity, albeit from a polemical point of view, in a communication of deep and gracious wisdom with its readers.

Dank is a Gudanji and Wakaja woman, author, academic, mother, sister and grandmother. As another First Nations author, Tara June Winch, writes: 'These are important biographical notes because this book is about all those qualifiers that not only make the author who she is, but root the overall story and guide its purpose' (2022). Melissa Lucashenko, also a First Nations author, writes that the book is the best she read in 2022. In 2022, the text was selected by the Grattan Institute as one of the books for the Prime Minister's Summer Reading List, an annual collection of six. Earlier this year, it was short-listed for no less than three NSW Premier Literary Awards (but winning four, including Book of the Year); and was one of six books short-listed for the 2023 Stella Prize, the annual literary award for writing by Australian women.

The text is one of a kind, meaning it is impossible to slot it into a slick, marketable genre. I have seen it on the shelves in bookstores under Memoir, Autobiography and Non-fiction. Discretely, it is none of these; perhaps a bit of each. I believe it is a deeply personal story performing as a collective narrative, and this is its strength and power. I learnt more about Australia and its First Nations from examining this text than I have in my whole life. It is an extraordinary foray into what Country actually means to our First Nations; how meaning and life and love and family is derived from it.

The book left me feeling bereft, that I, as a White, post-colonial and privileged academic, do not know how to be on Country the way our traditional owners, the oldest people in the world, do. I never 'came with this place' like our First Nations – my forebears arrived by boats from afar, pale-skinned strangers to these traditional owners.

The book is thick with the sounds and songs of the land and its inhabitants, both human and non-human. The desert country is its own entity, looming large in the lives of the young Debra and her two sisters, sitting around the campfire with their mum and dad; their ancestors dancing around them, always just a breath away. There are stories of their schooling and their mother's tenacious insistence on educating her girls; how she always carried books for herself and her daughters, but never for their father. Dank writes: 'He had no use for them because he did not read words on a paper. He heard them in the voices in the wind, whispering through the grasses; he saw them sitting in the hills and living in the outcrops and he felt them as he rode horses across all that big space ... his story-knowledge lived inside him and travelled in country, coming from the old people, through and on to us. He read stories in a landscape that was full of them' (p. 25).

There is her parents' constant pain of fearing their children could be removed from them, at any time. The harrowing tale of their father, witnessing a sexual assault of his beloved mother by White settlers, then running for his life from Gudanji land, literally; frontier power, violence and racism at its heightened, shameful worst. She writes: 'If you look carefully, it's possible to see the pain as it lies in the landscape. Can you hear the wail in the wind and see the blood running with the dust?' (p. 13).

Dank describes the book as a 'strange kind of letter, written to my place' (p. viii). Perhaps a love letter, to her family of origin, her own family now, her country and her ancestors. The text is imbued with a lyricism that makes you not want to put it down. But there is ubiquitous pain running through its seams. She writes: 'All of us know that terrible things happened here, and one day I hope we might be able to be smart and speak through that pain that curls into itself and keeps the words away, to let the words free and start to heal the pain. Listen well when this country is telling you our story. Listen with your feet in the sand and your heart in your hands and give it over to this country. She deserves it most' (p. 13).

Her parents' love story was one with flaws, like most, but these flaws were grown from childhoods blighted by intergenerational traumas. She writes: 'Trauma had made newer stories inside my dad, and he was still learning how to live with them as they pushed and jostled the old stories. Sometimes the newer stories became too big for Dad to keep them inside and they pushed their way out with a violence that mostly Mum but sometimes I, too, had to deal with' (p. 26). There is a visceral scene of domestic violence where the teenage Dank strikes her father after he has hit her mother. She is non-apologetic about her fury, as credible as only a teenage fury is. She then situates her father's cellular pain as reason, even though she does not accept it at the time (pp 191-198). The older Dank knows her parents' relationship was one of imperfect love, but it was a potent, protective and powerful love, surrounding her sisters as they grew.

There is a joyful warmth and humour woven around these dark collective family tales of pain. Juxtaposed against them is the story of the 10-year-old Dank as a reluctant fairy princess in a school play. She has only three words to say, twice – 'o deary me, o deary me'. Only speaking her own language Wakaja for the first decade of her life, she could read the words but pronunciation was another matter. She delivered her lines: 'o duri me, o duri me', not knowing at the time that what she was saying in her own language was 'o fuck me, o fuck me'. Only her parents and other First Nations in the audience knew what she said, and sat aghast. The White members of the audience clapped and smiled at 'the little brown girl, standing on stage in a pretty yellow dress' (p. 169).

This text made me smile, made me cry and then enclosed me in a deep shame almost all at once. Beautifully illustrated by her daughter, Gudanji/Wakaja artist Ryhia Dank (Nardurna), the telling is gracious and powerful, and Dank's craft sings off the pages. I believe this text should be mandatory reading within school curricula around the country. We as a nation have to know this story. We have to grow up, knowing this story. Only then can we hope to begin to understand.

Associate Professor Sue Joseph,
University of South Australia

An admirable point: A brief history of the exclamation mark!
Florence Hazrat
London, Profile Books, 2022 pp 175
ISBN: 9781800811973

Many writers have detested the exclamation mark. F. Scott Fitzgerald suggested that it is the equivalent of laughing at your own jokes while Terry Pratchett has a character in *Discworld* declaring that multiple !!!s are a 'sure sign of a diseased mind' (p. 11). Shakespeare was clearly not a fan using it just 350 times in his entire *Folio* (p. 38). Anton Chekhov even composed a short story, 'The exclamation point' (1885), in which a minor clerk, Perekladin, is driven to distraction by the problem of the ! (pp 73-75). In 1956, the German philosopher Theodore Adorno likened the exclamation mark to 'soundless clashing of cymbals' (p. 113).

But Florence Hazrat, the host of *Standing on points*, a podcast about dots and dashes, is an 'unapologetic' enthusiast and sets out in her text 'to reclaim the exclamation mark from its much maligned and misunderstood place at the bottom of the punctuation hierarchy' (p. 21). She achieves this with great panache!

Digging deep into the archives, Hazrat suggests that Florentine lawyer, humanist and politician Coluccio Salutati used the mark for the first time in his *De nobilitated legum et medicinae*, of 1399. For the earliest mention in English, she cites *The opening of the unreasonable writing of our English tongue* (1551) by the educator, John Hart (p. 30). He calls the ! 'the wonderer' while the ? is 'the asker'. A guide to rhetoric of 1656 first recorded the ! as a 'note of exclamation' while in his *Essay on punctuation* (1785), Joseph Robertson called the mark 'the voice of nature, when she is agitated, amazed, or transported' (p. 41). But the highly influential guide on English grammar and style, *The King's English* (1906), by Henry and Francis Fowler, warned that excessive use of exclamation marks is 'one of the things that betray the uneducated' (p. 45).

Hazrat devotes special attention to the use of punctuation in the long, medieval poem, *Beowulf*, by the poets John Donne, Gerald Manley Hopkins and e.e. cummings (pp 105-107) and by the pop artist Roy Lichtenstein, whose *Whaam*!, of 1963, shows a fighter pilot firing at an enemy plane (p. 115). She reflects: 'The best writers can work magic with a well-placed !, enhancing our physical sensation of what we read. Too often, though, the might of ! gets abused, turning punctuation into a handmaid of brainwashing, social division and destructive consumption' (p. 121). Later chapters look at the use of the exclamation mark in the political campaign posters of Barack Obama,

Rishi Sunak, Emmanuel Macron, Angela Merkel and Donald Trump (pp 126-135).

All in all, *An admirable point* (complete with a judicious sprinkling of illustrations) is a delight!

Richard Lance Keeble,
University of Lincoln

Violence
Toby Miller
Abingdon, Oxon, Routledge, 2021 pp 137
ISBN: 9780367197605

This lively, succinct, engaging and thought-provoking book reaches across disciplines, discourses and the globe to develop new understandings of violence, a 'universal problem', and its place in our lives, societies and institutions by seeking answers to a series of fundamental questions:

- how has violence been defined: historically, geographically?
- has it decreased or increased?
- which regions are the most violent?
- does violence correlate with economies, political systems and religions?
- what is the relationship of gender and violence?
- what role do the media play?

It is, of course, that final field of inquiry that draws our attention. But before we go there, some further context is called for. Miller argues here for a richer set of understandings than those confined to supposedly universal human traits: one informed by specificities of history, place and population – interrogated through a series of case studies and discourses and drawing on an analytical framework grounded in cultural materialism. Along the way we encounter Marx, Gramsci, Foucault, Althusser, Shakespeare, Dashiell Hammett, Raymond Chandler, James Bond, Jack Reach ... and more.

The core chapters focus on definitions and numbers; the psychology of violence; gender and masculinity (where James Bond, 'probably the most violent and lasting male in cultural history after God' appears on page 52); the nation state – and finally, the media. Each section provides a series of nuanced insights and explorations of connections that enrich our understanding in ways uncomfortable as well as enlightening. But our focus here is on chapter 5 and the analysis of the symbiotic relationship between violence and the media (pp 77-91).

The chapter begins by charting the fear among those in power that access to mass media by 'the worthless mob' would give rise to turmoil – and the brutal responses by states, industrialists and slave-owners to those in servitude becoming independent-minded. Yet, at the same time, new forms of mass media have also been welcomed as 'new forms of life that could bring peace by eliminating distance and bringing new understandings between nations'. The origins of social psychology, says Miller, can be traced to these anxieties (p. 77) and, in particular, the focus on the perceived effects of media and their role in 'encouraging or retarding violence among readers, listeners, viewers, and players' (p. 79).

The chapter provides an elegant summary, analysis and critique of the media effects tradition and its three dominant models:

- that screens offer 'how-to' guides to means and motivations for violence (social cognitive theory);
- that the media have reciprocal impacts on social conduct (distribution and cue analysis);
- that an individual's tendencies to violence are heightened by seeing it on screen (arousal theory).

Miller offers examples of these models being applied to social policy and responses to social problems around the world – and the damage this has caused and continues to cause. He laments this tradition's failure to account for cultural norms and politics, 'the arc of history and waves of geography that situate texts and the responses to them inside politics, war, ideology and discourse' (p. 81). And he highlights the need to problematise media texts – to 'track what happens *in* media texts and what happens to them as they travel, attenuating and developing links and discourses across their careers, for it is reductive to understand the media and violence via methods that are purely psy-orientated' (p. 83, original emphasis). To this end, he moves on to consider in detail two critical fields: violence and journalism, violence and fiction.

In journalism's case, he analyses coverage of the Iraq War of 2003 and the 'propaganda machine that distorts reality'. But he also considers journalism work and the intimidation, kidnapping, detention and murder they risk in direct relation to that work. Risks that are far from confined to war zones and war reporting: between 2002 and 2013, 93 per cent of murdered journalists were killed in their own countries, often by criminal gangs threatened by media exposure. Assaults on journalists' integrity and gender-based violence women journalists face include abuse, defamation, calumny, trolling and threats of sexual assault and murder.

Miller moves from war, conflict and violence to explore the interrelationships of media and violence in the 1993 case and its continuing resonance of the murder of two-year-old James Bulger in Liverpool, UK, by pre-teens Robert Thompson and Jon Venables. Video was said to have caused the crime (the killers watched violent and pornographic tapes); illustrated the boy's callousness (they watched cartoons after the murder); proved their guilt (CCTV). Ever since, video games, documentary and the marketing of true crime content have given rise to public outrage and offence to James Bulger's family, often reported by news media. The point Miller draws is that our consideration of media's problematic relationship with violence needs to encompass a far wider perspective than their possible effects as an incentive to violent behaviour.

In the case of fiction Miller highlights the field as a site where the legitimacy of states' monopoly on the exercise of violence in protection of private property, private morality and public safety is widely accepted. He also draws on a series of case studies to demonstrate a disturbing tendency to glamorise organised crime and its core violence. But again, he draws out the complexities in these representations. Narcos – drug traffickers – tend to embody upward mobility in societies where structural social and economic inequalities deny life chances to large swathes of the population.

Attempts to hold media accountable for violence, Miller argues, distract from more productive discussions which 'ensue from seeing meeting points of violence and media in terms of inadequate reporting due to nationalistic bigotry, perils of journalists, unworthy glamorisation of gangsters and complexities of drawing clear distinctions between fact and fiction' (p. 91).

This is an academic work, but it would appeal to anyone interested in more clearly understanding this 'universal problem', and it is of particular interest to journalism and media students and researchers, journalists and journalism educators.

Dr David Baines,
School of Arts and Cultures,
Newcastle University, UK

Listen world!: How the intrepid Elsie Robinson became America's most-read female

Julia Scheeres and Allison Gilbert

New York, Seal Press, 2022 pp 338

ISBN: 9781541674356 (hbk); 9781541674349 (ebk)

Elsie Robinson was an amazing journalistic phenomenon. During a forty-year career (1916-1956), she produced around nine thousand columns and articles. In the process she became a household name with more than twenty million loyal readers in the United States. In 1918, she launched a children's section in the *Oakland Tribune*, both writing and illustrating her articles. 'Aunt Elsie's magazine' proved an instant sensation spawning Aunt Elsie clubs for kids across California. By 1924, she was the highest paid woman writer in William Randolph Hearst's mighty press empire – her syndicated column, 'Listen, world!', tackling a vast range of topics: gender inequality, anti-racism, capital punishment, the rights of immigrants – and more.

Yet today, Elsie Robinson is largely forgotten. Not surprisingly, then, authors Julia Scheeres and Allison Gilbert state in the Introduction that their main aim is to restore her 'to her rightful place as a venerable American icon' (p. 6). They certainly succeed: this is fascinating, well-researched, entertaining and timely biography.

Robinson's extraordinary life story makes for riveting reading. For this the authors draw liberally (and perhaps too uncritically) from her columns and autobiography, *I wanted out*! (1934) – extracts always clearly marked in italics. Born in 1883 into a poor, working class family in the frontier town of Benicia, California (famed for its bars and brothels), Robinson is obliged to attend a puritan seminary before her marriage, aged just 19, to the wealthy businessman and widower Christie Crowell. All her feelings there of desperation are captured in this extract from her memoir:

> This dour Puritan Jehovah! This sour and all-pervading Sense of Sin! These people who seemingly lived but to suffer ... whose thoughts were bent on Sacrifice and Hard Labor ... who shuffled through life like a chain-gang, never rebelling, never rejoicing, never adventuring! ...If this be the way to Heaven I wanted to raise Hell (pp 60-61).

Moving to the mansion, Lindenhurst, in Brattleboro, Vermont, Robinson becomes increasingly frustrated in her loveless marriage (though a son, George Alexander, is born in 1904). In 1911, she meets Robert Wallace, a patient at the local lunatic asylum (as it was then known) who employs her to illustrate two of his children's books. Four years later, she joins Wallace and her brother Phil in the largely deserted gold mining town of Hornitos, in the Sierra Nevada, hoping that the air in the remote region will help George – an asthma sufferer throughout his short life. At times Scheeres and Gilbert write with a sort of Mills & Boonish gushiness. For instance, on Robinson's decision to move to Hornitos, they report:

> There was freedom in this paring down … in dispensing with the stuffy Victorian protocols that regulated everything from cutlery to conversation. There was beauty in falling asleep to a symphony of crickets or the wind swishing through the trees. Their days were quiet and slow, ruled by the simple rhythms of the earth (pp 134-135).

When Christie learns that his wife is living with Wallace he cuts off her allowance and files for divorce. So, ever-resourceful, Robinson goes down a hard-rock mine, not like George Orwell as a committed investigative journalist but in desperation – to earn money. In her memoir, she writes, movingly:

> I had crossed the wall – left woman's world behind me. Now I was with men … always with men … only men. I heard no other voices … knew no other problems. When they raced up the shaft – away from the shot – I ran with them. When they piled down into the shaft again – fumbled, gasping, through the half-cleared air to peer for the miracle of gold across the face of the rock, I piled and peered with them. … Scared? I was so scared that my toe nails would have curled if there'd been room!

Whilst slaving away as a miner, Robinson somehow finds time to bash out on a typewriter a few stories ('The little maverick', 'Buck Calhoun's woman' and 'Shall the woman tell?') which she sells to the magazines, *Black Cat, Breezy Stories* and *McClure's*. Leaving Wallace, she moves to San Francisco in 1918 and secures her first journalistic job – as a columnist – on the *Oakland Tribune*. Her first article, 'Trestle Glen secrets', named after a wooded area near Lake Merritt in downtown Oakland, is such a hit that on 11 May 1919, she is given a weekly, one-page feature. In the following year, 'Aunt Elsie's magazine' expands to two pages; by 1922 she is assigned a whole eight-page section for her children's stories (p. 193). In January 1921, her adult column 'Listen, world!', is syndicated in newspapers across the country by the George Matthew Adams News Service – and she is firmly on the road to journalistic fame (p. 198).

Hearst is also to exploit her writing skills as a news reporter – covering such stories as the 1932 kidnapping of the infant son of aviators Charles and Anne Lindbergh, the Bonus March later in the year when 40,000 jobless World War One veterans marched in protest to Washington, DC, only to be brutally attacked by police and troops – and the controversial 1940 Democratic Convention when President Roosevelt was nominated for an unprecedented third term (p. 234).

While Robinson's final years are covered over-rapidly, one of the most impressive features of this biography appears near the end (pp 283-319) in the long list of notes which provide evidence of exceptionally detailed research. Take, for instance, Elizabeth Pearson, Elsie's mother. Tracing her family background, the authors delve deep citing the State of California Department of Public Health Vital Statistics, the Ireland Civil Registration Indexes, the Custom House, Dublin, the 1889 and 1900 US censuses and Ancestry.com (p. 287). For the final years of Robert Wallace, the 1920 US federal census, Texas death certificates and health services, *Marshall News Messenger* and www.carthagetexas.us are mentioned (p. 308).

Moreover, Scheeres and Gilbert offer the longest acknowledgements section I've ever seen – over twelve pages (269-280).

In a chapter titled 'Remembering Elsie', the authors highlight the way in which sexism has operated effectively to eliminate her from the history of journalism. They write: 'When it comes to learning history in American public schools, a recent study by the National Women's History Museum found that only 24 per cent of all the historical figures studied from kindergarten through twelfth grade are women' (p. 249). This biography, then, stands as an important affirmation of women's too often overlooked place in history..

Richard Lance Keeble,
University of Lincoln

The International Journal
of Communication Ethics

Subscription information
Each volume contains four issues, published quarterly.

Annual Subscription (including postage)

Personal Subscription	Printed	Online
UK	£55	£25
Europe	£70	£25
RoW	£85	£25

Institutional Subscription	
UK	£185
Europe	£195
RoW	£210

Single Issue - Open Access £300

Enquiries regarding subscriptions and orders should be sent to:

Journals Fulfilment Department
Abramis Academic
ASK House
Northgate Avenue
Bury St Edmunds
Suffolk, IP32 6BB
UK

Tel: +44(0)1284 717884
Email: info@abramis.co.uk